SCIENCE ESSENTIALS

HIGH SCHOOL LEVEL

Lessons and Activities for Test Preparation

D1441632

SCIENCE ESSENTIALS

HIGH SCHOOL LEVEL

Lessons and Activities for Test Preparation

Jia Yao, Ren

Mark J. Handwerker, Ph.D.

JOSSEY-BASS
A Wiley Imprint
www.josseybass.com

Published by Jossey-Bass
A Wiley Imprint
989 Market Street, San Francisco, CA 94103-1741   www.josseybass.com

Jossey-Bass books and products are available through most bookstores. To contact Jossey-Bass directly call our Customer Care Department within the U.S. at (800) 956-7739, outside the U.S. at (317) 572-3986 or fax (317) 572-4002.

Jossey-Bass also publishes its books in a variety of electronic formats. Some content that appears in print may not be available in electronic books.

Library of Congress Cataloging-in-Publication Data

Handwerker, Mark J.
  [Ready-to-use science proficiency lessons & activities, 10th grade level]
  Science essentials, high school level / Mark J. Handwerker.—1st ed.
    p. cm.—(Science essentials)
  Originally published: Ready-to-use science proficiency lessons & activities, 10th grade
level. Paramus, NJ : Center for Applied Research in Education, c2002, in series: TestPrep
curriculum activities library.
    ISBN 0-7879-7575-3 (alk. paper)
    1. Science—Study and teaching (Secondary)—Activity programs—United States. I. Title.

Q183.3.A1H36 2004
507'.1'273–dc22

                                                              2004045125

FIRST EDITION
PB Printing 10 9 8 7 6 5 4 3 2 1

About This Science TestPrep Teaching Resource

Science Essentials gives high school classroom science teachers and science specialists a dynamic and progressive way to meet curriculum standards and competencies. The lessons actively engage students in learning about the natural and technological world in which we live by encouraging them to use their senses and intuitive abilities on the road to discovery. The lessons and activities have been developed and tested by professional science teachers who sought to provide students with enjoyable learning experiences while at the same time preparing them for district and statewide science proficiency exams.

For quick access and easy use, materials are printed in a big 8¼" × 10⅞" lay-flat format that folds flat for photocopying of over 100 student activity sheets and are organized into the following two sections:

I. BIOLOGY

Lessons 1 through 60 plus Sample Test Questions

II. CHEMISTRY

Lessons 61 through 107 plus Sample Test Questions

Each section includes detailed lessons with reproducible student handouts for teaching basic concepts and skills in one important area of science. All of the lessons and student handouts are complete and ready for use. Each lesson includes:

- the **Basic Principle** underlying the lesson and accompanying student activity

- the specific science **Competency** students will demonstrate

- **Materials** needed to complete the activity

- easy-to-follow, illustrated **Procedure** for presenting the lesson and accompanying student activity handout

- **Observation & Analysis** describing the desired results and answers to the student activity

- a two-page, illustrated **Student Handout** with step-by-step directions for carrying out the activity and recording observations and conclusions

The lessons in each section are followed by a variety of sample test questions focusing on the concepts and skills emphasized in that section. These are designed to help students prepare for the types of questions they will be asked in actual test situations and are followed by complete answer keys.

Science Essentials are also available from the publisher for the Elementary School and Middle School levels. The lessons, activities, and sample test items in all three grade-level volumes provide a stimulating and effective way to help students master basic science content and prepare to demonstrate their knowledge.

Mark J. Handwerker, Ph.D.

About the Author

Mark J. Handwerker (B.S., C.C.N.Y.; Ph.D. in Biology, U.C.I.) has taught secondary school science for 18 years in the Los Angeles and Temecula Valley Unified School Districts. As a mentor and instructional support teacher, he has trained scores of new teachers in the "art" of teaching science. He is also the author/editor of articles in a number of scientific fields and the coauthor of an earth science textbook currently in use.

Dr. Handwerker teaches his students that the best way to learn basic scientific principles is to become familiar with the men and women who first conceived them. His classroom demonstrations are modeled on those used by the most innovative scientists of the past. He believes that a familiarity with the history of science, an understanding of the ideas and methods used by the world's most curious people, is the key to comprehending revolutions in modern technology and human thought.

Contents

Science Essentials

HIGH SCHOOL LEVEL

I. BIOLOGY / 1

Basic Principle: Fundamental life processes depend on a variety of chemical reactions carried out in specialized cell organelles.
Science Competency: Students will show how a semipermeable membrane regulates a cell's interactions with its environment.
Reproducibles: Student Handout—Lesson 1

Basic Principle: Fundamental life processes depend on a variety of chemical reactions carried out in specialized cell organelles.
Science Competency: Students will show how enzymes catalyze biochemical reactions.
Reproducibles: Student Handout—Lesson 2

Basic Principle: Fundamental life processes depend on a variety of chemical reactions carried out in specialized cell organelles.
Science Competency: Students will show how prokaryotic cells, eukaryotic cells, and viruses differ in complexity and general structure.
Reproducibles: Student Handout—Lesson 3

Basic Principle: Fundamental life processes depend on a variety of chemical reactions carried out in specialized cell organelles.
Science Competency: Students will describe the flow of information from the transcription of RNA in the nucleus to the translation of proteins on ribosomes in the cytoplasm.
Reproducibles: Student Handout—Lesson 4

Basic Principle: Fundamental life processes depend on a variety of chemical reactions carried out in specialized cell organelles.
Science Competency: Students will describe the role of the endoplasmic reticulum and Golgi apparatus in the secretion of proteins.
Reproducibles: Student Handout—Lesson 5

Basic Principle: Fundamental life processes depend on a variety of chemical reactions carried out in specialized cell organelles.
Science Competency: Students will show that energy captured from sunlight by chloroplasts is stored in plants in the form of starch.
Reproducibles: Student Handout—Lesson 6

Contents

II. CHEMISTRY / 215

Contents

Science Competency: Students will use the Atomic-Molecular Theory of Matter to explain how solids differ from liquids and liquids differ from gas.
Reproducibles: Student Handout—Lesson 71

Basic Principle: The biochemical, chemical, and physical properties of matter result from the ability of atoms to form bonds based on electrostatic forces between electrons and protons and between atoms and molecules.
Science Competency: Students will draw Lewis-dot (i.e., electron-dot) structures of atoms and ions.
Reproducibles: Student Handout—Lesson 72

Basic Principle: The conservation of atoms in chemical reactions leads to the principle of conservation of matter and the ability to calculate the masses of products and reactants.
Science Competency: Students will show that matter is conserved in a chemical reaction.
Reproducibles: Student Handout—Lesson 73

Basic Principle: The conservation of atoms in chemical reactions leads to the principle of conservation of matter and the ability to calculate the masses of products and reactants.
Science Competency: Students will describe chemical reactions by writing balanced chemical equations.
Reproducibles: Student Handout—Lesson 74

Basic Principle: The conservation of atoms in chemical reactions leads to the principle of conservation of matter and the ability to calculate the masses of products and reactants.
Science Competency: Students will explain the concept of a "mole."
Reproducibles: Student Handout—Lesson 75

Basic Principle: The conservation of atoms in chemical reactions leads to the principle of conservation of matter and the ability to calculate the masses of products and reactants.
Science Competency: Students will determine the molar masses of a molecule from its chemical formula using a table of atomic masses.
Reproducibles: Student Handout—Lesson 76

Basic Principle: The conservation of atoms in chemical reactions leads to the principle of conservation of matter and the ability to calculate the masses of products and reactants.
Science Competency: Students will convert the mass of a molecular substance to moles.
Reproducibles: Student Handout—Lesson 77

Basic Principle: The conservation of atoms in chemical reactions leads to the principle of conservation of matter and the ability to calculate the masses of products and reactants.
Science Competency: Students will calculate the masses of reactants and products in a chemical reaction from the mass of one of the reactants or products.
Reproducibles: Student Handout—Lesson 78

Basic Principle: The Kinetic-Molecular Theory describes the motion of atoms and molecules, and explains the properties of gases.

Science Competency: Students will illustrate the random motion of molecules in a gas and their collisions to explain the observable pressure on that surface.
Reproducibles: Student Handout—Lesson 79

Basic Principle: The Kinetic-Molecular Theory describes the motion of atoms and molecules, and explains the properties of gases.
Science Competency: Students will illustrate the random motion of molecules to explain the phenomenon of diffusion.
Reproducibles: Student Handout—Lesson 80

Basic Principle: The Kinetic-Molecular Theory describes the motion of atoms and molecules, and explains the properties of gases.
Science Competency: Students will apply the gas laws relating to pressure, temperature, and volume of ideal gases and mixtures of ideal gases.
Reproducibles: Student Handout—Lesson 81

Basic Principle: The Kinetic-Molecular Theory describes the motion of atoms and molecules, and explains the properties of gases.
Science Competency: Students will define the values and meanings of standard temperature and pressure (STP).
Reproducibles: Student Handout—Lesson 82

Basic Principle: The Kinetic-Molecular Theory describes the motion of atoms and molecules, and explains the properties of gases.
Science Competency: Students will define the value and meaning of absolute zero: 0 Kelvin.
Reproducibles: Student Handout—Lesson 83

Basic Principle: The Kinetic-Molecular Theory describes the motion of atoms and molecules, and explains the properties of gases.
Science Competency: Students will convert temperatures from one scale to another: Celsius, Kelvin, Fahrenheit.
Reproducibles: Student Handout—Lesson 84

Basic Principle: Acids, bases, and salts are three classes of compounds that form ions in water solutions.
Science Competency: Students will list the properties of acids, bases, and salts.
Reproducibles: Student Handout—Lesson 85

Basic Principle: Acids, bases, and salts are three classes of compounds that form ions in water solutions.
Science Competency: Students will identify acids as hydrogen-ion-donating and bases as hydrogen-ion-accepting substances.
Reproducibles: Student Handout—Lesson 86

Basic Principle: Acids, bases, and salts are three classes of compounds that form ions in water solutions.

Science Competency: Students will solve problems of heat flow using known values of specific heat.
Reproducibles: Student Handout—Lesson 95

Basic Principle: Chemical reaction rates depend on factors that influence the frequency of collision among reactant molecules.
Science Competency: Students will explain that the rate of reaction is the decrease in concentration of reactants, or the increase in the concentration of products with time.
Reproducibles: Student Handout—Lesson 96

Basic Principle: Chemical reaction rates depend on factors that influence the frequency of collision among reactant molecules.
Science Competency: Students will show how reaction rates depend on such factors as concentration, temperature, and pressure.
Reproducibles: Student Handout—Lesson 97

Basic Principle: Chemical reaction rates depend on factors that influence the frequency of collision among reactant molecules.
Science Competency: Students will show how reaction rates depend on such factors as concentration, temperature, and pressure.
Reproducibles: Student Handout—Lesson 98

Basic Principle: Chemical equilibrium is a dynamic process at the molecular level.
Science Competency: Students will show that equilibrium is established when forward and reverse reaction rates are equal.
Reproducibles: Student Handout—Lesson 99

Basic Principle: Chemical equilibrium is a dynamic process at the molecular level.
Science Competency: Students will use Le Chatelier's Principle to predict the effect of changes in concentration, temperature, and pressure on chemical reactions in equilibrium.
Reproducibles: Student Handout—Lesson 100

Basic Principle: The bonding characteristics of carbon lead to many different molecules with varied sizes, shapes, and chemical properties, providing the chemical basis of life.
Science Competency: Students will show that large polymers such as carbohydrates, lipids, proteins, and nucleic acids are formed by repetitive combinations of smaller subunits.
Reproducibles: Student Handout—Lesson 101

Basic Principle: The bonding characteristics of carbon lead to many different molecules with varied sizes, shapes, and chemical properties, providing the chemical basis of life.
Science Competency: Students will identify the subunits of carbohydrates, lipids, proteins, and nucleic acids.
Reproducibles: Student Handout—Lesson 102

Basic Principle: Nuclear processes are those in which the atomic nucleus changes, including radioactive decay of naturally occurring and artificial isotopes, nuclear fission, and nuclear fusion.

SCIENCE ESSENTIALS

HIGH SCHOOL LEVEL

Lessons and Activities for Test Preparation

Section I: Biology

LESSONS AND ACTIVITIES

Lesson 1 Students will show how a semipermeable membrane regulates a cell's interactions with its environment.

Lesson 2 Students will show how enzymes catalyze biochemical reactions.

Lesson 3 Students will show how prokaryotic cells, eukaryotic cells, and viruses differ in complexity and general structure.

Lesson 4 Students will describe the flow of information from the transcription of RNA in the nucleus to the translation of proteins on ribosomes in the cytoplasm.

Lesson 5 Students will describe the role of the endoplasmic reticulum and Golgi apparatus in the secretion of proteins.

Lesson 6 Students will show that energy captured from sunlight by chloroplasts is stored in plants in the form of starch.

Lesson 7 Students will describe the role of mitochondria in making stored chemical bond energy available to cells by completing the breakdown of glucose to carbon dioxide.

Lesson 8 Students will explain how polysaccharides, macromolecules essential for the healthy functioning of living cells, are synthesized from a small collection of simple precursors.

Lesson 9 Students will explain how lipids, macromolecules essential for the healthy functioning of living cells, are synthesized from a small collection of simple precursors.

Lesson 10 Students will explain how proteins, macromolecules essential for the healthy functioning of living cells, are synthesized from a small collection of simple precursors.

Lesson 11 Students will explain how nucleic acids such as DNA, which carry the genetic code of living organisms, are synthesized from a small collection of simple precursors.

Lesson 12 Students will identify stages of mitosis.

Lesson 13 Students will identify stages of meiosis.

Lesson 14 Students will identify different types of chromosomal alterations.

Lesson 15 Students will explain how crossing over during meiosis increases the variability of traits within a species.

Lesson 16 Students will explain how male gametes form.

Biology-Contents *(Continued)*

BIOLOGY PRACTICE TEST

Lesson 1: Teacher Preparation

Basic Principle   Fundamental life processes depend on a variety of chemical reactions carried out in specialized cell organelles.

Competency   Students will show how a semipermeable membrane regulates a cell's interactions with its environment.

Materials   test tubes, Ehrlenmeyer flasks, ring stands with clamps, eyedroppers, wet cellophane or goldbeater's membranes, rubber bands, water, 1% solution of phenolphthalein indicator, ammonium hydroxide, goggles, apron

Procedure

1. Give students time to read the information on *Diffusion Across a Semipermeable Membrane*.
2. Draw the illustrations to show how a teaspoon of sugar diffuses in water to become an evenly mixed solution of sugar-water.
3. Give students time to complete the activity and the *Observations & Analysis* section.
4. Draw and discuss the illustration showing how oxygen and carbon dioxide diffuse across the semipermeable cell membrane of a single-celled amoeba.

Answers to Observations & Analysis

1. The phenolphthalein solution turned pink.
2. Vaporized molecules of ammonium hydroxide, a base containing hydroxide ions, diffused through the air and into the test tube filled with phenolphthalein. Since phenolphthalein turns pink in the presence of a base, the solution in the test tube turned pink.
3. The membrane must be porous to allow small molecules to move across it.
4. The membranes of living cells must also be porous to allow nutrients and gases, such as oxygen and carbon dioxide, to pass in and out of the cell.

DIFFUSION OF SUGAR IN WATER

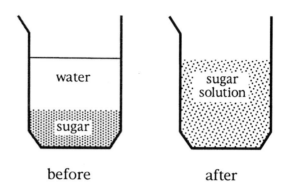

water

sugar

before

sugar
solution

after

DIFFUSION OF GASES ACROSS AN AMOEBA'S CELL MEMBRANE

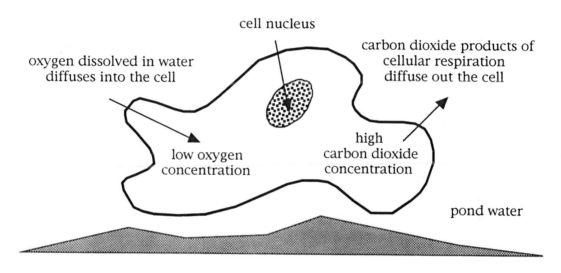

cell nucleus

oxygen dissolved in water
diffuses into the cell

carbon dioxide products of
cellular respiration
diffuse out the cell

low oxygen
concentration

high
carbon dioxide
concentration

pond water

Biology

STUDENT HANDOUT–LESSON 1

Basic Principle   Fundamental life processes depend on a variety of chemical reactions carried out in specialized cell organelles.

Objective   Show how a semipermeable membrane regulates a cell's interactions with its environment.

Materials   test tube, Ehrlenmeyer flask, ring stand with clamp, eyedropper, wet cellophane or goldbeater's membrane, rubber band, water, 1% solution of phenolphthalein indicator, ammonium hydroxide, goggles, apron

Procedure

1. Read the information section here.

Diffusion Across a Semipermeable Membrane

Diffusion is the random movement of molecules from regions of high concentration to regions of low concentration. For example, a teaspoon of sugar added to water will diffuse throughout the water until the concentration of sugar molecules is the same everywhere in solution. In living cells, diffusion is essential to the transport of nutrients and waste products across the cell membrane. The cell membranes of all living cells are composed of large macromolecules of lipid (i.e., fat), a substance present in the walls of soap bubbles, that allows smaller molecules (i.e., oxygen, carbon dioxide, glucose, amino acids) to pass in and out of the cell.

---

2. **WEAR GOGGLES AND AN APRON TO PREVENT INJURY AND DAMAGE TO CLOTHING.**

3. Fill the test tube with water and add a few drops of phenolphthalein indicator. Phenolphthalein, although clear in plain water, turns pink in the presence of a base containing hydroxide ions such as NaOH, $Ca(OH)_2$, or NH_4OH.

4. Cover the mouth of the test tube with wet cellophane or goldbeater's membrane, and secure the wrapping tightly with a rubber band. Invert and clamp the test tube to the ring stand as shown in the illustration.

5. Pour 200 mL of ammonium hydroxide, formula NH_4OH, into the Ehrlenmeyer flask, and place the flask directly under the test tube.

6. Complete the *Observations & Analysis* section.

Observations & Analysis

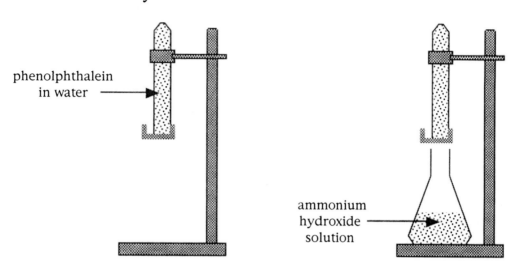

phenolphthalein
in water

ammonium
hydroxide
solution

1. Describe what happened when the ammonium hydroxide solution was placed directly under the inverted test tube.

   _____

   _____

2. Explain why this occurred.

   _____

   _____

   _____

3. Describe the characteristics of the membrane that allowed this phenomenon to take place.

   _____

   _____

   _____

4. Why is it important for the membranes of living cells to have a structure similar to the membrane used in this experiment?

   _____

   _____

   _____

   _____

Biology

Lesson 2: Teacher Preparation

Basic Principle   Fundamental life processes depend on a variety of chemical reactions carried out in specialized cell organelles.

Competency   Students will show how enzymes catalyze biochemical reactions.

Materials   500-mL beaker, 100-mL graduated cylinder, rubber tubing, glass tubing, 3 1-holed rubber stoppers to fit a large test tube, 3 large test tubes, test-tube rack, stopwatch, knife, turnips, beef liver, 3% hydrogen peroxide, water, goggles, apron

Procedure

1. Explain that enzymes are *biological catalysts* that change the rate of biochemical reactions. They are generally large protein molecules designed to change a specific substrate. A *substrate molecule* is a molecule that is changed in an enzymatic reaction.

2. Draw the illustration to show the *Lock and Key Model of Enzyme Activity*.

3. Give students time to read the information on *The Enzyme Catalase* and write the chemical equation for the *Decomposition of Hydrogen Peroxide* to illustrate the reactants and products of this particular enzymatic reaction.

4. Give students time to complete the activity and the *Observations & Analysis* section.

Answers to Observations & Analysis

1. Turnips usually contain more catalase than beef liver and should therefore produce oxygen at a faster rate. There should be no reaction in the test tube containing only hydrogen peroxide. Students' measurements should confirm these facts.

2. The catalase present in the turnip sample seemed to be more effective at causing the decomposition of hydrogen peroxide.

LOCK AND KEY MODEL OF ENZYME ACTIVITY

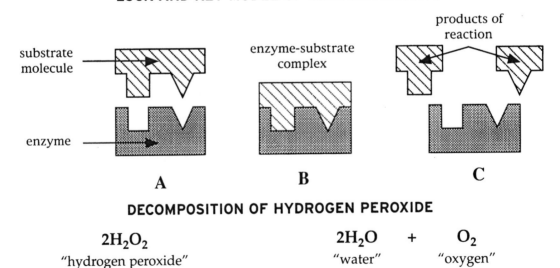

DECOMPOSITION OF HYDROGEN PEROXIDE

$$2H_2O_2 \qquad\qquad 2H_2O \quad + \quad O_2$$

"hydrogen peroxide"   "water"   "oxygen"

Name _____ **Date** _____

Biology

STUDENT HANDOUT–LESSON 2

Basic Principle Fundamental life processes depend on a variety of chemical reactions carried out in specialized cell organelles.

Objective Show how enzymes catalyze biochemical reactions.

Materials 500-mL beaker, 100-mL graduated cylinder, rubber tubing, glass tubing, 3 1-holed rubber stoppers to fit a large test tube, 3 large test tubes, test-tube rack, stopwatch, knife, turnips, beef liver, 3% hydrogen peroxide, water, goggles, apron

Procedure

1. Read the information section here.

The Enzyme Catalase

An *enzyme* is a protein molecule that changes the rate of a biochemical reaction. An iron-containing enzyme called *catalase* protects cells by preventing the buildup of hydrogen peroxide (H_2O_2), a toxic product of cellular metabolism. The enzyme is present in nearly all animal and plant cells, and accelerates the conversion of hydrogen peroxide molecules to harmless water and oxygen. The catalytic ability of the enzyme is truly amazing: A single molecule brings about the decomposition of 5,000,000 molecules of hydrogen peroxide per minute at 0°C. While iron atoms alone can split hydrogen peroxide into water and oxygen at a much slower rate, it would take three centuries for a single iron atom to do the work done in one second by a single catalase molecule.

---

2. WEAR GOGGLES AND AN APRON TO PREVENT INJURY AND DAMAGE TO CLOTHING.

3. Use a knife to carefully mince marble-sized pieces of turnip and beef liver.

4. Fill the 500-mL beaker two-thirds full of water. Fill the 100-mL graduated cylinder with water. Invert the cylinder into the beaker, making sure that no air leaks into the cylinder. Insert the free end of the rubber tubing into the inverted cylinder as shown in the illustration showing the *Experimental Setup*.

5. Fill the first large test tube one-third full with a fresh 3% hydrogen peroxide solution and secure it in a test-tube rack.

6. Place the minced turnip into the first hydrogen peroxide solution and immediately cap the tube with the rubber stopper. Record the time it takes for a fixed amount of oxygen (i.e., 10 mL) to bubble into the cylinder. Or, record the amount of oxygen in the cylinder after a fixed amount of time (i.e., 5 minutes).

7. Repeat Steps 3 through 5 with the second hydrogen peroxide solution using minced beef liver instead of minced turnip.

8. Repeat Steps 3 through 5 using only the hydrogen peroxide solution.

9. Complete the *Observations & Analysis* section.

EXPERIMENTAL SETUP

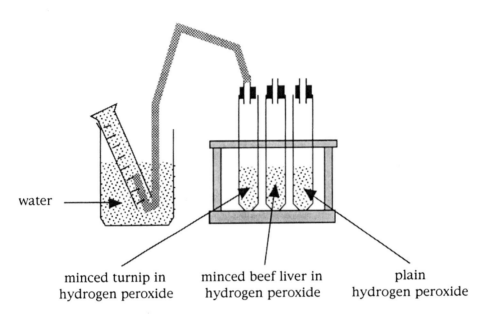

water

minced turnip in
hydrogen peroxide

minced beef liver in
hydrogen peroxide

plain
hydrogen peroxide

Observations & Analysis

1. Describe your observations of the reaction that took place in each test tube. Include the measurements you made using the stopwatch and graduated cylinder.

_____

_____

_____

2. Compare and contrast the effectiveness of the catalase present in turnips to the effectiveness of the catalase present in beef liver.

_____

_____

_____

 **Biology**

Lesson 3: Teacher Preparation

Basic Principle   Fundamental life processes depend on a variety of chemical reactions carried out in specialized cell organelles.

Competency   Students will show how prokaryotic cells, eukaryotic cells, and viruses differ in complexity and general structure.

Procedure

1. Give students time to read the information on *Prokaryotic Cells, Eukaryotic Cells, and Viruses.*

2. Introduce the work of the English scientist Robert Hooke (1635–1702). Hooke's microscopic observations of "cella" or "small compartments" in living tissue convinced him that living organisms were composed of clearly open cavities or "vesicles" which he called *cells*. Point out that the reductionist notion of chemists and physicists of the time guided biologists to a "globular theory" of living tissue which suggested that living matter was a composite of proteinaceous globules as small as 0.003 millimeters in diameter. The French physiologist Henri Dutrochet (1776–1847) combined the "vesicular" and "globule theories" into a more general theory of living microstructure; but, his ideas were largely abandoned in the face of enormous diversity among microscopic structures observed in plants and animals. The idea that all organisms could be composed of a common structural unit seemed ludicrous to biologists of his time. The German biologists Theodor Schwann (1810–1882) and Matthias Jakob Schleiden (1804–1881) finally proposed the "cell theory" in 1839, based on Schleiden's examination of germinal plant tissues. In 1838, Schleiden announced that plant organs were derived from plant cells, an idea that Schwann expanded to animals the following year. The German botanist Hugo von Mohl (1805–1872) coined the term "protoplasm" to describe the fluid material inside cells and was the first to describe the *cell membrane* and *nucleus* as structures common to all cells. Mohl also described the movement of water across the cell membrane and the cell's ability to govern its internal environment by this process of *osmosis*. The invention of the *electron microscope* in 1933 by the German physicist Ernst August Friedrich Ruska (1906–1988) caused a revolution in cellular biology by permitting the detailed examination of the multitude of *cellular organelles*: mitochondria, chloroplasts, and endoplasmic reticulum.

3. Give students time to complete the *Observations & Analysis* section.

Answers to Observations & Analysis

1. Paragraphs will vary, but should include the following main points: Prokaryotes do not have a well-defined nucleus and few, if any, of the specialized cell organelles present in eukaryotes. Eukaryotes have a well-defined nucleus and other cell organelles that carry out specific metabolic functions. A virus is merely a set of hereditary instructions enclosed in a protective shell.

2. A virus is unlike a living cell because it can neither sense nor respond, grow nor repair itself; and, it requires a host cell to supply it with the materials it needs to reproduce.

Biology

STUDENT HANDOUT–LESSON 3

Basic Principle Fundamental life processes depend on a variety of chemical reactions carried out in specialized cell organelles.

Objective Show how prokaryotic cells, eukaryotic cells, and viruses differ in complexity and general structure.

Procedure

1. Read the information section.

Prokaryotic Cells, Eukaryotic Cells, and Viruses

Cells are membrane-bound pieces of living matter that organize matter and energy in their environment in order to accomplish the following life-defining chores: (1) Living cells sense the conditions of their environment; (2) they respond to environmental conditions in an effort to maintain *homeostasis*; (3) they grow and repair injuries; and (4) they reproduce. Cells are the basic unit of all living things formed by the division of "parent" cells. Cells may work together to create *multicellular organisms* such as plants and animals comprised of many millions of individual cells. The essential features of a cell are its *membrane*, which regulates the flow of matter in and out of the cell; the *cytoplasm*, a jelly-like mixture of life-sustaining nutrients and *cell organelles* subserving particular metabolic functions; *ribosomes*, ribonucleoprotein particles that serve as the site of protein synthesis; and *deoxyribonucleic acid* (or DNA), which forms the hereditary material that determines the structure of enzymes and the overall architecture of the organism. *Prokaryotes* are single-celled organisms that lack specialized organelles such as *nuclei, mitochondria,* or *chloroplasts*. The DNA of a prokaryote forms rings called *plasmids*, instead of *chromosomes*, and is not confined in a cell nucleus. All *bacteria* and *cyanobacteria* are prokaryotes. All other living organisms are *eukaryotes*, characterized by a well-defined cell nucleus bound by a *nuclear membrane*. The DNA of a eukaryote is stored in its cell nucleus. Eukaryote cells may also contain a variety of specialized cell organelles such as mitochondria and chloroplasts. A *virus* is an infectious particle of matter consisting primarily of hereditary information (i.e., either DNA or RNA—*ribonucleic acid*) enclosed in a *glycoprotein* shell. A virus does little more than reproduce itself and requires a host organism to supply it with the matter and energy necessary to accomplish this task. In the process of reproduction, a virus disrupts the metabolic activity of its host cell, causing any number of diseases including chickenpox, herpes, rabies, and AIDS.

---

2. Examine the handout illustrations. Then complete the *Observations & Analysis* section.

PROKARYOTE BACILLUS

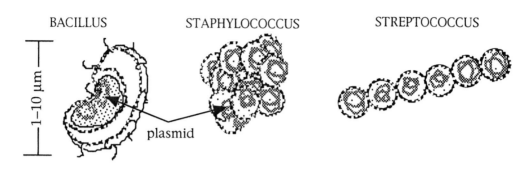

BACILLUS   STAPHYLOCOCCUS   STREPTOCOCCUS

1–10 μm

plasmid

EUKARYOTE PROTISTS

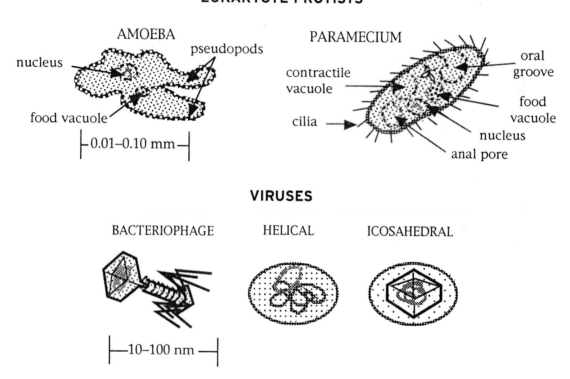

AMOEBA

nucleus

pseudopods

food vacuole

0.01–0.10 mm

PARAMECIUM

contractile vacuole

cilia

oral groove

food vacuole

nucleus

anal pore

VIRUSES

BACTERIOPHAGE   HELICAL   ICOSAHEDRAL

10–100 nm

Observations & Analysis

1. On the back of this sheet, write a short paragraph that compares and contrasts the defining characteristics of prokaryotes, eukaryotes, and a virus.

2. Which of the three is most unlike a living cell? Explain your answer on the back of this sheet.

Lesson 4: Teacher Preparation

Basic Principle   Fundamental life processes depend on a variety of chemical reactions carried out in specialized cell organelles.

Competency   Students will describe the flow of information from the transcription of RNA in the nucleus to the translation of proteins on ribosomes in the cytoplasm.

Procedure

1. Give students time to read the information on *Transcription and Translation of Genetic Information*.

2. Point out that the rediscovery of Gregor Mendel's (1822–1884) work in 1900 by Dutch botanist Hugo Marie de Vries (1848–1935) and its subsequent popularization by English geneticist William Bateson (1861–1926) marked the rebirth of the science of genetics. The discovery inspired American geneticists Thomas Hunt Morgan (1866–1945) and Herman Muller (1890–1967) to examine the effects of X-rays and toxic chemicals on the chromosomes of the common fruit fly *Drosophila melongaster*. They discovered that damage to chromosomes was the direct cause of genetic mutations. While many geneticists sought to further understand the role of chromosomes in the transmission of hereditary information and the mutation process, others sought to elucidate the biochemical structure of the chromosome. The pioneering work of English biochemist Dorothy Mary Crowfoot Hodgkin (1910–1994) in the field of X-ray crystallography allowed microbiologists to deduce the three-dimensional structure of a variety of organic molecules such as calciferol (i.e., vitamin D2) and cholesterol. With the assistance of the brilliant biophysicist and X-ray crystallographer Rosalind Elsie Franklin (1920–1958), molecular biologists James Dewey Watson (b. 1928) and H.C. Francis Crick (b. 1916) succeeded in constructing a three-dimensional model of deoxyribonucleic acid (DNA). Their model of the double helix allowed molecular biologists to elucidate how genetic information is "transcribed" in the nucleus, then "translated" into the production of proteins in the cytoplasm.

3. Give students time to complete the *Observations & Analysis* section.

Answer to Observations & Analysis

Paragraphs will vary, but should include the following main points: The term "transcription" refers to the transfer of coded information from DNA to mRNA. This occurs in the nucleus of living cells. The term "translation" refers to the manufacture of proteins on the ribosome using the information encoded in mRNA. This latter process occurs in the cytoplasm.

Name _____ Date _____

Biology

STUDENT HANDOUT–LESSON 4

Basic Principle   Fundamental life processes depend on a variety of chemical reactions carried out in specialized cell organelles.

Objective   Describe the flow of information from the transcription of RNA in the nucleus to the translation of proteins on ribosomes in the cytoplasm.

Procedure

1. Read the information section.

Transcription and Translation of Genetic Information

The central dogma of molecular biology outlines the biochemical mechanisms by which genetic information stored in the nucleic acid, *deoxyribonucleic acid (DNA)*, is translated into the production of *proteins*. Proteins comprise the vast variety of macromolecules that give living things their structure (i.e., collagens that form connective tissue) and regulate metabolic activity (i.e., enzymes). In all living cells, DNA molecules store the codes required to guide the manufacture of specific proteins. Each code is comprised of a sequence of biochemical units called *nucleotides* arranged in a specified order. Each nucleotide consists of three smaller units, a *deoxyribose sugar*, a *phosphate*, and any one of four *nitrogenous bases* (i.e., the *purines*, *adenine* and *guanine*, and the *pyrimidines*, *thymine* and *cytosine*). In the nucleus of every cell, nucleotides along an exposed strand of DNA lure matching nucleotides floating free in the nucleoplasm by electromagnetic van der Waals' forces (i.e., hydrogen bonding). The attracted nucleotides form a complimentary strand of *ribonucleic acid (RNA)* that carries the "transcribed" genetic message. This process is called *transcription*. A strand of RNA is composed of ribose sugars, rather than deoxyribose sugars, phosphates, and a sequence of nucleic acids: adenine, guanine, *uracil*, and cytosine. A strand of RNA does not contain thymine. Adenine on DNA is complimentary to uracil; thymine on DNA matches adenine; and guanine is attracted to cytosine. The finished strand of RNA, called *messenger RNA (mRNA)*, exits the nucleus. In the cytoplasm, a strand of mRNA is attracted to the surface of a ribonucleoprotein called a *ribosome*. Short segments of RNA, called *transfer RNA (tRNA)*, float free in the cytoplasm around the ribosome. Each segment of tRNA is linked to one of 20 amino acids (i.e., glycine, alanine, valine, leucine, etc.). The tRNA molecules are attracted to the complimentary nucleotide sequence on the mRNA that is stuck to the ribosome. The ribosome behaves like an "assembly-line enzyme" connecting the amino acids on the tRNA, one to another, in the proper sequence transcribed from the genetic code. This step in the process of protein synthesis is called *translation*.

---

2. Examine the handout illustrations. Then complete the *Observations & Analysis* section.

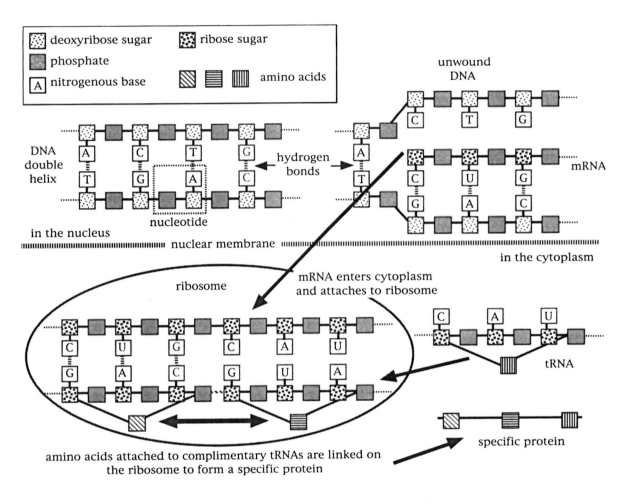

Observations & Analysis

Explain how "transcription" differs from "translation" in terms of molecular biology.

Lesson 5: Teacher Preparation

Basic Principle   Fundamental life processes depend on a variety of chemical reactions carried out in specialized cell organelles.

Competency   Students will describe the role of the endoplasmic reticulum and Golgi apparatus in the secretion of proteins.

Procedure

1. Give students time to read the information on *Endoplasmic Reticulum and Golgi Apparatus*.
2. Point out that the Golgi apparatus is named for the Italian anatomist Camillo Golgi (1843–1926) who first described it in 1898.
3. Give students time to complete the *Observations & Analysis* section.

Answers to Observations & Analysis

1. Paragraphs will vary, but should include the following main points: The endoplasmic reticulum is a membranous network of laminae and cisternae, continuous with the nuclear membrane. The primary function of the endoplasmic reticulum is to transport and secrete proteins manufactured on the ribosomes that cover its surface.
2. Paragraphs will vary, but should include the following main points: The Golgi apparatus is flattened pouches containing vesicles for the absorption and secretion of store proteins such as hormones.

Biology

STUDENT HANDOUT–LESSON 5

Basic Principle   Fundamental life processes depend on a variety of chemical reactions carried out in specialized cell organelles.

Objective   Describe the role of the endoplasmic reticulum and Golgi apparatus in the secretion of proteins.

Procedure

1. Read the information section.

Endoplasmic Reticulum and Golgi Apparatus

The *endoplasmic reticulum (ER)* is a cell organelle comprised of a folded, double-layered membranous network present in the cytoplasm of all eucaryotic cells. It is continuous with the nuclear membrane and is comprised of tubules, swollen vacuoles called *cisternae*, and flattened membranes called *lamellae*. Ribosomes containing messenger ribonucleic acid (mRNA) responsible for protein synthesis cover the ER lamellae. The ER secretes proteins manufactured on the ribosome for use by the rest of the cell. The Golgi apparatus is a cell organelle found in the cytoplasm of all eukaryotic cells. It may serve as a storage site for newly synthesized proteins and can be thought of as a "packaging" system for hormone secretions. The Golgi apparatus consists of a series of flattened pouches and round membranous vesicles. The apparatus absorbs the products of the endoplasmic reticulum by accepting them into small vesicles. It then transports these proteinaceous products to larger vesicles where they are delivered to other parts of the cell.

---

2. Study the handout illustrations and complete the *Observations & Analysis* section.

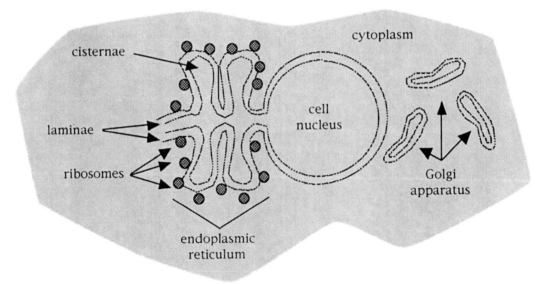

Observations & Analysis

1. Describe the structural features and primary function of the endoplasmic reticulum.

_____

_____

_____

_____

_____

_____

2. Describe the structural features and primary function of the Golgi apparatus.

_____

_____

_____

_____

_____

_____

Lesson 6: Teacher Preparation

Basic Principle   Fundamental life processes depend on a variety of chemical reactions carried out in specialized cell organelles.

Competency   Students will show that energy captured from sunlight by chloroplasts is stored in plants in the form of starch.

Materials   hot plates, 150-mL beakers, 500-mL beakers, water, Lugol's solution, petri dish, healthy green leafy plant, aluminum foil, tape, tongs, ethyl alcohol, eyedroppers, goggles, heat-resistant gloves, apron

Procedure

1. Prepare for this lesson several days in advance. (1) Tape aluminum foil across one half of a sufficient number of the healthy green leaves of a living plant (e.g., geranium leaves work great) so that each group of students can have one leaf. (2) Place the plant in sunlight, or two feet from a bright 75-watt bulb, for 24–48 hours (i.e., 12 hours light, then 12 hours dark). (3) Prepare Lugol's solution by dissolving 10 grams of potassium iodide (e.g., KI) in 100 mL of distilled water, then add 5 grams of iodine crystals. Lugol's solution tests for the presence of starch and can be purchased from any laboratory supply house.

2. Give students time to read the information on *Photosynthesis*.

3. Begin discussion by pointing out that all living things organize energy to perform basic life activities. Review how all plants obtain their energy from the Sun, trapping the energy in chlorophyll located in chloroplasts.

4. Draw the illustration of a *Chloroplast* to identify structures involved in photosynthesis.

5. Write the chemical equation that describes photosynthesis and be sure students understand the formulas for the reactants and products.

$$\underset{6CO_2}{\overset{\text{"carbon dioxide"}}{}} \quad + \quad \underset{6H_2O}{\overset{\text{"water"}}{}} \quad \xrightarrow{\text{sunlight}} \quad \underset{C_6O_{12}O_6}{\overset{\text{"sugar"}}{}} \quad + \quad \underset{6O_2}{\overset{\text{"oxygen"}}{}}$$

6. Point out that the element iodine present in Lugol's solution can be used to identify starch present in plant or animal tissue.

7. Give students time to complete the activity and the *Observations & Analysis* section.

Answers to Observations & Analysis

1. Drawings will vary with the positions of starch deposits, but should indicate more stain in the part of the leaf that was not covered with foil.

2. The aluminum foil taped over the leaf prevented that part of the leaf from producing starch.

3. The fact that the leaf could not manufacture starch in the half that was covered with foil indicates that plants require sunlight to successfully produce starch.

CHLOROPLAST

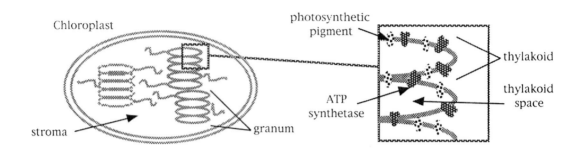

Chloroplast

photosynthetic pigment

thylakoid

ATP synthetase

thylakoid space

stroma

granum

EXPERIMENTAL SETUP

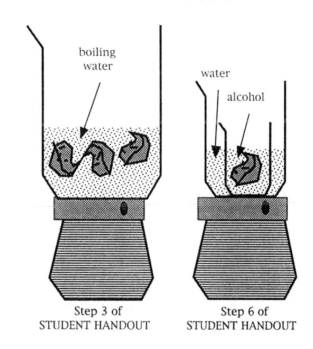

boiling water

water

alcohol

Step 3 of
STUDENT HANDOUT

Step 6 of
STUDENT HANDOUT

SAMPLE LEAF STAINED WITH LUGOL'S SOLUTION

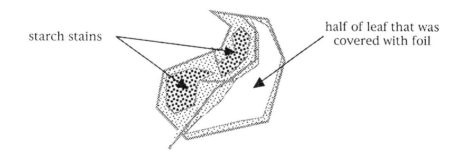

starch stains

half of leaf that was covered with foil

Biology

STUDENT HANDOUT–LESSON 6

Basic Principle   Fundamental life processes depend on a variety of chemical reactions carried out in specialized cell organelles.

Objective   Show that energy captured from sunlight by chloroplasts is stored in plants in the form of starch.

Materials   hot plate, 150-mL beaker, 500-mL beaker, water, Lugol's solution, petri dish, healthy green leafy plant, aluminum foil, tape, tongs, ethyl alcohol, eyedropper, goggles, heat-resistant gloves, apron

Procedure

1. Read the information on *Photosynthesis*.

Photosynthesis

The cells of green plants have incorporated an organelle called a *chloroplast* that contains a remarkable molecule called *chlorophyll*. Chlorophyll has the ability to absorb and store solar energy. Plants use the stored energy absorbed by chlorophyll molecules to promote the production of sugar and molecular *oxygen* and *sugar* from *water* and *carbon dioxide*. The process is called *photosynthesis*. The sugar is later polymerized to form macromolecules of starch.

---

2. **WEAR GOGGLES, HEAT-RESISTANT GLOVES, AND AN APRON. BOILING WATER AND ALCOHOL CAN CAUSE SERIOUS INJURY.** Be sure you are familiar with the proper way to use the hot plate.

3. Carefully remove the aluminum foil from the leaf provided by your instructor and place it in the large beaker of boiling water on the instructor's lab table.

4. While waiting for the leaf to boil 5 minutes, pour 250 mL water into a large 500-mL beaker and place the beaker on a hot plate on medium-high setting.

5. Pour 100 mL of ethyl alcohol into a 150-mL beaker and place the smaller beaker into the larger beaker on the hot plate.

6. Place the boiled leaf into the 150-mL beaker of alcohol and wait 5–10 minutes for the leaf to lose its green color.

7. Use tongs to remove the wet leaf from the alcohol and turn off the hot plate.

8. Rinse the leaf and place it in a petri dish.

9. Use an eyedropper to soak the leaf with Lugol's solution for 3–5 minutes before rinsing the leaf again.

10. Hold the leaf up to the light and examine the blackish areas of starch remaining in the leaf.

11. Complete the *Observations & Analysis* section.

Observations & Analysis

1. Draw the leaf before and after it has been stained with Lugol's solution.

2. How did the aluminum foil taped over the leaf effect the leaf's ability to produce starch?

   _____

   _____

   _____

   _____

   _____

   _____

3. Explain how this experiment gives evidence that plants require sunlight to successfully produce starch.

   _____

   _____

   _____

   _____

   _____

   _____

Lesson 7: Teacher Preparation

Basic Principle   Fundamental life processes depend on a variety of chemical reactions carried out in specialized cell organelles.

Competency   Students will describe the role of mitochondria in making stored chemical bond energy available to cells by completing the breakdown of glucose to carbon dioxide.

Procedure

1. Give students time to read the information on *Mitochondria*.

2. Point out that mitochondria are the site of *oxidative phosphorylation*. Following glycolysis, the conversion of glucose to pyruvate in the cytoplasm of the cell, mitochondria employ molecular oxygen, and a number of membrane-bound enzymes, to add energy-rich phosphate groups to molecules of adenosine diphosphate and guanosine triphosphate. The energy stored in the chemical bonds comprising these two molecules is used to drive cellular metabolism. Cells may contain from several hundred to several hundred thousand mitochondria depending upon the size of the host cell.

3. Assist students in identifying the membranous structures of the mitochondria and associated ATP, GDP, and CO_2 production sites.

4. Write the chemical equation describing the process of *aerobic respiration* to illustrate the relationship between that process and the function of mitochondria.

5. Give students time to complete the activity and the *Observations & Analysis* section.

Answer to Observations & Analysis

Paragraphs will vary, but should include the following main points: Mitochondria are sites of oxidative phosphorylation where pyruvate, the product of glycolysis, is converted to a series of molecules during the production of the energy-rich substances ATP and GTP. The energy stored in the chemical bonds comprising these two molecules is used to drive cellular metabolism.

AEROBIC RESPIRATION AND MITOCHONDRIA

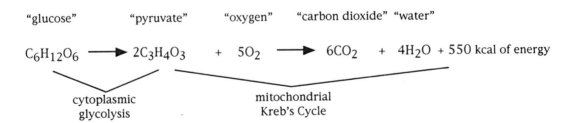

"glucose"   "pyruvate"   "oxygen"   "carbon dioxide" "water"

$$C_6H_{12}O_6 \longrightarrow 2C_3H_4O_3 \ + \ 5O_2 \longrightarrow 6CO_2 \ + \ 4H_2O + 550 \text{ kcal of energy}$$

cytoplasmic
glycolysis

mitochondrial
Kreb's Cycle

This summary of the Kreb's Cycle shows that 1 mole of glucose is converted to 2 moles of pyruvate, which in combination with 5 moles of molecular oxygen is transformed to 6 moles of carbon dioxide, 4 moles of water, and 550 kilocalories of energy stored in the chemical bonds of ATP and GTP.

Name _____   Date _____

Biology

STUDENT HANDOUT–LESSON 7

Basic Principle   Fundamental life processes depend on a variety of chemical reactions carried out in specialized cell organelles.

Objective   Describe the role of mitochondria in making stored chemical bond energy available to cells by completing the breakdown of glucose to carbon dioxide.

Procedure

1. Read the information on *Mitochondria*.

Mitochondria

Mitochondria are cell organelles that provide living organisms with energy through the process of aerobic respiration. Mitochondria contain enzymes capable of converting *pyruvate*, the product of glucose metabolism which begins in the cytoplasm, to *adenosine triphosphate (ATP)* and *guanosine triphosphate (GTP)*. These two molecules contain energy-rich chemical bonds that can be broken to release the energy that drives the cell's metabolic activities. The organelles are similar in size to bacteria, measuring 5 to 10 micrometers in length and 0.5 to 1 micrometer in width. They are comprised of a smooth outer membrane and a folded inner membrane called the *matrix*. The fluid within the matrix contains numerous enzymes, ribosomes, and strands of both RNA and DNA. The fact that mitochondria contain their own DNA suggests that these organelles are the descendents of ancient prokaryotes that formed a symbiotic relationship with neighboring primeval cells. Although cellular respiration begins in the cytoplasm with glycolysis, the breakdown of glucose to form pyruvate, the process is completed along the folded *cristae* of the matrix where the Kreb's Cycle and electron transport produce ATP and GTP.

---

2. Examine the handout illustrations. Then complete the *Observations & Analysis* section.

STRUCTURE OF A MITOCHONDRION

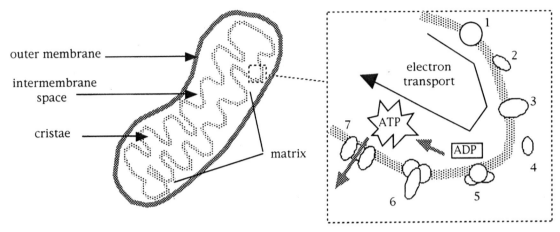

Enzymes associated with electron transport

1. NADH Reductase
2. Coenzyme Q
3. Cytochrome B
4. Cytochrome C
5. Cytochrome Oxidase
6. ATP Synthetase
7. Channel protein

KREB'S CYCLE

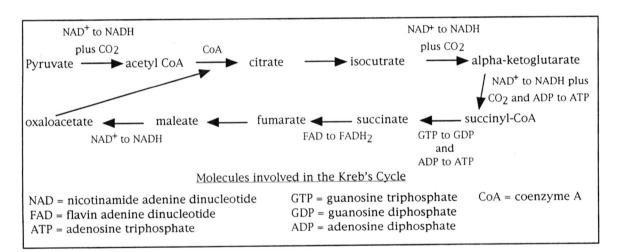

Molecules involved in the Kreb's Cycle

NAD = nicotinamide adenine dinucleotide
FAD = flavin adenine dinucleotide
ATP = adenosine triphosphate

GTP = guanosine triphosphate
GDP = guanosine diphosphate
ADP = adenosine diphosphate

CoA = coenzyme A

Observations & Analysis

Write a brief paragraph describing the primary function of mitochondria.

_____

_____

_____

_____

_____

_____

Lesson 8: Teacher Preparation

Basic Principle   Fundamental life processes depend on a variety of chemical reactions carried out in specialized cell organelles.

Competency   Students will explain how polysaccharides, macromolecules essential for the healthy functioning of living cells, are synthesized from a small collection of simple precursors.

Materials   molecular modeling kits *or* modeling clay and toothpicks

Procedure

1. Give students time to read the information on *Polysaccharides*.
2. Emphasize the fact that polysaccharides, like the other molecules of life (i.e., proteins, lipids, and nucleic acids) are all formed by dehydration synthesis.
3. Assist students in completing the activity and the *Observations & Analysis* section.

Answers to Observations & Analysis

1. Polysaccharides are formed by the linking of smaller saccharides in a reaction called dehydration synthesis. Dehydration synthesis involves the loss of a water molecule between the small saccharide molecules that link to form the larger polysaccharide.
2. See the diagram.

A SIMPLE POLYSACCHARIDE

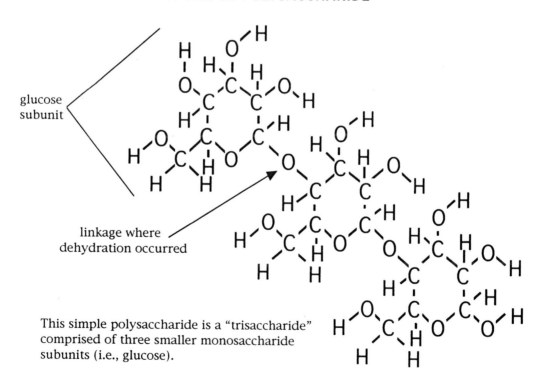

This simple polysaccharide is a "trisaccharide" comprised of three smaller monosaccharide subunits (i.e., glucose).

27

Biology

STUDENT HANDOUT–LESSON 8

Basic Principle   Fundamental life processes depend on a variety of chemical reactions carried out in specialized cell organelles.

Objective   Explain how polysaccharides, macromolecules essential for the healthy functioning of living cells, are synthesized from a small collection of simple precursors.

Materials   molecular modeling kits *or* modeling clay and toothpicks

Procedure

1. Read the information on *Polysaccharides*.

Polysaccharides

Polysaccharides are long-chain *carbohydrates* composed of hundreds or thousands of linked simple sugars called *monosaccharides*. The simplest saccharide is glucose ($C_6H_{12}O_6$). Monosaccharides combine in a chemical reaction called *dehydration synthesis*. During dehydration synthesis, a molecule of water (i.e., 2 hydrogen atoms and 1 oxygen atom) is removed from two monosaccharide molecules to form a polysaccharide chain. Polysaccharides are natural polymers, serving primarily as an energy source in both plants (i.e., starch) and animals (i.e., glycogen). They also give the cell walls of plant cells their sturdy structure (i.e., cellulose) and form the hard exoskeleton of insects (i.e., chitin).

---

2. Use the materials provided by your instructor to build a ringed molecule of glucose like the one shown in the handout illustration.

3. Link your molecule with the molecules of other students to create a small polysaccharide chain by dehydration synthesis.

4. Examine the handout illustration. Then complete the *Observations & Analysis* section.

SYNTHESIS OF A POLYSACCHARIDE

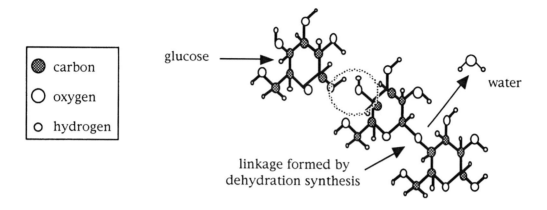

carbon
oxygen
hydrogen

glucose

water

linkage formed by
dehydration synthesis

Observations & Analysis

1. A synthesis reaction is a reaction in which two or more elements or compounds form a more complex compound. Explain how the synthesis of a polysaccharide differs from that of most other synthesis reactions.

   _____

   _____

   _____

   _____

2. Draw a structural diagram for the short polysaccharide you built with the aid of your classmates.

Lesson 9: Teacher Preparation

Basic Principle Fundamental life processes depend on a variety of chemical reactions carried out in specialized cell organelles.

Competency Students will explain how lipids, macromolecules essential for the healthy functioning of living cells, are synthesized from a small collection of simple precursors.

Materials molecular modeling kits *or* modeling clay and toothpicks

Procedure

1. Give students time to read the information on *Lipids*.
2. Emphasize the fact that lipids, like the other molecules of life (i.e., polysaccharides, proteins, and nucleic acids) are all formed by dehydration synthesis.
3. Assist students in completing the activity and the *Observations & Analysis* section.

Answers to Observations & Analysis

1. Answers will vary but should contain the following main points: Both lipids and polysaccharides are formed by dehydration synthesis. However, the subunits that form lipids are fatty acids and glycols; while the subunits that form polysaccharides are saccharides.
2. See the diagram.

A SIMPLE LIPID

fatty acids

glycerol

linkages where
dehydration occurred

Name _____ **Date** _____

Biology

STUDENT HANDOUT–LESSON 9

Basic Principle   Fundamental life processes depend on a variety of chemical reactions carried out in specialized cell organelles.

Objective   Explain how lipids, macromolecules essential for the healthy functioning of living cells, are synthesized from a small collection of simple precursors.

Materials   molecular modeling kits *or* modeling clay and toothpicks

Procedure

1. Read the information on *Lipids*.

Lipids

Fats—also called *lipids*—help to form an organism's protective tissues. Fats also serve as a secondary source of energy after an organism's carbohydrate supply has been exhausted. Like carbohydrates, fats are also produced by dehydration synthesis. The illustration shows three hydrocarbon chains called "fatty acids" and a molecule of "glycerol" ($C_3H_8O_3$) combining to make a lipid molecule.

---

2. Use the materials provided by your instructor to build a fatty acid or glycerol molecule.

3. Link your molecule with the molecules of other students to create a small lipid by dehydration synthesis.

4. Examine the handout illustration. Then complete the *Observations & Analysis* section.

SYNTHESIS OF A LIPID

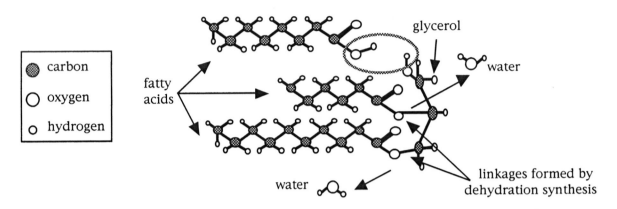

Observations & Analysis

1. Compare and contrast the synthesis of a lipid to that of a polysaccharide.

   _____

   _____

   _____

   _____

   _____

   _____

   _____

2. Draw a structural diagram for the lipid you built with the aid of your classmates.

 **Biology**

Lesson 10: Teacher Preparation

Basic Principle   Fundamental life processes depend on a variety of chemical reactions carried out in specialized cell organelles.

Competency   Students will explain how proteins, macromolecules essential for the healthy functioning of living cells, are synthesized from a small collection of simple precursors.

Materials   molecular modeling kits *or* modeling clay and toothpicks

Procedure

1. Give students time to read the information on *Proteins*.
2. Emphasize the fact that proteins, like the other molecules of life (i.e., polysaccharides, lipids, and nucleic acids) are all formed by dehydration synthesis.
3. Assist students in completing the activity and the *Observations & Analysis* section.

Answers to Observations & Analysis

1. Answers will vary but should contain the following main points: Proteins, lipids, and polysaccharides are all formed by dehydration synthesis. But while proteins are made of smaller subunits called amino acids, the subunits that form lipids are fatty acids and glycols. The subunits that form polysaccharides are saccharides.
2. See the diagram.

A SIMPLE PROTEIN

valine   alanine   glycine

(diagram of a tripeptide molecule showing valine, alanine, and glycine with peptide bonds indicated)

peptide bonds
where dehydration occurred

This simple protein is a polypeptide (i.e., a tripeptide) composed of three amino acids: valine, alanine, and glycine.

Biology

STUDENT HANDOUT–LESSON 10

Basic Principle   Fundamental life processes depend on a variety of chemical reactions carried out in specialized cell organelles.

Objective   Explain how proteins, macromolecules essential for the healthy functioning of living cells, are synthesized from a small collection of simple precursors.

Materials   molecular modeling kits *or* modeling clay and toothpicks

Procedure

1. Read the information on *Proteins*.

Proteins

Proteins give organisms their structure. All organs, including muscle and bone, are made of protein. The building blocks of proteins are molecules called *amino acids*. There are about 20 different amino acids in nature. Different combinations of amino acids give rise to the millions of proteins that exist in nature. As shown in the handout illustration, the amino acids *valine, alanine,* and *glycine* are joined by dehydration synthesis to produce a protein. The linkage between the amino ($^-NH_2$) group of one amino acid and the acid group (^-COOH) of another amino acid is called a *peptide bond*. For this reason, proteins are also referred to as *polypeptides*.

---

2. Use the materials provided by your instructor to build one or more amino acid like the one shown in the handout illustration.

3. Link your amino acids with those of other students to create a small protein chain by dehydration synthesis.

4. Examine the handout illustration. Then complete the *Observations & Analysis* section.

SYNTHESIS OF A PROTEIN

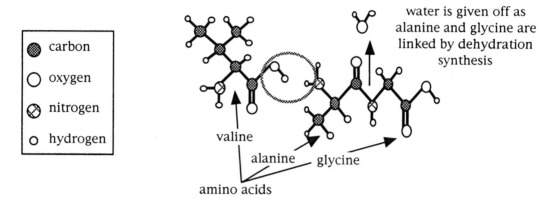

water is given off as
alanine and glycine are
linked by dehydration
synthesis

carbon

oxygen

nitrogen

hydrogen

valine

alanine   glycine

amino acids

Observations & Analysis

1. Compare and contrast the synthesis of a protein to that of a lipid and polysaccharide.

_____

_____

_____

_____

_____

_____

2. Draw a structural diagram for the protein you built with the aid of your classmates.

Lesson 11: Teacher Preparation

Basic Principle   Fundamental life processes depend on a variety of chemical reactions carried out in specialized cell organelles.

Competency   Students will explain how nucleic acids such as DNA, which carry the genetic code of living organisms, are synthesized from a small collection of simple precursors.

Materials   molecular modeling kits *or* modeling clay and toothpicks

Procedure

1. Give students time to read the information on *Nucleic Acids*.

2. Emphasize the fact that nucleic acids, like the other molecules of life (i.e., polysaccharides, lipids, and proteins) are all formed by dehydration synthesis.

3. Point out that the individuals of a given species share about 99% of their genetic material. All humans, for example, share about 99.9% of their genes. Single-letter differences in the DNA sequences that comprise our more than 100,000 genes (i.e., differences in the sequence of nitrogenous bases, A = adenine, C = cytosine, G = guanine, and T = thymine, that make up the genetic code) account for our individual variability. These single-letter differences are called *single nucleotide polymorphisms*, or *SNPs* ("snips").

4. Assist students in completing the activity and the *Observations & Analysis* section.

Answers to Observations & Analysis

1. Answers will vary but should contain the following main points: Nucleic acids, proteins, lipids, and polysaccharides are all formed by dehydration synthesis. However, each kind of macromolecule is composed of different kinds of subunits. Nucleic acids are made of nucleotides built from simple sugars, phosphates, and nitrogenous bases. Proteins are made of amino acids. Lipids are made of fatty acids and glycols. Polysaccharides are made of smaller saccharides.

2. See the diagram.

A SIMPLE NUCLEIC ACID

deoxyribose
sugar

phosphate

adenine

cytosine

guanine

thymine

Biology

STUDENT HANDOUT–LESSON 11

Basic Principle   Fundamental life processes depend on a variety of chemical reactions carried out in specialized cell organelles.

Objective   Explain how nucleic acids such as DNA, which carry the genetic code of living organisms, are synthesized from a small collection of simple precursors.

Materials   molecular modeling kits *or* modeling clay and toothpicks

Procedure

1. Read the information on *Nucleic Acids*.

Nucleic Acids

Nucleic acids carry the "hereditary features" of every living organism. The instructions for assembling the particular proteins that determine an organism's unique physical characteristics (i.e., eye color, hair color, body shape) are passed from one generation to the next by these long-chained organic compounds. Nucleic acids are formed by dehydration synthesis from smaller units called *nucleotides*. Nucleotides are arranged in a coded sequence and held together on a chain made of *phosphates* and *sugars*. In the handout illustration, water molecules are released during the joining of deoxyribose sugars and phosphates that serve as the "backbone" of the larger nucleic acid. Molecules called *nitrogenous bases*, the *purines* (i.e., *adenine* and *guanine*) and *pyrimidines* (i.e., *thymine* and *cytosine*), attach to the deoxyribose-phosphate molecule to form a nucleotide. The nucleotides are then joined to form a large macromolecule called *deoxyribonucleic acid (DNA)*. The sequence of nucleotides along the DNA macromolecule determines the proteins that a living organism will synthesize.

---

2. Use the materials provided by your instructor to build a phosphate, deoxyribose, purine, or pyrimidine molecule.

3. Link your molecule with the molecules of other students to create a small section of a DNA macromolecule by dehydration synthesis.

4. Examine the handout illustration. Then complete the *Observations & Analysis* section.

SYNTHESIS OF A NUCLEIC ACID

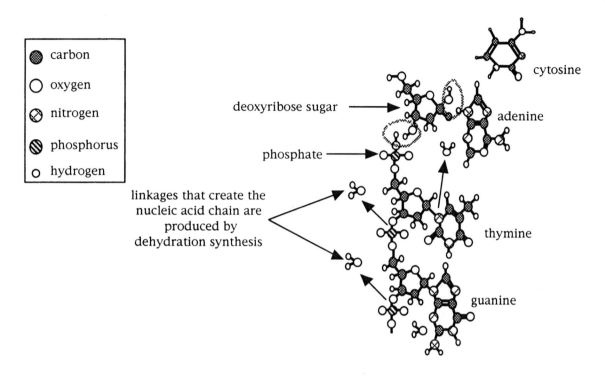

- ● carbon
- ○ oxygen
- ⊘ nitrogen
- ◍ phosphorus
- ○ hydrogen

deoxyribose sugar

phosphate

cytosine

adenine

thymine

guanine

linkages that create the
nucleic acid chain are
produced by
dehydration synthesis

Observations & Analysis

1. Compare and contrast the synthesis of a nucleic acid to that of a lipid, polysaccharide, and protein.

   _____

   _____

   _____

   _____

   _____

   _____

   _____

2. Draw a structural diagram for the nucleic acid you built with the aid of your classmates.

Lesson 12: Teacher Preparation

Basic Principle   All living organisms are composed of cells capable of reproduction.

Competency   Students will identify stages of mitosis.

Procedure

1. Give students time to read the information on *Mitosis*.

2. Point out that a clear understanding of how cells reproduce was not possible until the development of adequate staining techniques and the construction of microscopes able to magnify and resolve images on the order of several thousand times. It was not until the 1860s that biologists could clearly see cells dividing to form "daughter cells," having first accomplished a division of the "parent cell's" nuclear material. The German biologist Walther Flemming (1843–1905) is recognized for his accomplishments in this line of study. Flemming is credited for coining the term "mitosis" and for describing the duplication of the easily stained "threadlike" nuclear structures called chromosomes (i.e., meaning "colored bodies"). By 1879, Flemming had described several stages of mitosis although the terminology he used has since been changed. Flemming also reported that reproductive cells, gametes like sperm and eggs, divided without reproducing their chromosomes first, a process he called "meiosis." This observation was later explained by the German botanist Eduard Adolf Strasburger (1844–1912). Strasburger clarified the role of chromosomes in heredity by concluding that fertilization required the joining of "haploid" cells: cells having a single set of chromosomes instead of the usual duplicate set present in diploid cells. Strasburger is also credited for coining the terms "nucleoplasm" (i.e., the region inside the cell nucleus), "cytoplasm" (i.e., the region outside the cell nucleus), and "chloroplast" (i.e., the structure in which photosynthesis takes place).

3. Assist students in completing the activity and the *Observations & Analysis* section.

Answer to Observations & Analysis

See the diagram.

STAGES OF MITOSIS

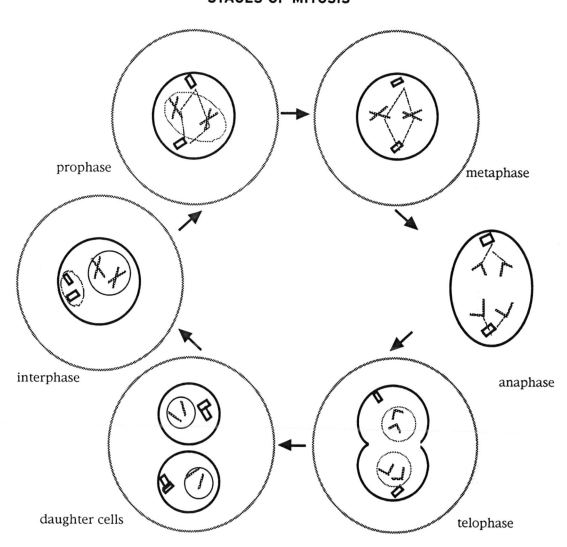

prophase

metaphase

interphase

anaphase

daughter cells

telophase

Biology

STUDENT HANDOUT–LESSON 12

Basic Principle   All living organisms are composed of cells capable of reproduction.

Objective   Identify stages of mitosis.

Procedure

1. Read the information on *Mitosis*.

Mitosis

All multicellular organisms grow and repair injuries by reproducing the cells that comprise their body tissues. This is accomplished by the division of healthy cells that grow to replace injured cells. The process of cell division is called *mitosis*. Mitosis occurs in stages: *interphase, prophase, metaphase, anaphase, telophase,* and *cytokinesis*. Beginning at interphase, the chromosomes carrying the hereditary information of the parent cell are duplicated within the confines of the nuclear membrane. In prophase, the nuclear membrane begins to dissolve and tiny cylindrical-shaped *centrioles* escape the confines of a structure called a *centrosome*. The centrioles spread apart and throw out spindle fibers that attach to freed chromosomes. During metaphase the centrioles move to opposite poles of the cell as chromosomes align at the midline of the cell. During anaphase, the duplicated chromosomes split apart and are dragged to opposite poles of the cell. A *cleavage furrow* begins to form around the equator of the cell at the start of telophase and begins to pinch the cell in half. The final division and separation into two completely independent *daughter cells* is called cytokinesis (i.e., meaning "cells in motion"). Each daughter cell begins a life cycle of its own.

---

2. Examine the handout illustrations. Then complete the *Observations & Analysis* section.

Observations & Analysis

1. Examine the diagrams representing different phases of mitosis.
2. Redraw the diagrams in their correct sequence.

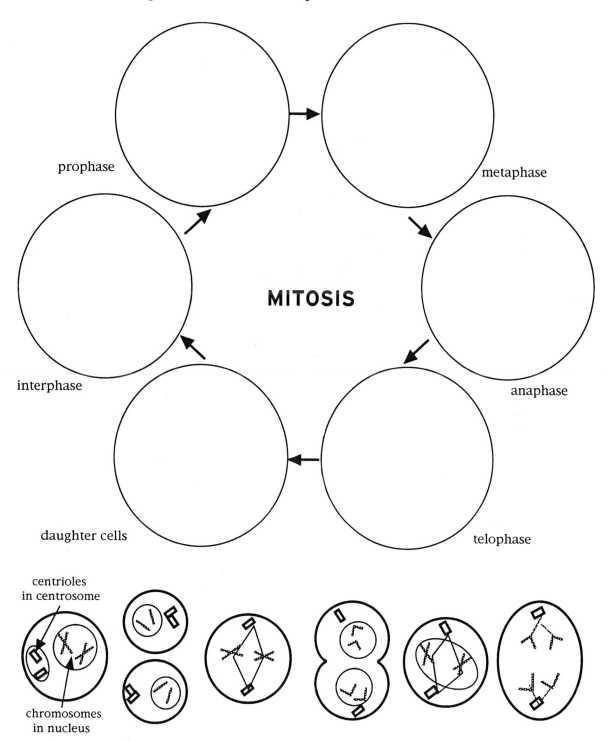

Lesson 13: Teacher Preparation

Basic Principle   Mutation and sexual reproduction lead to genetic variation in a population.

Competency   Students will identify stages of meiosis.

Procedure

1. Give students time to read the information on *Meiosis*.
2. Assist students in completing the *Observations & Analysis* section.

Answers to Observations & Analysis

1. Answers will vary, but should include the following main points: Meiosis results in the production of haploid sex cells containing half the number of chromosomes present in all the other cells of an organism. Mitosis results in the production of cells with the same number of chromosomes as the parent cell.

2. Answers will vary, but should include the following main points: Meiosis A resembles mitosis in that the phase begins with the duplication of chromosomes. At the start of Meiosis B, the germ cell fails to duplicate its chromosomes and divides, leaving the daughter cells with half as much genetic material.

Biology

STUDENT HANDOUT–LESSON 13

Basic Principle   Mutation and sexual reproduction lead to genetic variation in a population.

Objective   Identify stages of meiosis.

Procedure

1. Read the information on *Meiosis*.

Meiosis

Meiosis is the process of cell division that results in the formation of sex cells called *gametes*. The process occurs in the cells of reproductive organs and is sometimes called *reduction division* since the gametes produced contain half the number of chromosomes of the parent cell. A parent cell that contains a full complement of chromosomes is a *diploid* cell. Sex cells contain only half that number of chromosomes and are, therefore, referred to as *haploid* cells. The *zygote*, or "offspring" cell, formed at fertilization by the fusion of a male (i.e., sperm) and female (i.e., egg) gamete is a diploid cell. Meiosis occurs in stages similar to the stages of *mitosis* (i.e., diploid cell division to produce diploid daughter cells): prophase, metaphase, anaphase, and telophase. The process involves two cycles of cell division: Meiosis A and Meiosis B. During Meiosis A a reproductive *germ cell* divides mitotically to produce two diploid daughter cells. At the start of Meiosis B, the daughter cells fail to duplicate their chromosomes and divide again to produce haploid cells. These haploid cells then differentiate into male sperm or female eggs depending upon the gender instructions carried in the genetic code.

---

2. Examine the handout illustrations. Then complete the *Observations & Analysis* section.

MEIOSIS A

centrioles
in centrosome

duplicated
chromosomes
in nucleus

prophase   metaphase   anaphase   telophase

MEIOSIS B OF A SINGLE DAUGHTER GERM CELL

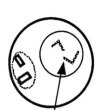  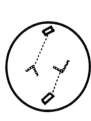   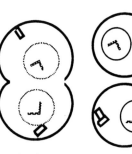

chromosomes
fail to duplicate

prophase   metaphase   anaphase   telophase

Observations & Analysis

1. Explain how meiosis differs from mitosis.

   _____

   _____

   _____

   _____

   _____

2. Explain how Meiosis A differs from Meiosis B.

   _____

   _____

   _____

   _____

   _____

Lesson 14: Teacher Preparation

Basic Principle   Mutation and sexual reproduction lead to genetic variation in a population.

Competency   Students will identify different types of chromosomal alterations.

Procedure

1. Give students time to read the information on *Chromosomal Alterations*.
2. Assist students in completing the *Observations & Analysis* section.

Answer to Observations & Analysis

Answers will vary, but should include the following main points: During deletion, gene "D" was lost. During inversion, gene segment "BC" was flipped to change the sequence of genetic information. During translocation, gene segments "CD" and "HI" exchanged places on their respective chromosomes. During duplication, gene "C" was replicated and the reproduced segment was incorporated into the same chromosome.

Biology

STUDENT HANDOUT–LESSON 14

Basic Principle   Mutation and sexual reproduction lead to genetic variation in a population.

Objective   Identify different types of chromosomal alterations.

Procedure

1. Read the information on *Chromosomal Alterations*.

Chromosomal Alterations

Mutations are alterations in the genetic instructions that give organisms their particular physical traits. Mutations that increase the number of variations of a particular trait are caused by different types of *chromosomal alterations*. These alterations include *deletion, inversion, translocation,* and *duplication*. When chromosomal alterations occur in sperm or egg cells, they may be passed on from one generation to the next. Deletion results in the loss of a *gene*, a section of chromosome (i.e., genetic information) responsible for the production of a protein underlying a specific trait. Inversion involves the "flipping" of a section of chromosome which changes the sequence of genetic instructions. Translocation results in the transfer of a gene from one chromosome to another. Duplication involves the "doubling" of a gene segment. Chromosomal alterations play an important role in evolution by increasing the variety of traits that come under selective pressure through the mechanism of natural selection.

---

2. Examine the handout illustrations. Then complete the *Observations & Analysis* section.

TYPES OF CHROMOSOMAL ALTERATIONS

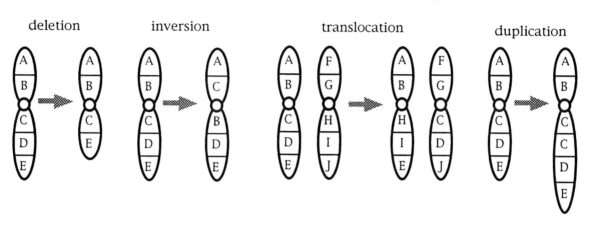

Observations & Analysis

Use the lettered "genes" to explain precisely what occurred during each type of chromosomal alteration.

_____

_____

_____

_____

_____

_____

_____

_____

_____

_____

_____

_____

_____

_____

_____

_____

_____

_____

_____

 **Biology**

Lesson 15: Teacher Preparation

Basic Principle   Mutation and sexual reproduction lead to genetic variation in a population.

Competency   Students will explain how crossing over during meiosis increases the variability of traits within a species.

Procedure
1. Give students time to read the information on *Crossing Over*.
2. Assist students in completing the *Observations & Analysis* section.

Answers to Observations & Analysis
1. Answers will vary, but should include the following main points: Gene segments "DE" and "IJ" exchanged positions to alter the sequence of genetic instructions on two of the chromosomes comprising the tetrad.
2. Answers will vary, but should include the following main points: By altering the sequence of genetic instructions, making them different from those of the chromosomes in the parent cell, new proteins underlying new traits might be expressed in the next generation of offspring.

Biology

STUDENT HANDOUT–LESSON 15

Basic Principle   Mutation and sexual reproduction lead to genetic variation in a population.

Objective   Explain how crossing over during meiosis increases the variability of traits within a species.

Procedure

1. Read the information on *Crossing Over*.

Crossing Over

Crossing over occurs during the production of gametes. During the first prophase of meiosis, duplicated chromosome pairs form *tetrads* (i.e., groups of four chromosomes) that can become entangled. Entangled gene segments may translocate and become incorporated into other tetrad partners. As meiosis proceeds, the chromosomes separate and come to reside in separate gametes having chromosomes whose sequence of genetic instructions is unlike that of the original germ cell. Like other forms of chromosomal alteration, crossing over increases the variety of trait combinations within a given species.

---

2. Examine the handout illustrations. Then complete the *Observations & Analysis* section.

CROSSING OVER

site of gene crossover

duplicated pairs
of chromosomes

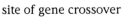

crossover occurs
in the tetrad

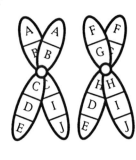

resulting tetrad

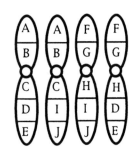

separated chromosomes
that will form haploid
gametes

Observations & Analysis

1. Use the lettered "genes" to explain precisely what occurred during this crossover.

_____

_____

_____

_____

_____

_____

_____

2. Explain how crossover increases the variety of traits within a species.

_____

_____

_____

_____

_____

_____

_____

_____

_____

Lesson 16: Teacher Preparation

Basic Principle   Mutation and sexual reproduction lead to genetic variation in a population.

Competency   Students will explain how male gametes form.

Procedure

1. Give students time to read the information on *Spermatogenesis*.
2. Assist students in completing the *Observations & Analysis* section.

Answers to Observations & Analysis

1. Answers will vary, but should contain the following main points: Primary spermatocytes, like most other cells of the organism, are diploid and contain twice the number of chromosomes as that of haploid secondary spermatocytes.
2. Answers will vary, but should contain the following main points: Secondary spermatocytes lack the motility of sperm cells which have a head, body, and tail.

Biology

STUDENT HANDOUT–LESSON 16

Basic Principle   Mutation and sexual reproduction lead to genetic variation in a population.

Objective   Explain how male gametes form.

Procedure

1. Read the information on *Spermatogenesis.*

Spermatogenesis

The formation of male gametes is called *spermatogenesis.* It takes place in the *seminiferous tubules* within the *testes* and results in the formation of haploid sex cells called *sperm.* Diploid germ cells called *spermatogonia* divide to form *primary spermatocytes* that undergo meiosis to form *secondary spermatocytes.* The secondary spermatocytes undergo a second meiosis and go on to form sperm cells. Every sperm cell has a head, body, and tail. The head incorporates a nucleus, containing genetic information from the male parent. The body contains mitochondria that provide the sperm with energy. The tail, comprised of microfilaments, enables the cell to move.

---

2. Examine the handout illustrations. Then complete the *Observations & Analysis* section.

SPERM CELL

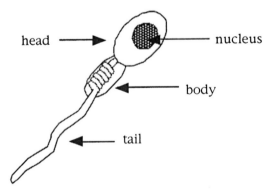

SPERMATOGENESIS–FIRST MEIOSIS

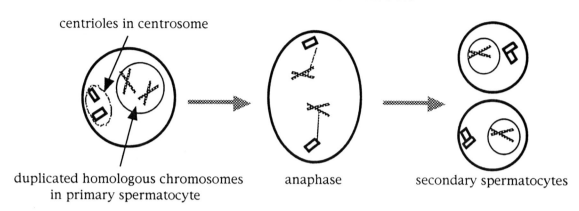

centrioles in centrosome

duplicated homologous chromosomes in primary spermatocyte

anaphase

secondary spermatocytes

SPERMATOGENESIS–SECOND MEIOSIS

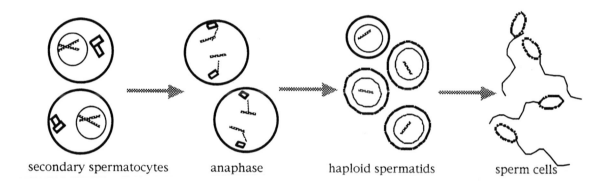

secondary spermatocytes

anaphase

haploid spermatids

sperm cells

Observations & Analysis

1. Explain how primary spermatocytes differ from secondary spermatocytes.

   _____

   _____

   _____

   _____

   _____

2. Explain how secondary spermatocytes differ from sperm cells.

   _____

   _____

   _____

   _____

   _____

Biology

Lesson 17: Teacher Preparation

Basic Principle   Mutation and sexual reproduction lead to genetic variation in a population.

Competency   Students will explain how female gametes form.

Procedure

1. Give students time to read the information on *Oogenesis*.
2. Assistant students in completing the *Observations & Analysis* section.

Answer to Observations & Analysis

Answers will vary, but should contain the following main points: Oogenesis results in the production of female gametes, while spermatogenesis results in the production of male gametes. A single egg cell is produced during oogenesis from one primary oocyte. In spermatogenesis, four sperm are produced from a single primary spermatocyte.

Name _____   **Date** _____

Biology

STUDENT HANDOUT–LESSON 17

Basic Principle   Mutation and sexual reproduction lead to genetic variation in a population.

Objective   Explain how female gametes form.

Procedure

1. Read the information on *Oogenesis*.

Oogenesis

The formation of female gametes is called *oogenesis*. It takes place in the *ovaries* and results in the formation of haploid sex cells called *eggs*. A diploid germ cell called a *primary oocyte* divides to form a *polar body* and a *secondary oocyte*. The polar body divides into two more polar bodies while the secondary oocyte undergoes a second meiotic division to form an egg cell and a third polar body. The three polar bodies have no functional value and disintegrate.

---

2. Examine the handout illustrations. Then complete the *Observations & Analysis* section.

OOGENESIS–FIRST MEIOSIS

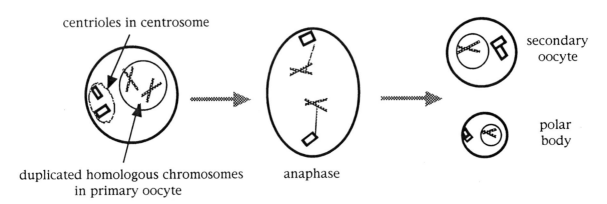

centrioles in centrosome

duplicated homologous chromosomes
in primary oocyte

anaphase

secondary
oocyte

polar
body

OOGENESIS–SECOND MEIOSIS

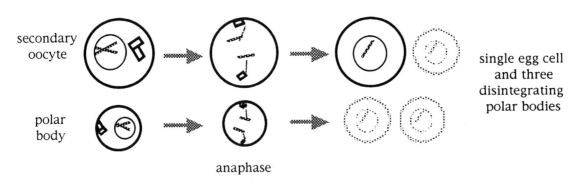

secondary
oocyte

polar
body

anaphase

single egg cell
and three
disintegrating
polar bodies

Observations & Analysis

Explain how oogenesis differs from spermatogenesis.

_____

_____

_____

_____

_____

_____

_____

_____

_____

_____

 **Biology**

Lesson 18: Teacher Preparation

Basic Principle   Mutation and sexual reproduction lead to genetic variation in a population.

Competency   Students will describe the process of fertilization.

Procedure

1. Give students time to read the information on *Fertilization*.
2. Assist students in completing the *Observations & Analysis* section.

Answers to Observations & Analysis

1. Answers will vary, but should contain the following main points: The zygote must contain the full complement of chromosomes appropriate to its species. Since fertilization involves the fusion of male and female sex cells, both sex cells must contain half that number of chromosomes.
2. Answers will vary, but should contain the following main points: Though organisms of the same species share the vast majority of traits, each parent has a unique set of individual traits inherited from their parents. The fusion of sperm and egg creates a new individual having a mixture of different traits from two different male grandparents and two different female grandparents.

Name _____   Date _____

Biology

STUDENT HANDOUT–LESSON 18

Basic Principle   Mutation and sexual reproduction lead to genetic variation in a population.

Objective   Describe the process of fertilization.

Procedure

1. Read the information on *Fertilization*.

Fertilization

The term *fertilization* refers to the stage of sexual reproduction in which a male gamete (i.e., sperm) fuses with a female gamete (i.e., egg). The resulting *zygote* (i.e., fertilized egg) contains a mixture of the genetic information from both parent cells. A sperm cell penetrating the outer membrane of the egg cell forms an *entrance cone*. The tail of the sperm is left outside the cell to be engulfed by leucocytes in the vaginal epithelium. The head of the sperm cell swells to become a *male pronucleus* which unites with the *female pronucleus*. The fusion of the two pronuclei gives the newly fertilized cell a unique combination of genetic material that increases the number of possible variations available to the gene pool of the species. Fertilization is followed, in either plants or animals, by the development of an *embryo*. During development, embryonic cells differentiate into a variety of specialized cells that comprise the tissues of a multicellular organism. Development continues throughout the life of the organism from birth into infancy, childhood, adolescence, and adulthood.

---

2. Examine the handout illustrations. Then complete the *Observations & Analysis* section.

STAGES OF FERTILIZATION

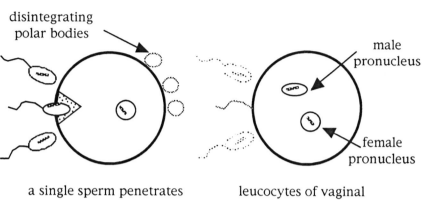
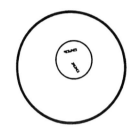

a single sperm penetrates the egg, creating an entrance cone

leucocytes of vaginal epithelium engulf remaining sperm

zygote with genetic information from both parents

Observations & Analysis

1. Explain why it is necessary for male and female gametes to be haploid.

_____

_____

_____

_____

_____

_____

_____

2. Explain why the fusion of sperm and egg increases the number of variations available to the gene pool of the species.

_____

_____

_____

_____

_____

_____

_____

Lesson 19: Teacher Preparation

Basic Principle A multicellular organism develops from a single zygote.

Competency Students will identify the stages of human embryonic development.

Procedure

1. Give students time to read the information on *Human Embryonic Development*.

2. Begin discussion with a brief introduction to the science of embryology. In 1651, the English physician William Harvey (1578–1657), who discovered the workings of the human circulatory system, published *On the Generation of Animals* in which he argued that the characteristics of all offspring were carried in the "primordial ovum" of the female. His views were supported by the discovery of egg follicles in the ovaries of both animals and human females (i.e., cadavers). By the end of the 18th century, sexual reproduction was considered the major method of procreation for all organisms of the Animal Kingdom. The Swedish botanist Carolus Linnaeus (1707–1778) identified the sexual organs of plants (i.e., male anthers, female ovules) and described the cells they contained (i.e., pollen and seeds) as analogous to the reproductive cells of humans that had been identified as "spermatic animalcules" and "seedlings" by the Dutch microscopist Anton von Leeuwenhoek (1632–1723). Leeuwenhoek had incorrectly argued that sperm carried the "preformed" human embryo, merely requiring the female womb as the site of complete development. Linnaeus argued that both male and female sex cells contributed the characteristics of the respective parents to their offspring. It was not until the work of the German zoologist Wilhelm August Oscar Hertwig (1849–1922) that it was clearly shown that fertilization involved the fusion of a sperm and an egg. The work of German zoologist Ernst Heinrich Philipp August Haekel (1834–1919) showed that the developing embryo passes through a series of stages that oddly resemble the evolutionary transitions made by living organisms from ancestral reptilian to human form. His view that "ontogeny recapitulates phylogeny" ultimately proved false, but stimulated much research in the area by laying a foundation for further embryological study.

3. Give students time to complete the *Observations & Analysis* section.

Answers to Observations & Analysis

1. See the diagram.

2. Answers will vary, but should contain the following main point: Since the blood of the mother intermingles with that of the developing embryo in the placenta, most anything that the mother ingests will reach the tissues of her unborn child.

STAGES OF HUMAN EMBRYONIC DEVELOPMENT

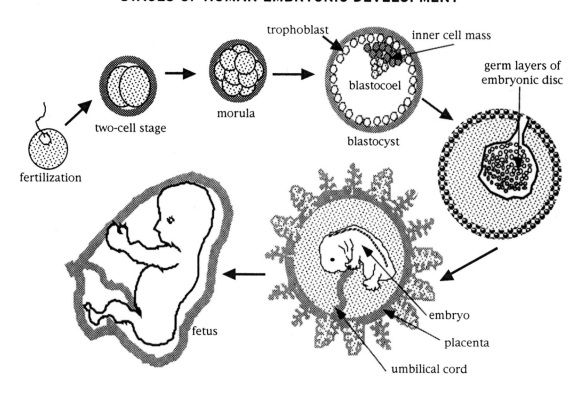

Biology

STUDENT HANDOUT–LESSON 19

Basic Principle   A multicellular organism develops from a single zygote.

Objective   Identify the stages of human embryonic development.

Procedure

1. Read the information on *Human Embryonic Development*.

Human Embryonic Development

Following the fusion of a male sperm and female egg during the act of fertilization, the fertilized egg, called a *zygote*, begins the process of *embryonic development*. Within the next several days, the zygote undergoes mitosis to form two cells, then four, then eight. The cells continue to divide, maintaining their size to become a tightly packed mass of about 32 cells called a *morula*. Division continues, increasing the number of cells to as many as 2,000. At this stage the cell complex is called a *blastocyst* and is comprised of cells that migrate to different positions around a central cavity called a *blastocoel*. The cells on one side of the blastocoel form the *trophoblast* which later becomes the *placenta*, or lining of the womb, where the embryo's capillaries intermingle with those of the mother's circulatory system. Nutrients filter from the mother to the embryo while embryonic wastes pass into the mother's circulation. The cells on the other side of the blastocoel, called the *inner cell mass*, become the *embryonic disc* which forms the developing embryo. The cells within the embryonic disc differentiate into three *germ layers* (i.e., ectoderm, mesoderm, endoderm) which eventually form the various organ systems of the body (i.e., nervous system, digestive system, skeletal and muscular systems). A four-week-old embryo with its *umbilical cord* firmly attached to the wall of the placenta is about 5 millimeters in length. By five weeks the embryo has developed a head, nerve cord, and limb buds. The first bones are formed at the end of the eighth to tenth week marking the start of the *fetal stage*. The developing fetus gestates for approximately another 28 weeks, its bones remaining soft for *parturition* (i.e., birth).

---

2. Complete the *Observations & Analysis* section.

STAGES OF HUMAN EMBRYONIC DEVELOPMENT

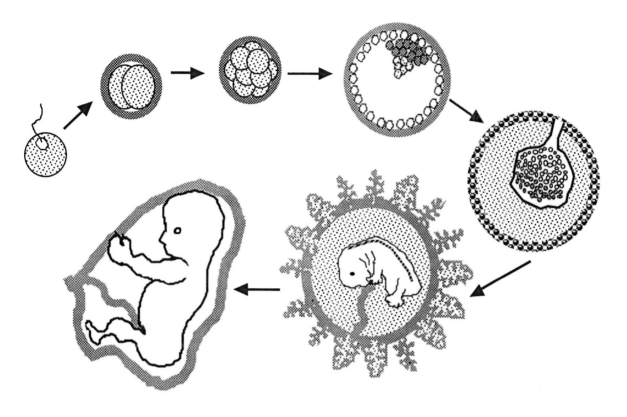

Observations & Analysis

1. Label the diagrams to identify the stages of human embryonic development.

2. Write a brief paragraph explaining why the eating habits of a pregnant woman have a direct impact on the developing embryo and fetus.

_____

_____

_____

_____

_____

_____

_____

_____

_____

_____

_____

 **Biology**

Lesson 20: Teacher Preparation

Basic Principle   A multicellular organism develops from a single zygote.

Competency   Students will identify the primordial germ layers that give rise to the organ systems of the body.

Procedure

1. Give students time to read the information on *Embryonic Germ Layers*.

2. Introduce the work of Russian scientists Christian Heinrich Pander (1794–1865) and Karl Ernst von Baer (1792–1876). These two embryologists were the first to maintain that an embryo has different structural layers (i.e., germ layers) which give rise to physiologically distinct adult tissues. They argued that development occurs "epigenetically" rather than by "preformation." William Harvey (1578–1657) used the term "epigenesis" in his book *On the Generation of Animals* to describe how germ material took on form in a gradual, step-by-step process. He believed that a uniform pattern of development took place in the egg after activation by an inseminating sperm. Other 17th-century scientists, on the other hand, believed that organisms existed in a "preformed" state that unfolded in the course of development. The argument was eventually resolved by Robert Remak (1815–1865) whose work emphasized the fact that the formation of germ layers and the later differentiation of tissues were both products of cell division.

3. Give students time to complete the *Observations & Analysis* section.

Answers to Observations & Analysis

1. Diagrams will vary, but should include the following drawings and labels: The left-hand fetus should include the esophagus, stomach, small intestine, large intestine, liver and gallbladder, pancreas, inner lining of lungs, and most endocrine glands; the center fetus should include skeletal bones, skeletal muscles, heart, arteries and veins, outer lining of lungs, and kidneys; the right-hand fetus should include skin and hair, nails and teeth, brain, spinal cord, nerves, sensory organs, and the pituitary gland.

2. Answers will vary, but should contain the following main point: The term "differentiation" refers to how cells become more and more different throughout embryonic development, becoming specialized to give rise to complex structures having particular functions within the organism.

Biology

STUDENT HANDOUT–LESSON 20

Basic Principle   A multicellular organism develops from a single zygote.

Objective   Identify the primordial germ layers that give rise to the organ systems of the body.

Procedure

1. Read the information about *Embryonic Germ Layers*.

Embryonic Germ Layers

By the third week of human embryonic development, cells begin to specialize their function in a process called *differentiation*. The cells of the embryonic disc form three distinguishable layers of cells that will eventually comprise the different organ systems of the body. These *germ layers* are the *ectoderm, mesoderm,* and *endoderm*. Some of the derivative organs of these germ layers are listed below.

ECTODERM	**MESODERM**	**ENDODERM**
skin and hair	skeletal bones	esophagus
nails and teeth	skeletal muscles	stomach
brain	heart	small intestine
spinal cord	arteries and veins	large intestine
nerves	outer lining of lungs	liver and gallbladder
sensory organs	kidneys	pancreas
pituitary gland		inner lining of lungs
		most endocrine glands

---

2. Study the handout illustrations. Then complete the *Observations & Analysis* section.

EMBRYONIC GERM LAYERS

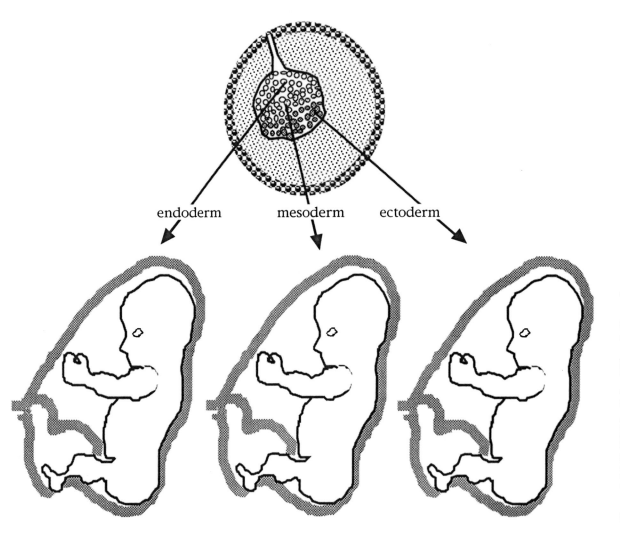

Observations & Analysis

1. Draw and label the derivative organs of each embryonic germ layer in the appropriate fetal diagram.

2. Explain what is meant by the term "differentiation."

_____

_____

_____

_____

_____

_____

Lesson 21: Teacher Preparation

Basic Principle   The phenotype of an organism depends on its genotype which is established at fertilization.

Competency   Students will use a Punnett Square to determine the genotypes and phenotypes of an organism resulting from a monohybrid cross.

Procedure

1. Give students time to read the information on *Mendelian Genetics*.

2. Inform students that hybridization in plants was a major curiosity of 18th-century biologists including Carolus Linneaus (1707–1778) who created the binomial system of classification. Linneaus believed that only a few members of every genus had been "divinely created" and that the rest were generated by the "crossing" of slightly different strains. According to Linneaus, hybridization was the basis of variation. Hybridization experiments continued until the middle of the 19th century when they were largely abandoned following Charles Darwin's (1809–1882) proposal that natural selection was the primary mechanism responsible for the diversity of species. However, Darwin could not account for the mechanism that gave rise to new variations. The practical uses of hybridization continue to this day, however, benefiting horticulturists and agriculturists in the search for new plant and breeding stock variations. In 1865, Gregor Mendel published a report entitled *Experiments in Plant Hybridization* in which he established the basic laws of of inheritance. The key point of his work was the assertion that reproductive cells carried "factors" that embodied the organic characters of living organisms (i.e., the gene concept). Mendel reported that some strains of pea plants bred true to their characteristics. That is, their offspring exhibited characteristics identical to those of the parent. Mendel noted that other strains, however, gave rise to offspring with variations that were a departure from the parents' traits, although they could be found elsewhere in members of related populations. By careful mathematical analysis of the plant populations he hybridized, Mendel was able to determine the statistical probability of producing particular traits in any population of offspring. He had, in effect, discovered the laws that governed the passing of traits from one generation to the next: the laws of heredity.

3. Give students time to complete the activity and the *Observations & Analysis* sections.

Answers to Observations & Analysis

1. See the Punnett Square. The offspring of the first and third plants of the second generation would be 50% hybrid tall and 50% purebred tall.

2. See the Punnett Square. The offspring of the second and fourth plants of the second generation would be 50% purebred short and 50% hybrid tall.

MONOHYBRID CROSS OF THE FIRST AND THIRD OFFSPRING
OF THE SECOND GENERATION

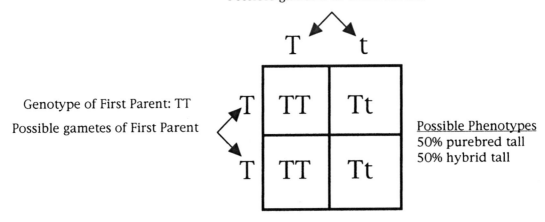

Genotype of Third Parent: Tt
Possible gametes of Third Parent

Genotype of First Parent: TT
Possible gametes of First Parent

Possible Phenotypes
50% purebred tall
50% hybrid tall

MONOHYBRID CROSS OF THE SECOND AND FOURTH OFFSPRING
OF THE SECOND GENERATION

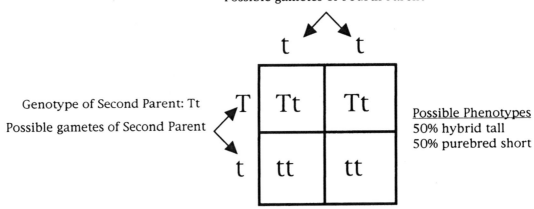

Genotype of Fourth Parent: tt
Possible gametes of Fourth Parent

Genotype of Second Parent: Tt
Possible gametes of Second Parent

Possible Phenotypes
50% hybrid tall
50% purebred short

Biology

STUDENT HANDOUT–LESSON 21

Basic Principle   The phenotype of an organism depends on its genotype, which is established at fertilization.

Objective   Use a Punnett Square to determine the genotypes and phenotypes of an organism resulting from a monohybrid cross.

Procedure

1. Read the information on *Mendelian Genetics*.

Mendelian Genetics

In the middle of the 18th century, an Austrian monk named Gregor Mendel (1822–1884) sought to understand how the traits of organisms are passed from one generation to the next. He defined a *trait* as any characteristic of an organism that makes it different from other organisms: such as the number of arms or legs an organism has; whether or not it has hair; whether or not it has skin, scales, or feathers. All members of a species have the same *species traits*. Species traits are those traits common to every member of a species (i.e., All trout have scales). *Individual traits* are variations of a trait among individuals of a particular species. Blue eyes and brown eyes, for example, are two individual traits for eye color, which is a species trait. Mendel discovered that traits were inherited in units that he called *genes*. Gene variations of a particular species trait (i.e., blue or brown eye pigment) he called *alleles*. Today, biologists know that genes, and their various alleles, are biochemically based units of information stored in the chromosomes of living cells. *Heredity* refers to the passing of those units from parents to offspring while the study of heredity is called *genetics*. Mendel's research was done mainly on common pea plants. He found that certain traits always passed from parents to their offspring while other traits "skipped" one or more generations before showing up in a descendant. Traits that are always passed from one generation to the next are called *dominant traits*. Traits that skip generations are called *recessive traits*. An organism that carries both dominant and recessive alleles for a trait is called a *hybrid*. An organism that has only dominant alleles or recessive alleles for a particular trait is *purebred* for that particular trait. The combination of genes present in the cells of an organism is called the organism's *genotype*. Traits "expressed" by genes, and visible to anyone who looks at the organism, is the organism's *phenotype*. Mendel summarized his ideas in three laws known today as *Mendel's Laws*: (1) Inherited traits can be either dominant or recessive. (2) Many traits are inherited in pairs. (3) Hybrids do not breed true.

---

2. Study the handout illustrations. Then complete the *Observations & Analysis* section.

A MONOHYBRID CROSS IN MENDEL'S PEA PLANTS

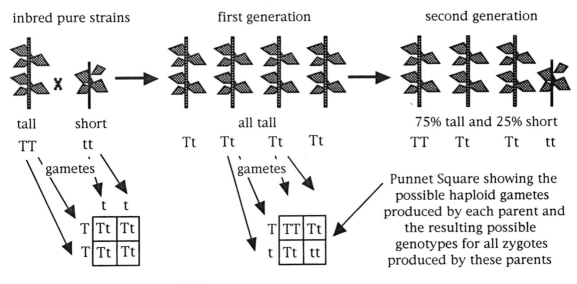

inbred pure strains   first generation   second generation

tall   short   all tall   75% tall and 25% short
TT   tt   Tt   Tt   Tt   Tt   TT   Tt   Tt   tt

gametes   gametes

	t	t
T	Tt	Tt
T	Tt	Tt

	T	t
T	TT	Tt
t	Tt	tt

Punnet Square showing the possible haploid gametes produced by each parent and the resulting possible genotypes for all zygotes produced by these parents

Crossing of pure strains results in hybrid offspring

Crossing of hybrids results in 25% purebred tall, 25% purebred short, and 50% hybrid tall offspring

Observations & Analysis

1. Use a Punnett Square to illustrate all possible genotypes and phenotypes of the offspring that could result from a crossing of the first and third offspring of the second generation. Note that "tall" is the dominant allele (T) for this particular "height" trait. What percentage of offspring will be hybrid tall?

2. Use a Punnett Square to illustrate all possible genotypes and phenotypes of the offspring that could result from a crossing of the second and fourth offspring of the second generation. Note that "tall" is the dominant allele (T) for this particular "height" trait. What percentage of offspring will be purebred short?

Lesson 22: Teacher Preparation

Basic Principle   The phenotype of an organism depends on its genotype which is established at fertilization.

Competency   Students will use a Punnett Square to determine the genotypes and phenotypes of an organism resulting from a dihybrid cross.

Procedure

1. Give students time to read the information on *Mendel's Law of Independent Assortment*.

2. Give students time to complete the *Observations & Analysis* section.

Answers to Observations & Analysis

1. There is a 3 in 16 chance that the offspring of the parents in the example will have wrinkled-yellow seeds (i.e., rrYY, rrYy, or rrYy). There is a 1 in 16 chance that the offspring of the parents in the example will have wrinkled-green seeds (i.e., rryy).

2. Male genotype: EEHh; female genotype: eehh. See the Punnett Square.

3. None of the offspring from this dihybrid cross will be two-eyed, one-horned Andromedans, since the male parent is purebred for the dominant one-eyed trait. All of his offspring must, therefore, be one-eyed.

POSSIBLE GENOTYPES OF A DIHYBRID CROSS

female genotype
(eehh)

female
gametes

		eh	eh	eh	eh
	EH	EeHh	EeHh	EeHh	EeHh
	EH	EeHh	EeHh	EeHh	EeHh
	Eh	Eehh	Eehh	Eehh	Eehh
	Eh	Eehh	Eehh	Eehh	Eehh

male genotype (EEHh)   male gametes

Name _____   Date _____

Biology

STUDENT HANDOUT–LESSON 22

Basic Principle   The phenotype of an organism depends on its genotype which is established at fertilization.

Objective   Use a Punnett Square to determine the genotypes and phenotypes of an organism resulting from a dihybrid cross.

Procedure

1. Read the information on *Mendel's Law of Independent Assortment*.

Mendel's Law of Independent Assortment

The results of Mendel's experiments using pea plants with more than one allele for each or several traits (i.e., plant height either tall or short, seed shape either round or wrinkled, seed color either yellow or green) led him to his *Law of Independent Assortment*. The law states that the inheritance of a pair of alleles (i.e., round or wrinkled) for a particulat trait (i.e., seed shape) occurs independently of the inheritance of another pair of alleles (i.e., yellow or green) of a different trait (i.e., seed color). Mendel used dihybrid crosses (i.e., crossing two parents that are hybrid for different traits) to examine the inheritance pattern of his pea plants' multiple characteristics. The illustration shows the pattern of inheritance over several generations of pea plants beginning with purebred grandparents. One grandparent in this first cross is purebred for round (RR) and yellow (YY) seeds. The other grandparent is purebred for wrinkled (rr) and green (yy) seeds. The offspring of these purebred strains of grandparent plants must all have hybrid round-yellow seeds (i.e., RrYy). The genotypes of the next generation of offspring, however, are more varied since there are four possible combinations of gametes for each hybrid parent.

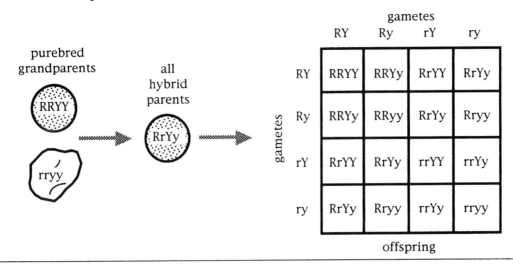

2. Study the handout illustrations. Then complete the *Observations & Analysis* section.

Copyright © 2005 by John Wiley & Sons, Inc.

Observations & Analysis

1. What are the chances that the offpring of the parents shown in the example will have wrinkled-yellow seeds? Wrinkled-green seeds?

   _____

   _____

2. Use a Punnett Square to illustrate all possible genotypes and phenotypes of the offspring resulting from the mating of the two Andromedans described below.

   > A male purebred one-eyed (EE), hybrid one-horned (Hh) Andromedan met and mated a purebred two-eyed (ee), purebred two-horned (hh) female. Andromedan alleles for particular traits (i.e., Andromedans can have either one or two eyes and one or two horns) are inherited in pairs. Show the genotypes of both male and female Andromedans. Determine the possible gametes for each parent and use a Punnett Square to show all possible genotypes of their offspring.
   >
   > male genotype: __ __ __ __   female genotype: __ __ __ __

3. What percentage of the offspring from this dihybrid cross will be two-eyed, one-horned Andromedans? Explain your answer.

   _____

   _____

   _____

   _____

Lesson 23: Teacher Preparation

Basic Principle   The phenotype of an organism depends on its genotype which is established at fertilization.

Competency   Students will explain the role of chromosomes in determining an organism's gender.

Procedure

1. Give students time to read the information on *Sex Chromosomes*.
2. Assist students in completing the activity and the *Observations & Analysis* section.

Answer to Observations & Analysis

See the Punnett Square.

PUNNETT SQUARE ILLUSTRATING SEX DETERMINATION

female genotype: XX

female gametes

	X	X	
X	XX	XX	50% female offspring
Y	XY	XY	50% male offspring

male genotype (XY)

male gametes

Biology

STUDENT HANDOUT–LESSON 23

Basic Principle   The phenotype of an organism depends on its genotype which is established at fertilization.

Objective   Explain the role of chromosomes in determining an organism's gender.

Procedure

1. Read the information on *Sex Chromosomes*.

Sex Chromosomes

With the exception of individuals with an inherited genetic disorder (i.e., *Down syndrome, Klinefelter syndrome*, etc.), all humans have 46 chromosomes in 23 homologous pairs. Each homologous pair of chromosomes can be distinguished from the other pairs by their size, appearance, and the position of their centromere which binds the chromosomes together. Homologous pairs of chromosomes carry alleles for particular traits, although the alleles for any particular trait may vary (i.e., brown pigment versus blue pigment for eye color). Geneticists can photograph chromosomes and arrange the pairs in order according to size to simplify the identification of genetic anomolies. This kind of arrangement is called a *karyotype*. The first 22 pairs of chromosomes are called *autosomes*. The 23rd pair is a set of *sex chromosomes*. Unlike autosomes, the sex chromosomes can be different in appearance. In a female, the chromosomes of the 23rd pair resemble one another and are referred to as *X-chromosomes* (i.e., female genotype, XX). In a male, however, the 23rd pair is comprised of one large X-chromosome and a smaller *Y-chromosome* (i.e., male genotype, XY). Female gametes can contain only X-chromosomes, whereas, male gametes can contain either an X-chromosome or a Y-chromosome. It is the Y-chromosome that determines male primary and secondary sexual characteristics; and it is the male parent who determines the gender of the offspring at fertilization.

---

2. Complete the *Observations & Analysis* section.

Observations & Analysis

Use a Punnett Square to show why the chances of being either a male or a female are 1 in 2.

Lesson 24: Teacher Preparation

Basic Principle   The phenotype of an organism depends on its genotype which is established at fertilization.

Competency   Students will predict the possible outcomes of genotypes and phenotypes in a cross involving an X-linked disease.

Procedure

1. Give students time to read the information on *Sex-Linked Traits*.

2. Make sure students understand the distribution of offspring and the characteristics associated with them: 1 in 4 offspring is a normal female; 1 in 4 offspring is a female "carrier" who does not have the disease; 1 in 4 offspring is a normal male; and 1 in 4 offspring is a male with the disorder.

3. Assist students in completing the activity and the *Observations & Analysis* section.

Answer to Observations & Analysis

All hemophiliac females are purebred (i.e., homozygous) for that defect. In order for one or more of Queen Victoria's female descendents to become a hemophiliac, they would need to be the offspring of a "carrier" who mates with a hemophiliac male. Or, one of Queen Victoria's hemophiliac male descendents must mate with a female "carrier" from their own or another family. A mating between any hemophiliac male and a hemophiliac female will produce all hemophiliac offspring. See the Punnett Square for one example of how this might occur.

A FEMALE HEMOPHILIAC

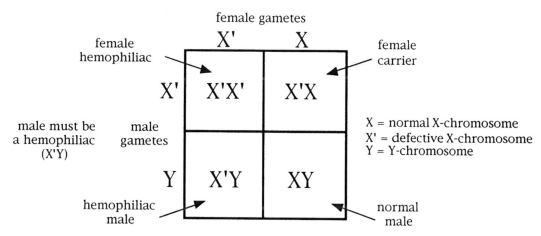

Biology

STUDENT HANDOUT–LESSON 24

Basic Principle   The phenotype of an organism depends on its genotype which is established at fertilization.

Objective   Predict the possible outcomes of genotypes and phenotypes in a cross involving an X-linked disease.

Procedure

1. Read the information on *Sex-Linked Taits*.

Sex-Linked Traits

X-linked disorders, sometimes called *sex-linked traits*, refer to the tendency of some characteristics to be expressed exclusively, or in the vast majority of cases, in one gender. The most widely known examples of sex-linked traits are *colorblindness* and *hemophilia*, both anomolies found predominantly in males. Since the Y-chromosome carries little more than instructions for producing male primary and secondary sexual characteristics, the instructions to counteract the deleterious effects of a defective allele found on the X-chromosome in a male offspring (i.e., genotype XY), are lacking. A female (i.e., genotype XX) with at least one healthy X-chromosome would have the instructions necessary to counteract such a defect. In the illustration, a female "carrier" of a defective gene that can result in colorblindness mates with a normal male. In this example, the chances are 1 in 2 that any male child born to this couple will be colorblind.

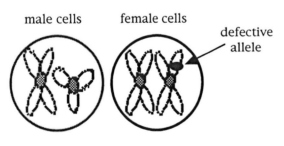

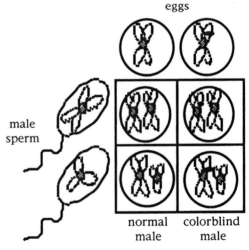

Note that one female offspring is normal while the other is a "carrier." One male offspring is normal while the second carries a defective gene that will be expressed for lack of a matching healthy gene.

---

2. Complete the *Observations & Analysis* section.

Observations & Analysis

The 19th-century British monarch Queen Victoria was a carrier of the bleeding disorder hemophilia. Since the disorder is an X-linked disease, many of her male descendents, including Prince Alexis, son of the last Russian monarch, Czar Nicolaus II, had the disease. Use a Punnett Square to illustrate how it would have been possible for female descendents of Queen Victoria to have hemophilia. Note that a female "carrier" of a defective gene that can give rise to hemophilia in her offspring may not necessarily have the disease herself.

Biology

Lesson 25: Teacher Preparation

Basic Principle   Genes are a set of instructions encoded in the DNA of each organism.

Competency   Students will construct a model of a DNA molecule.

Materials   handout illustrations, scissors, T-pins, tape, construction paper, pipe cleaners, clay, marking pen

Procedure

1. Make sufficient copies of *Constructing a Chromosome* for distribution.
2. Give students time to read the information on *Deoxyribonucleic Acid.*
3. Point out that the pioneering work of English biochemist Dorothy Mary Crowfoot Hodgkin (1910–1994) in the field of X-ray crystallography allowed microbiologists to deduce the three-dimensional structure of many organic compounds. With the assistance of the brilliant biophysicist and X-ray crystallographer Rosalind Elsie Franklin (1920–1958), molecular biologists James Dewey Watson (b. 1928) and H.C. Francis Crick (b. 1916) constructed a model of DNA in 1953 for which they shared a Nobel Prize in 1961.
4. Give students time to construct their DNA-histone composite and complete the *Observations & Analysis* section.

Answers to Observations & Analysis

1. nitrogenous base, deoxyribose sugar, phosphate
2. The purines adenine and guanine are double-ringed structures. The pyrimidines thymine and cytosine are single-ringed structures.
3. Answers will vary, but should contain the following main points: A nitrogenous base is a subunit of a nucleotide. A nucleic acid, such as DNA, is composed of a chain of nucleotides containing nitrogenous bases.

Constructing a Chromosome

1. Cut out small strips of construction paper about 2–3 cm in length and label them with letter combinations representing matched pairs of purines and pyrimidines (i.e., adenine, A, bonds to thymine, T; and guanine, G, bonds to cytosine, C).

2. Use a T-pin to poke holes near the ends of each strip.

3. Slide the strips along the lengths of two pipe cleaners. Each pipe cleaner represents a chain of deoxyribose-phosphate links that comprise the backbone of the DNA molecule.

4. Twist the two ends of the ladder in opposite directions to create a double helix.

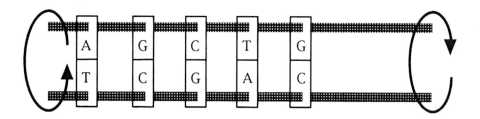

5. Roll small bits of clay into balls about 1 cm in diameter. Each ball represents a histone protein.

6. Combine eight of the histone proteins into a larger ball representing a histone complex. Make two or three histone complexes.

7. Wind the double helix around the histone complexes.

8. Combine your section of DNA-histone with those of other classmates by attaching the pipe cleaners end-to-end.

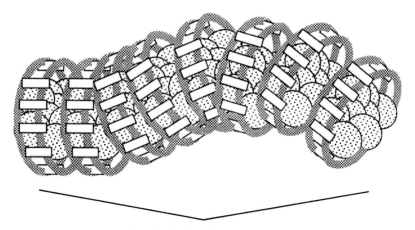

Model of a Chromosome
(DNA-histone complex)

Biology

STUDENT HANDOUT–LESSON 25

Basic Principle   Genes are a set of instructions encoded in the DNA of each organism.

Objective   Construct a model of a DNA molecule.

Materials   handout illustrations, scissors, T-pins, tape, construction paper, pipe cleaners, clay, marking pen

Procedure

1. Read the information on *Deoxyribonucleic Acid*.

Deoxyribonucleic Acid

Deoxyribonucleic acid (DNA) is a complex macromolecule that incorporates the chemically coded information required to construct, control, and coordinate the activities of a living organism. DNA molecules, organized into *chromosomes* found in the nuclei of cells, serve as the basis of genetic inheritance. DNA is a double-stranded, ladderlike *nucleic acid* composed of matched pairs of *nitrogenous bases* called *purines* (i.e., *adenine* and *guanine*) and *pyrimidines* (i.e., *thymine* and *cytosine*). The purines and pyrimidines are held together by *hydrogen bonding* (i.e., *van der Waals' forces*). The nitrogenous bases are attached to *deoxyribose sugars* linked together in a chain by *phosphate* molecules. The deoxyribose-phosphate links form the backbone of the DNA molecule. Each nitrogenous base–deoxyribose–phosphate group is called a *nucleotide*. The sequence of nucleotides in a particular DNA molecule determines the kind of structural and regulatory proteins made by an organism. In eukaryotic cells, long strands of DNA form a twisted *double helix* that becomes wrapped around proteins called *histone*. Histones are small, tightly packed proteins that help to bundle the double helix into its chromosomal form.

---

2. Examine the handout illustrations and use the information on *Constructing a Chromosome* provided by your instructor to build a small composite model of the DNA double helix wrapped around histone proteins.

3. Attach your DNA-histone composite to those of other students to make a small section of a chromosome.

4. Complete the *Observations & Analysis* section.

HOW THE DOUBLE HELIX FORMS A CHROMOSOME

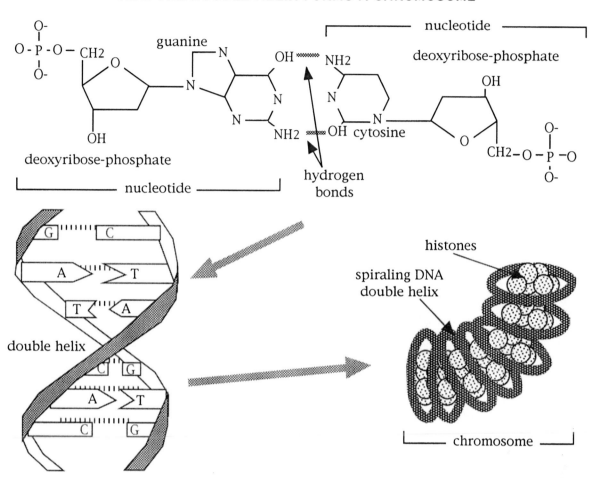

Observations & Analysis

1. List the subunits of a nucleotide.

   _____

   _____

2. Describe one major structural difference between purines and pyrimidines.

   _____

   _____

3. Explain the difference between nucleotides and nitrogenous bases; nitrogenous bases and nucleic acids.

   _____

   _____

   _____

Lesson 26: Teacher Preparation

Basic Principle   Genes are a set of instructions encoded in the DNA of each organism.

Competency   Students will explain how DNA replicates itself.

Materials   model constructed in LESSON 25

Procedure

1. Give students time to read the information on *DNA Replication*.
2. Assist students in using the model of DNA they constructed in LESSON 25 to visualize how DNA replicates itself in the nucleus.

Answers to Observations & Analysis

1. Answers will vary, but should contain the following main point: Deoxyribose sugars link to phosphates to form the backbone of the DNA molecule.
2. TTAGCTACGATCGATC
3. Answers will vary, but should contain the following main point: In order for daughter cells to contain the same amount of DNA as the parent cell, DNA must replicate itself before division of the parent cell begins.

Biology

STUDENT HANDOUT–LESSON 26

Basic Principle   Genes are a set of instructions encoded in the DNA of each organism.

Objective   Explain how DNA replicates itself.

Materials   model constructed in LESSON 25

Procedure

1. Read the information on *DNA Replication.*

DNA Replication

The division of cells (i.e., mitosis) to form new cells is preceded by the duplication of DNA molecules. The duplication of DNA is called *replication.* DNA replication occurs during interphase and takes advantage of the fact that the building blocks used to construct DNA (i.e., deoxyribose sugars, phosphates, and nitrogenous bases) are all present in the nucleus of the cell. DNA replication begins with the separation, or uncoiling, of the two strands of the double helix. The uncoiling of the double helix exposes the purines (i.e., adenine and guanine) and pyrimidines (i.e., thymine and cytosine) fixed to each uncoiled strand to their matching nucleotides floating free in the nucleoplasm. During replication, nucleotides containing adenine are attracted to nucleotides containing thymine, while nucleotides containing guanine are attracted to nucleotides containing cytosine. The deoxyribose sugar on one nucleotide links by dehydration synthesis to the phosphate molecule on an adjacent nucleotide to form the backbone of a complementary strand of nucleic acid.

---

2. Examine the handout illustrations and the model you constructed in LESSON 25 before completing the *Observations & Analysis* section.

REPLICATING A DNA MOLECULE

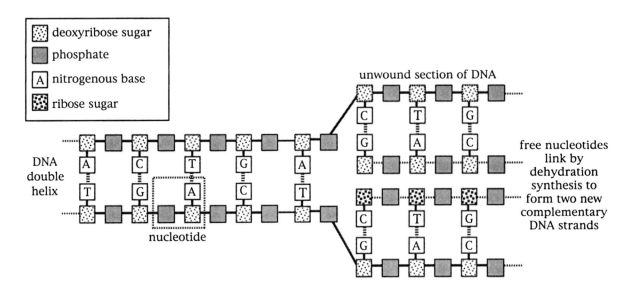

Observations & Analysis

1. Which two molecules link by dehydration synthesis to form the backbone of a new complementary strand of DNA?

2. Write the complementary sequence of nitrogenous bases that would be formed by the following genetic sequence: AATCGATGCTAGCTAG.

3. Explain why it is necessary for DNA to replicate itself before the prophase stage of mitosis.

Lesson 27: Teacher Preparation

Basic Principle   Genes are a set of instructions encoded in the DNA of each organism.

Competency   Students will examine the functions of RNA molecules in helping DNA to execute the genetic code.

Procedure

1. Give students time to read the information on *Ribonucleic Acid*.

2. Point out the structural differences between DNA and RNA.

3. Explain that the molecular diagrams on STUDENT HANDOUT 27 are not to scale and that both mRNA and tRNA are small enough to bind to the larger ribosomal RNA (i.e., ribosomes). Refer students to the diagrams in LESSON 4 which depict transcription and translation.

4. Draw all or part of the chart listing *Amino Acid Abbreviations and Codons* to illustrate how the genetic code is transcribed from DNA, then translated into the production of proteins (i.e., linked amino acids).

5. Assist students in completing the *Observations & Analysis* section.

Answers to Observations & Analysis

1. Answers will vary, but should contain the following main points: The DNA backbone is comprised of deoxyribose-phosphate links while the RNA backbone is made of ribose-phosphate links. DNA is a double-stranded molecule, while RNA is a single-stranded molecule. RNA contains the nitrogenous base uracil, while DNA contains the nitrogenous base thymine.

2. Answers will vary, but should contain the following main points: Messenger RNA transcribes the genetic code from DNA and takes the code out of the nucleus and into the cytoplasm. Transfer RNA molecules transport amino acids to the ribosome. Ribosomes are made of large and smaller subunits of ribosomal RNA which serves as the site of translation where protein synthesis takes place.

AMINO ACID ABBREVIATIONS AND CODONS

Ala   =   alanyl

Arg   =   arginyl

Asp   =   aspartyl

Asn   =   asparaginyl

Csy   =   cysteinyl

Gln   =   glutaminyl

Gly   =   glycyl

His   =   histidyl

Hyl   =   hydroxylysyl

Hyp   =   hydroxypropyl

Ile   =   isoleucyl

Leu   =   leucyl

Lys   =   lysyl

Met   =   methionyl

Phe   =   phenylalanyl

Pro   =   prolyl

Ser   =   seryl

Thry   =   threonyl

Trp   =   tryptophanyl

Try   =   tyrosyl

Val   =   valyl

	Second Position				
First Position	U	C	A	G	Third Position
U	Phe	Ser	Tyr	Cys	U
	Phe	Ser	Tyr	Cys	C
	Leu	Ser	*	*	A
	Leu	Ser	*	Try	G
C	Leu	Pro	His	Arg	U
	Leu	Pro	His	Arg	C
	Leu	Pro	Gln	Arg	A
	Leu	Pro	Gln	Arg	G
A	Ile	Thr	Asn	Ser	U
	Ile	Thr	Asn	Ser	C
	Ile	Thr	Lys	Arg	A
	Met	Thr	Lys	Arg	G
G	Val	Ala	Asp	Gly	U
	Val	Ala	Asp	Gly	C
	Val	Ala	Glu	Gly	A
	Val	Ala	Glu	Gly	G

*refers to the chain-terminating codon for the carboxyl-end (⁻COOH) of the polypeptide chain

Name _____   Date _____

Biology

STUDENT HANDOUT–LESSON 27

Basic Principle   Genes are a set of instructions encoded in the DNA of each organism.

Objective   Examine the functions of RNA molecules in helping DNA to execute the genetic code.

Procedure

1. Read the information on *Ribonucleic Acid.*

Ribonucleic Acid

Ribonucleic acid (RNA) acts as an intermediary between the DNA code and the proteins it is designed to construct. The discoveries that (1) DNA is confined to the nucleus and (2) that proteins are synthesized in the cytoplasm prompted scientists to search for substances that linked the genetic code to actual sites of protein synthesis. In the 1940s, molecular biologists discovered that cells in the active process of manufacturing proteins contained higher amounts of ribonucleic acid than less active cells. RNA differs structurally from DNA in two important ways. First, one of the nitrogenous bases in RNA differs from that found in DNA: DNA's thymine is replaced by RNA's *uracil*. Second, the sugar-phosphate links comprising the backbone of the RNA molecule are made of *ribose sugars* rather than deoxyribose sugars. Further work in the field established three different types of RNA as integral to the expression of the genetic code. A single-stranded molecule called *messenger RNA (mRNA)* "transcribes" the genetic code from DNA. Messenger RNA then moves across the nuclear membrane into the cytoplasm. In the cytoplasm, mRNA attaches to *ribosomal RNA*, the actual site of protein synthesis. Ribosomal RNA is composed of a large and smaller subunit that work together to bind other molecules involved in protein synthesis (i.e., translation). Molecules of *transfer RNA (tRNA)* carry amino acids to the ribosome where they are linked together in the correct sequence to form proteins according to the instructions encoded in DNA.

---

2. Examine the handout illustrations. Then complete the *Observations & Analysis* section.

THREE TYPES OF RIBONUCLEIC ACID

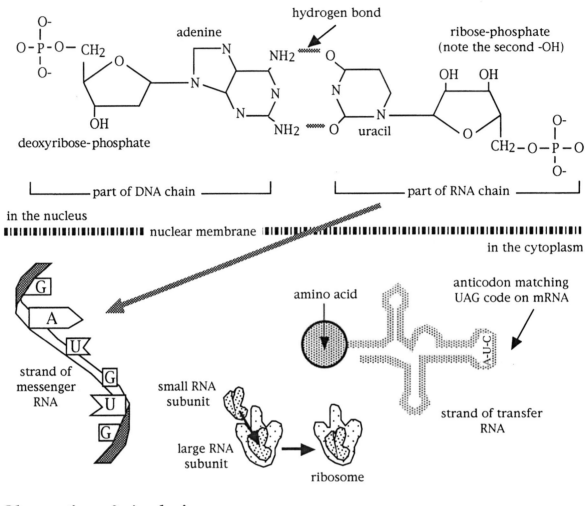

Observations & Analysis

1. Describe the structural differences between DNA and RNA.

_____

_____

_____

2. Describe the three different types of RNA involved in the decoding of DNA and protein synthesis.

_____

_____

_____

_____

Lesson 28: Teacher Preparation

Basic Principle   Genes are a set of instructions encoded in the DNA of each organism.

Competency   Students will explain how genes can be regulated.

Procedure

1. Give students time to read the information on *Gene Regulation*.

2. Introduce the French biochemist Jacques Lucien Monod (1910–1976) who shared the Nobel Prize in 1965 with his associates André Lwoff (b. 1902) and François Jacob (b. 1920). The three scientists discovered a class of genes in bacteria (i.e., *Escherichia coli*) that regulates other genes. Their model proposed the existence of specific messenger RNAs that lead to the production of "operator genes" that regulate the activity of other mRNAs by affecting their transcription.

3. Draw the diagram showing *A Typical Feedback Pathway* to illustrate that gene regulation is a "feedback mechanism."

4. Give students time to complete the *Observations & Analysis* section.

Answers to Observations & Analysis

Answers will vary, but should include the following main points: The regulation of lactose metabolism involves the binding of lactose to a repressor protein that ordinarily inhibits the production of lactose-digesting proteins. The result is the "disabling" of the repressor protein and the continued production of lactose-digesting proteins. Tryptophan regulates metabolic pathways by binding with, and thereby "enabling," a repressor molecule to halt further transcription of critical RNA messengers.

A TYPICAL FEEDBACK PATHWAY

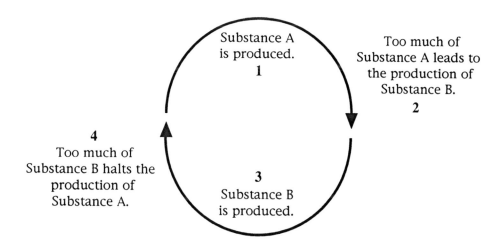

Substance A is produced.
1

Too much of Substance A leads to the production of Substance B.
2

4
Too much of Substance B halts the production of Substance A.

3
Substance B is produced.

Name _____   Date _____

Biology

STUDENT HANDOUT–LESSON 28

Basic Principle   Genes are a set of instructions encoded in the DNA of each organism.

Objective   Explain how genes can be regulated.

Procedure

1. Read the information on *Gene Regulation.*

Gene Regulation

The transcription of messenger RNA from DNA in the nucleus is essential for the eventual synthesis of proteins in the cytoplasm. The process of blocking the transcription of specific messengers, therefore, serves to regulate the production of needed proteins in the cell. In the 1940s, the French biochemists François Jacob (b. 1920), Jacques Lucien Monod (1910–1976), and André Lwoff (b. 1902) discovered two types of *gene regulation* controlling cellular metabolism. In the first type of gene regulation, a *regulator gene* produces a *repressor protein* that binds to a section of DNA that codes for a particular protein or set of proteins (i.e., proteins necessary for the proper digestion of lactose). The repressor protein works at the "encoding site" by blocking the enzyme *RNA polymerase* which catalyzes transcription. The synthesis of mRNA needed to translate needed proteins is halted. However, the presence of a substance, such as lactose, can "disable" a repressor protein, thereby leading to the transcription of those mRNA strands that allow the translation of needed proteins to take place (i.e., proteins necessary for the proper digestion of lactose). In the second type of gene regulation, a regulator protein combines with a substance, such as the amino acid tryptophan, to form a *repressor complex* that can bind to a given DNA site. The DNA site is blocked from using RNA polymerase and transcription of specific RNA messengers is stopped. In the absence of tryptophan, however, the repressor protein cannot bind to DNA, and RNA polymerase remains free to do its work on that section of the gene. Gene regulation is a "feedback mechanism." For example, excess lactose in a cell leads to the synthesis of proteins that help to digest lactose, whereas a short supply of lactose keeps the concentration of lactose-digesting proteins low. An excess of tryptophan halts specific metabolic activities, while too little tryptophan allows those metabolic activities to proceed.

---

2. Examine the handout illustrations. Then complete the *Observations & Analysis* section.

GENE REGULATION OF LACTOSE METABOLISM

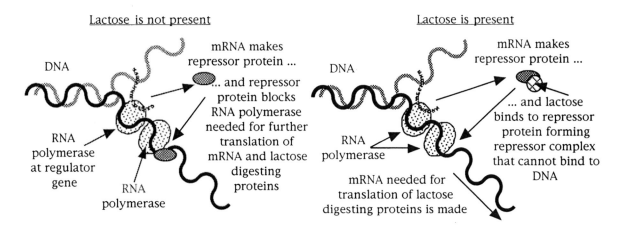

Lactose is not present

DNA

RNA polymerase at regulator gene

RNA polymerase

mRNA makes repressor protein ...

... and repressor protein blocks RNA polymerase needed for further translation of mRNA and lactose digesting proteins

Lactose is present

DNA

RNA polymerase

mRNA makes repressor protein ...

... and lactose binds to repressor protein forming repressor complex that cannot bind to DNA

mRNA needed for translation of lactose digesting proteins is made

TRYPTOPHAN REGULATION OF METABOLISM

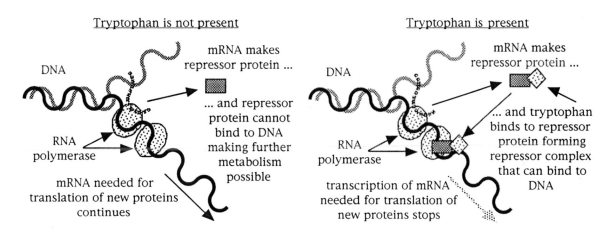

Tryptophan is not present

DNA

RNA polymerase

mRNA makes repressor protein ...

... and repressor protein cannot bind to DNA making further metabolism possible

mRNA needed for translation of new proteins continues

Tryptophan is present

DNA

RNA polymerase

mRNA makes repressor protein ...

... and tryptophan binds to repressor protein forming repressor complex that can bind to DNA

transcription of mRNA needed for translation of new proteins stops

Observations & Analysis

Explain how gene regulation of lactose metabolism differs from the regulation of metabolism by the amino acid tryptophan.

_____

_____

_____

_____

_____

_____

_____

_____

 **Biology**

Lesson 29: Teacher Preparation

Basic Principle   Genes are a set of instructions encoded in the DNA of each organism.

Competency   Students will explain how genetic mutations occur.

Materials   chart from LESSON 27

Procedure

1. Make sufficient copies of the *Amino Acid Abbreviations and Codons* chart from LESSON 27 for distribution to students.
2. Give students time to read the information on *Genetic Mutations* before completing the *Observations & Analysis* section using the chart from LESSON 27.

Answers to Observations & Analysis

1. See the diagram.
2. Answers will vary, but should include the following main points: Chromosomal alterations such as translocation result in recombinations of existing alleles. This type of mutation increases the number of combinations of traits within a species. A genetic mutation caused by ultraviolet rays, however, may result in the production of an entirely new allele encoding the instructions for a new structural or functional protein. This type of mutation might result in an individual having a trait that is not present in the other members of its species.

A GENETIC MUTATION

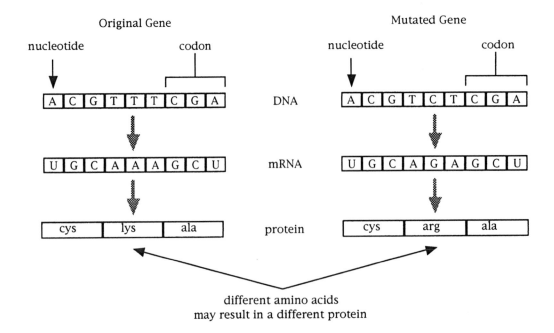

Name _____ Date _____

Biology

STUDENT HANDOUT–LESSON 29

Basic Principle   Genes are a set of instructions encoded in the DNA of each organism.

Objective   Explain how genetic mutations occur.

Materials   chart from LESSON 27

Procedure

1. Read the information on *Genetic Mutations*.

Genetic Mutations

Genetic mutations are changes in the genetic instructions that give organisms their particular physical traits. Unlike other forms of chromosomal alterations (i.e., deletion, inversion, translocation, and duplication), some genetic mutations—caused by environmental agents such as toxic chemicals and ultraviolet rays—are "unregulated alterations" that can affect the phenotype of an organism. Mutations of this kind do not merely increase the number of possible combinations of mixed traits within a species (i.e., tall green peas, tall yellow peas, short green peas, short yellow peas), they also change the nature of the species' pool of variations (i.e., tall *red* peas). Unregulated genetic mutations result in the formation of entirely new traits (i.e., red pigment). They serve as the basis of evolution by creating whole new physical and functional adaptations. The replacement of a single nitrogenous base (i.e., A, G, T, or C) by another nitrogenous base alters the codon giving instructions for the placement of a particular amino acid in a particular protein. Replacing one amino acid with another may result in the synthesis of a protein different from the protein encoded in the original DNA strand. A gene encoding instructions for a particular eye or skin pigment, for example, might be altered by a toxic chemical. The altered (i.e., mutated) instruction might then direct the synthesis of a dysfunctional pigment that produces no color. A person carrying such an allele might be albino (i.e., have no eye or skin pigment). Because the mutation occurs in DNA, the new trait can be passed on to the next generation.

---

2. Examine the handout illustrations. Then complete the *Observations & Analysis* section.

Observations & Analysis

1. Complete the diagram to show how the mutated gene will cause the synthesis of a new protein. Use the handout of *Amino Acids Abbreviations and Codons* provided by your instructor to fill in the illustrations of the respective mRNA strands and amino acid sequences that give rise to each protein.

A GENETIC MUTATION

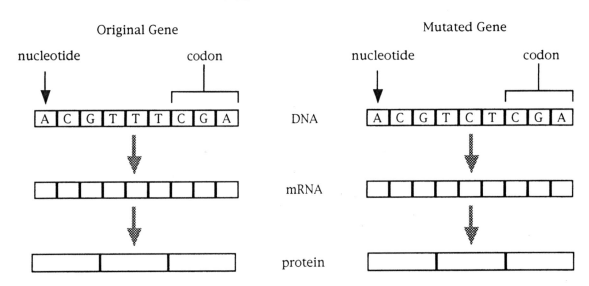

2. Explain how a genetic mutation caused by ultraviolet rays effects the gene pool of a species in a manner different from that of a chromosomal alteration such as translocation.

_____

_____

_____

_____

_____

_____

_____

_____

_____

_____

_____

_____

_____

Lesson 30: Teacher Preparation

Basic Principle   Genes are a set of instructions encoded in the DNA of each organism.

Competency   Students will explain how recombinant DNA is synthesized.

Procedure

1. Give students time to read the information on *Recombinant DNA* before completing the *Observations & Analysis* section.

2. Point out that recombinant DNA technology, also called genetic engineering, is the purposeful manipulation of chromosomal material by biochemical techniques. This is accomplished by splitting the DNA fragments of different organisms (i.e., virus, bacteria, etc.) and recombining them to form new genetic combinations. Genetic engineering can be conducted for pure research or in an effort to synthesize proteins needed for medical use (i.e., human insulin, human growth hormone, and vaccines).

Answer to Observations & Analysis

Answers will vary, but should include the following main point: Recombinant DNA technology involves the designing and constructing of new DNA fragments. It is the engineering of genes that can be used to produce desired proteins. For this reason, recombinant DNA technology is also called genetic engineering.

Biology

STUDENT HANDOUT–LESSON 30

Basic Principle   Genes are a set of instructions encoded in the DNA of each organism.

Objective   Explain how recombinant DNA is synthesized.

Procedure

1. Read the information on *Recombinant DNA*.

Recombinant DNA

In the 1970s, scientists developed techniques for splicing and recombining segments of DNA. The technique utilizes enzymes called *restriction enzymes* extracted from the bacterium *Escherichia coli*. Restriction enzymes are used to cleave a DNA molecule at a specific site called a *recognition site*. The desired portions of DNA can then be isolated. With the help of a second enzyme called a *ligase enzyme*, the nitrogenous bases at the ends of an isolated DNA fragment can be matched to the complementary nitrogenous bases at the ends of another DNA fragment. DNA from different organisms can be "recombined" in this manner to form *recombinant DNA*. This new technology is called *genetic engineering*. Recombinant DNA technology, or genetic engineering, has numerous uses in pharmacology, medicine, and agriculture.

---

2. Examine the handout illustrations. Then complete the *Observations & Analysis* section.

HOW RECOMBINANT DNA TECHNOLOGY WORKS

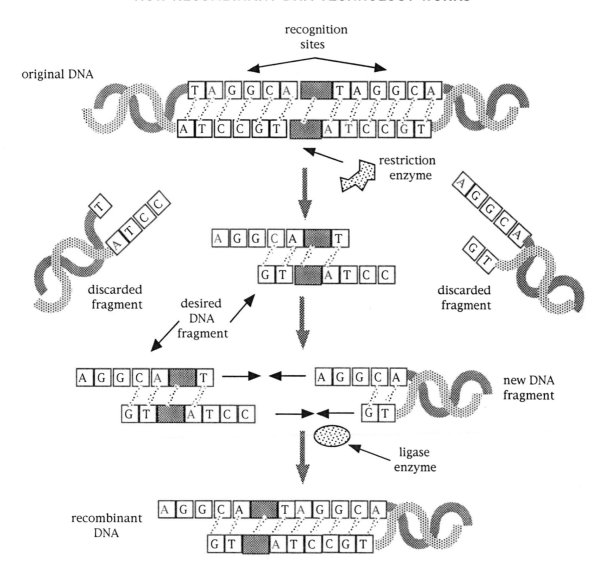

Observations & Analysis

Explain why recombinant DNA technology is also called genetic engineering.

_____

_____

_____

_____

_____

_____

Lesson 31: Teacher Preparation

Basic Principle   Genes are a set of instructions encoded in the DNA of each organism.

Competency   Students will explain how bacteria are used to help synthesize human proteins.

Procedure

1. Give students time to read the information on *Genetic Engineering Using Bacteria* before completing the *Observations & Analysis* section.

2. Begin by asking students to report on any recent news they have heard about genetic engineering. Explain that this revolutionary new technique allows pharmaceutical firms to produce drugs such as insulin for the treatment of diabetes. The new procedures are much less expensive than those used only a few years ago to isolate animal insulin formerly used in the treatment of the disease. Less than a few decades ago, diabetics used purified animal insulin to control their blood-sugar levels. Today, they use genuine human insulin extracted from bacteria! Explain that genetic engineers first locate the site on human DNA that codes for the synthesis of human insulin. They then isolate that DNA fragment. Next, they isolate bacterial plasmids that can incorporate the human DNA. Bacteria multiply quickly; and, within days, there are millions of bacteria carrying the gene that codes for the synthesis of human insulin.

Answers to Observations & Analysis

1. Answers will vary, but should include the following main point: The recombinant DNA in this bacteria carries the genetic instructions for the synthesis of human insulin.

2. Answers will vary, but should include the following main points: Identify the site on human DNA that codes for the synthesis of human growth hormone. Isolate that DNA fragment using restriction enzymes along with bacterial plasmids able to incorporate the human DNA. Use ligase enzyme to splice the human DNA into the bacterial plasmid. Reinsert the plasmids into the bacteria. Allow the bacteria to multiply, then extract the human growth hormone they synthesize.

Biology

STUDENT HANDOUT–LESSON 31

Basic Principle   Genes are a set of instructions encoded in the DNA of each organism.

Objective   Explain how bacteria are used to help synthesize human proteins.

Procedure

1. Read the information on *Genetic Engineering Using Bacteria*.

Genetic Engineering Using Bacteria

The new science of *genetic engineering* takes advantage of the fact that chromosomes can be "dissected apart," then "teased back together." By inserting sections of human DNA into the chromosomes of bacteria (i.e., *Escherichia coli*), scientists can induce the bacteria to manufacture human proteins. The DNA constructed for this purpose is called "recombined" or *recombinant DNA*. The science of genetic engineering is changing the way researchers and physicians think about disease and treatment. This revolutionary technology is already being used to correct birth defects and treat genetically related illness.

---

2. Examine the handout illustrations. Then complete the *Observations & Analysis* section.

HOW BACTERIA CAN MAKE HUMAN INSULIN

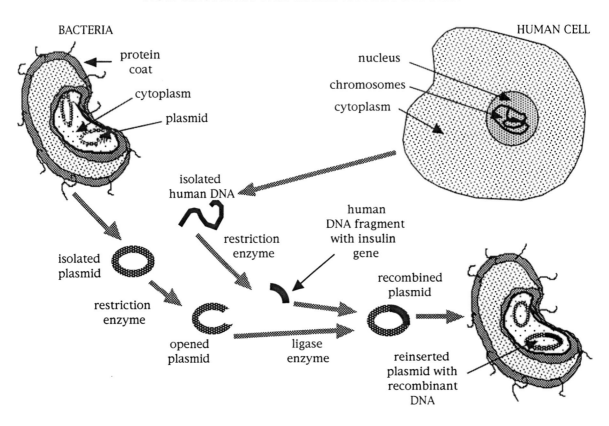

Observations & Analysis

1. Why is the bacteria containing the recombinant DNA in this example able to synthesize human insulin?

    _____

    _____

    _____

2. Briefly outline the procedure for engineering a bacteria able to synthesize human growth hormone.

    _____

    _____

    _____

    _____

    _____

    _____

    _____

    _____

 **Biology**

Lesson 32: Teacher Preparation

Basic Principle   Genes are a set of instructions encoded in the DNA of each organism.

Competency   Students will explain how criminal investigators use DNA fingerprinting to help solve crimes.

Procedure   Give students time to read the information on *DNA Fingerprinting* before completing the *Observations & Analysis* section.

Answers to Observations & Analysis

1. The RFLP migration pattern of suspect #2 matches the pattern of the sample retrieved from the crime scene. Suspect #2 was more than likely at the crime scene.

2. Answers will vary. Accept any logical arguments such as the following: The suspect is also a relative of the person whose home was burglarized and has been in the home on several occasions.

Biology

STUDENT HANDOUT–LESSON 32

Basic Principle   Genes are a set of instructions encoded in the DNA of each organism.

Objective   Explain how criminal investigators use DNA fingerprinting to help solve crimes.

Procedure

1. Read the information on *DNA Fingerprinting*.

DNA Fingerprinting

DNA fingerprinting is an extremely useful investigative technique. It requires only small organic samples from a crime scene and suspects (i.e., blood, hair, skin) in order to lead to a reliable conclusion. The samples are treated with *restriction enzymes* that split the DNA fragments into pieces. The sample pieces are called *restriction fragment length polymorphisms (RFLPs)*. The RFLPs are then placed in *agarose*, a gelatinous material that can be layered into sheets and examined by *gel electrophoresis*. In this procedure, a sheet of agarose is placed between electrical poles that produce a current. The pieces of DNA migrate from one pole to another traveling at different rates according to their size. Smaller fragments move more quickly than larger fragments. The sheet is then layered with a nylon membrane that absorbs the repositioned fragments. A *mixed DNA probe* containing *radioactive markers* is poured over the membrane, and the radiaoactive signals from the markers are photographed to record the pattern of migration made by each set of DNA fragments. By comparing the migration patterns left by the RFLPs, investigators can reasonably conclude whether or not a given suspect was present at a crime scene.

---

2. Examine the handout illustrations. Then complete the *Observations & Analysis* section.

HOW TO CATCH A THIEF USING DNA FINGERPRINTING

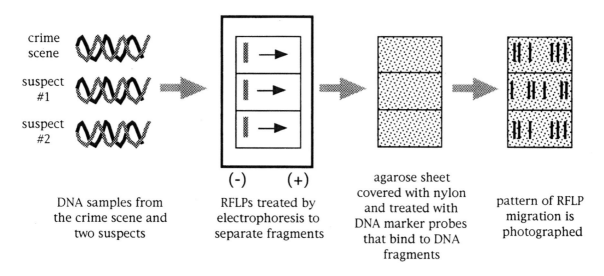

| DNA samples from the crime scene and two suspects | RFLPs treated by electrophoresis to separate fragments | agarose sheet covered with nylon and treated with DNA marker probes that bind to DNA fragments | pattern of RFLP migration is photographed |

Observations & Analysis

1. Which suspect in the example above was probably at the crime scene? Explain your conclusion.

   _____

   _____

   _____

   _____

   _____

   _____

2. As the defense attorney for the suspect accused of this crime, based on this DNA evidence, what arguments would you submit to help acquit your client?

   _____

   _____

   _____

   _____

   _____

   _____

   _____

   _____

Lesson 33: Teacher Preparation

Basic Principle   Genes are a set of instructions encoded in the DNA of each organism.

Competency   Students will explain how gene therapy works.

Procedure

1. Give students time to read the information on *Gene Therapy Using a Retrovirus* before completing the *Observations & Analysis* section.

2. Point out that gene therapy is the product of recombinant-DNA technology. Its primary goal is to find cures for the vast variety of genetically based human diseases. Working genes are introduced directly into cells having faulty genes using both physical and biochemical techniques. The use of retroviruses to treat genetic disorders is only one of these methods. Gene-therapy trials began in 1990 in an attempt to treat a child who could not produce the enzyme adenosine deaminase (ADA), an enzyme crucial to the development of the immune system. Lymphocytes were removed from the child's blood and treated with retroviruses containing recombinant RNA having a working ADA gene. The cells were then returned to the child's bloodstream. Since then, more than a thousand individuals have undergone one form of genetic therapy or another. Experimental treatments have been designed for a number of disorders: cystic fibrosis, hemophilia, and hypercholesterolemia. So far, these procedures have been somewhat successful in alleviating disease symptoms, although none of the treatments has resulted in a complete cure.

Answer to Observations & Analysis

Answers will vary, but should include the following main points: A healthy gene is isolated and inserted into a retrovirus. The retrovirus is then inserted into faulty cells taken from the patient. The retroviral RNA produces a complementary DNA strand encoding the instructions to synthesize working proteins. The patient's treated cells, now carrying the working genes, can be reintroduced into the patient.

Name _____   Date _____

Biology

STUDENT HANDOUT–LESSON 33

Basic Principle   Genes are a set of instructions encoded in the DNA of each organism.

Objective   Explain how gene therapy works.

Procedure

1. Read the information on *Gene Therapy Using a Retrovirus.*

Gene Therapy Using a Retrovirus

The goal of *gene therapy* is the replacement of defective genes with working genes. A disease such as *cystic fibrosis*, symptomatized by the buildup of sticky mucus in the lungs, is caused by a faulty gene that fails to regulate the passage of ions across the membranes of lung cells. In an attempt to relieve the disorder, a working form of the gene is isolated and inserted into a virus called a *retrovirus*. A blood sample is taken from the patient, and the retrovirus is inserted into the patient's cells. The retroviral RNA employs a strategy of "reverse transcription" to manufacture new DNA. DNA normally is transcribed to produce RNA. However, a retrovirus can force a cell to synthesize DNA from viral RNA. The new DNA is then incorporated into the cell nuclei of the patient's cells where it codes for the synthesis of working proteins. The working proteins improve the regulation of ion transfer across the membranes of the lung cells; following treatment, the sticky mucus lining the patient's lungs begins to dissolve.

---

2. Examine the handout illustrations. Then complete the *Observations & Analysis* section.

TREATING DISEASE WITH A RETROVIRUS

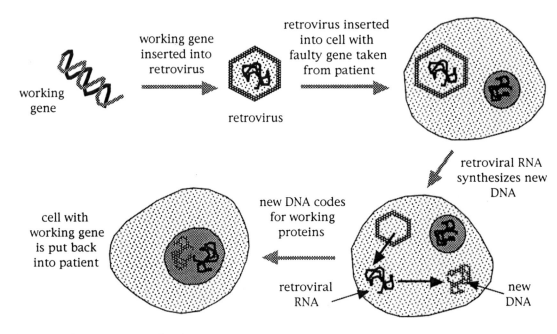

Observations & Analysis

Write a brief description of the procedure you might try to treat a genetically inherited disorder using a retrovirus.

_____

_____

_____

_____

_____

_____

_____

_____

_____

_____

_____

_____

_____

_____

Lesson 34: Teacher Preparation

Basic Principle   Stability in an ecosystem is a balance of competing effects.

Competency   Students will give examples of biodiversity within ecological communities.

Materials   pictures of living organisms shown here

Procedure   Give students time to read the information on *Biodiversity within Ecological Communities* before completing the *Observations & Analysis* section.

Answers to Observations & Analysis

1. *Inhabitants of the aquatic habitat:* frog, newt, turtle, shark, grass, fur seal, sea cow, sea turtle, pelican, salmon, whale, alligator. *Inhabitants of the terrestrial habitat:* woodpecker, frog, newt, earthworm, grasshopper, turtle, spider, moth, wolf, sycamore, daisy, grass, fern, deer, opossum, bat, pelican, bear, calf, lion.

2. Answers will vary, but should contain the following main points: Organisms that reside in an aquatic habitat spend most of their time in water. Organisms that reside in a terrestrial habitat spend most of their time on land.

3. Answers will vary, but should contain the following main points: Since most insects fall prey to the same predators and consume the same kinds of plant and animal resources, the extinction of a single species of insect in an ecosystem supporting several hundred species of insect would probably not result in the complete collapse of that ecosystem. The surviving species of insect would remain to serve as prey for needy predators and to stabilize the populations of existing consumables.

woodpecker

frog

newt

earthworm

grasshopper

moth

turtle

spider

shark

wolf

sycamore

daisy

grass

fern

deer

fur seal

sea cow

opossum

whale

bat

pelican

salmon

sea turtle

alligator

bear

calf

lion

Name _____ Date _____

Biology

STUDENT HANDOUT–LESSON 34

Basic Principle   Stability in an ecosystem is a balance of competing effects.

Objective   Give examples of biodiversity within ecological communities.

Materials   pictures of living organisms supplied by your instructor

Procedure

1. Read the information on *Biodiversity within Ecological Communities*.

Biodiversity within Ecological Communities

Ecology is the branch of biology that studies the relationship between living organisms and their environment. The term *biodiversity* refers to the sum total of living organisms in an ecosystem. An *ecosystem* is a unit of *biotic* (i.e., living) and *abiotic* (i.e., nonliving) things that share environmental resources. All organisms interact with their environment, and changes in the environment, due to biotic or abiotic components, effect the kind and quantity of organisms that inhabit it. The place where an organism lives is called its *habitat*. There are two major habitats in nature: the *aquatic* (i.e., water) habitat and the *terrestrial* (i.e., land) habitat. An organism's "place" in the community (i.e., its physical, chemical, and biological impact on its habitat) is called its *niche*. Organisms that are hunters are called *predators*. Organisms that become the food of predators are called *prey*. Most biotic and abiotic resources in an ecosystem are used over and over again (i.e., recycled) while others may become depleted. Depletion of resources can upset the balance of nature within an ecosystem. Removing a particular rodent species from an ecosystem, for example, might allow the insects normally eaten by that species of rodent to over-populate. The growing population of insects might destroy the vegetation in the ecosystem, causing the extinction of life forms dependent upon that resource. The ecosystem would be destroyed. The greater the biodiversity within an ecosystem, the less likely it is to suffer complete collapse.

---

2. Examine the pictures provided by your instructor. Then complete the *Observations & Analysis* section.

Observations & Analysis

1. Identify the habitat of each organism shown on the handout provided by your instructor. Does the organism reside in an aquatic or terrestrial habitat?

    _____

    _____

    _____

    _____

    _____

    _____

    _____

2. List ten more organisms that add to the diversity of these habitats.

    _____

    _____

    _____

    _____

    _____

    _____

3. Explain why the extinction of a single species of insect in an ecosystem supporting several hundred species of insect would probably not cause the collapse of that ecosystem.

    _____

    _____

    _____

    _____

    _____

    _____

    _____

    _____

    _____

    _____

 **Biology**

Lesson 35: Teacher Preparation

Basic Principle   Stability in an ecosystem is a balance of competing effects.

Competency   Students will analyze changes in an ecosystem resulting from climatic change.

Materials   pictures of living organisms shown here

Procedure   Give students time to read the information on *Terrestrial Biomes and Climatic Change* before completing the *Observations & Analysis* section.

Answers to Observations & Analysis

Answers will vary, but should contain the following main point: The warming of the Earth's atmosphere and rising sea level will lead to the shifting global and local climates that would challenge the adaptability of organisms within existing biomes.

woodpecker

frog

lion

turtle

wolf

bear

cow

deer

pelican

opossum

whale

salmon

alligator

shark

Name _____   Date _____

Biology

STUDENT HANDOUT–LESSON 35

Basic Principle   Stability in an ecosystem is a balance of competing effects.

Objective   Analyze changes in an ecosystem resulting from climatic change.

Materials   pictures of living organisms provided by your instructor

Procedure

1.   Read the information on *Terrestrial Biomes and Climatic Change*.

Terrestrial Biomes and Climatic Change

Living things inhabit a narrow zone of our planet's surface where conditions are adequate to support them. Biologists call this zone the *biosphere*. The biosphere is limited to the watery environments of the world, a portion of Earth's crust, and the lower elevations of the atmosphere. Because climate and land features differ around the world, the organisms that adapt to inhabit a particular geographical region can be very different from those of other regions. A large community of living things that inhabit a particular geographical region is called a *biome*. Biomes arise as a result of the interactions between climate, land features, and the activities of other organisms. The major biomes studied by biologists include *tundra, forests, grasslands, deserts, marine, mountain,* and *fresh-water* biomes. The tundra, characterized by low temperatures, a short growing season, and very little rainfall, spreads across North America, Northern Europe, and Northern Asia. These regions are populated by many migratory species that move south during the harsh winter months. *Coniferous, deciduous,* and *tropical* forests found south of the tundra stretch across North America, Europe, and Asia. Coniferous forests (i.e., taiga) are inhabited by evergreen conifers that are green all year long. Deciduous forests are found in more temperate climatic regions and are populated by fruit-and-nut-producing trees (e.g., oak and maple) that lose their leaves in winter. Tropical forests, located along the equatorial regions of Central and South America, Central Africa, Southeast Asia, and New Guinea, have the greatest biodiversity. Tropical biomes are characterized by heavy rainfall which supports dense vegetation rising to a canopy layer more than 30 meters above the forest floor. Grassland biomes comprise the prairies and grazing pastures of the Midwestern United States, Australia, Argentina, and southern Russia. The African *savannah* found north of that continent's central tropical rain forest and south of the Sahara Desert is also a grassland biome. Desert biomes are scattered across the equatorial and temperate regions of the globe wherever rainfall falls below 25 centimeters per year. Vegetation is sparse and plants have thick and spiney outer layers to prevent water loss. Burrowing animals such as kangaroo rats and pocket mice that live in desert biomes have adapted ways to extract water from buried seeds and water-filled cactus. The salty sea, or marine biome, is divided into an *oceanic* zone and a *neritic* zone. The oceanic zone refers to the open ocean off the continental shelf that surrounds every continent. It is the deep ocean: inhabited by a vast variety of organisms living near the surface and others adapted to the extreme pressures of the wide abyssal plain. The primary food and oxygen producers of the world, called *phytoplankton*, inhabit the first few meters of ocean surface. All ocean-dwelling organisms feed directly on phytoplankton or on other organisms that do. The neritic zone refers to the shallow waters along the continental shelf. Boney fishes, crustacea, sea turtles, seals, and cetaceans inhabit the neritic biome. These creatures are dependent upon the warm water, high salt content, and plentiful food on the shelf. Mountain biomes are found in mountainous regions around the world such as the Rockies, Andes, and Himalayan mountain ranges. The extreme cold at high elevations limits plant and animal life. However, melting fresh snow during the spring and summer months produces fresh-water biomes where water flows from the mountains to the sea. Fresh-water biomes are diverse in plant and animal populations because they exist within the confines of other land biomes. They are also the least stable and change rapidly as temperature and rainfall change slightly from year to year.

2. Examine the pictures supplied by your instructor. Then complete the *Observations & Analysis* section.

Observations & Analysis

Choose one organism provided by your instructor and describe the biome in which the organism lives. Write a brief paragraph describing how the life of that organism would change as the result of a runaway *greenhouse effect*. The greenhouse effect is a phenomenon of Earth's atmosphere by which solar radiation normally absorbed by the Earth's surface and re-emitted into space becomes trapped by carbon dioxide and other atmospheric gases. The result is the warming of Earth's atmosphere and the elevation of sea level resulting from the melting of arctic and antarctic ice.

_____

_____

_____

_____

_____

_____

_____

_____

_____

_____

Lesson 36: Teacher Preparation

Basic Principle   Stability in an ecosystem is a balance of competing effects.

Competency   Students will analyze changes in an ecosystem resulting from human activity.

Procedure   Give students time to read the information on *Deforestation* before completing the *Observations & Analysis* section.

Answers to Observations & Analysis

1. Answers will vary, but should contain the following main point: Destruction of forests removes a multivaried depository of resources from local ecosystems.

2. Answers will vary, but should contain the following main point: The physical and chemical characteristics of the soil (i.e., integrity and porosity) in a biome are largely attributable to the kinds of plant life inhabiting an area. Plants are also essential to the carbon cycle which is integral to biochemical respiration and photosynthesis. The wholesale destruction of plant life in an area, therefore, can significantly change the characteristics of a biome.

Biology

STUDENT HANDOUT–LESSON 36

Basic Principle   Stability in an ecosystem is a balance of competing effects.

Objective   Analyze changes in an ecosystem resulting from human activity.

Procedure

1. Read the information on *Deforestation*.

Deforestation

Forest resources have been consumed by humans for thousands of years all over the world. In tropical regions, where soils are quickly replenished by the recycling of the forest's abundant biotic elements, new growth and harvesting occurs at a rapid rate. In regions of Africa, where soils are easily eroded and the climate is variable, forests are diminishing in size. In addition, poor agricultural practices practiced in response to increasing human populations have resulted in deforestation. Ecologists are attempting to involve local government officials in forest management in these regions and are seeking the assistance of wealthy nations to help developing countries. But even in those wealthy nations, the problem has become acute. In the United States less than 5 percent of the forests that once covered the nation still remain. As the population increases and industrialization continues, environmental activists are on constant watch to ensure that remaining forests are conserved. As scientific knowledge of forest growth expands and a record of the detrimental effects of human activity is compiled, conservationists work to prevent the destruction of forests. Their efforts are being applied around the world to prevent the exploitation, neglect, and devastation of forests.

---

2. Complete the *Observations & Analysis* section.

Observations & Analysis

1. Explain why the destruction of forests resulting from exploitation by humans might have a significant effect on local ecosystems.

   _____

   _____

   _____

   _____

   _____

   _____

   _____

2. Explain why the destruction of forests resulting from exploitation by humans might have a significant effect on large terrestrial biomes. Consider the integral role of plants (i.e., physical, chemical, biological effects) in ecosystems.

   _____

   _____

   _____

   _____

   _____

   _____

   _____

Biology

Lesson 37: Teacher Preparation

Basic Principle   Stability in an ecosystem is a balance of competing effects.

Competency   Students will analyze changes in an ecosystem resulting from the introduction of a nonnative species.

Procedure   Give students time to read the information on *Killer Bees* before completing the *Observations & Analysis* section.

Answer to Observations & Analysis

Answers will vary, but should contain the following main point: Killer bees can interfere with the pollination of crops ordinarily serviced by more efficient domestic bees.

Biology

STUDENT HANDOUT–LESSON 37

Basic Principle   Stability in an ecosystem is a balance of competing effects.

Objective   Analyze the changes in an ecosystem resulting from the introduction of a nonnative species.

Procedure

1. Read the information on *Killer Bees*.

Killer Bees

Killer bees are known to fatally attack humans and other animals. They are a hybrid strain resulting from a cross between wild bees and the African honeybee, *Apis mellifera scutellata*. Accidentally released in Brazil in 1956, killer bees have spread to distant regions thousands of miles from their original habitat. They are aggressive and often attack in swarms. Unlike domestic honeybees, killer bees are poor pollinators and produce limited quantities of honey. They inhabited northern Mexico by the late 1980s and crossed into the southwestern United States in the 1990s. Despite efforts to control their spread, killer bees now pose an agricultural threat to this part of the world.

---

2. Complete the *Observations & Analysis* section.

Observations & Analysis

Explain why killer bees pose an agricultural threat to northern Mexico and the southwestern United States.

_____

_____

_____

_____

_____

_____

_____

_____

_____

Lesson 38: Teacher Preparation

Basic Principle Stability in an ecosystem is a balance of competing effects.

Competency Students will show how population size fluctuates due to birth rate, immigration, emigration, and death.

Materials graph of *Human Population Age-Sex Distributions*

Procedure Give students time to read the information on *Human Population Ecology* before completing the *Observations & Analysis* section.

Answers to Observations & Analysis

1. Answers will vary, but should contain the following main point: The population of Mexico is likely to increase as the graph has a broad base showing a large pre-sexual group that will soon reach puberty.

2. Answers will vary, but should contain the following main point: The population of the United States is relatively stable compared with that of Mexico as the graph has a narrow base, although its birth rate has changed over the years as indicated by two bulges in the 20–24 and 55–59 age ranges.

3. Answers will vary, but should contain the following main point: The population of Sweden is likely to decrease as the graph has a very narrow base as compared with those of the other nations.

4. Answers will vary, but should contain the following main point: Should the borders between the two countries be open to the free migration of the two populaces, it is likely that the population density of the more affluent United States will increase due to the immigration of increasing numbers of individuals from its poorer, more densely populated, neighbor.

HUMAN POPULATION AGE-SEX DISTRIBUTION

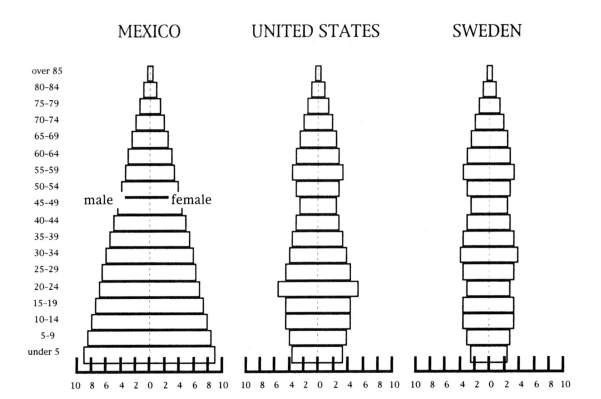

MEXICO   UNITED STATES   SWEDEN

over 85
80–84
75–79
70–74
65–69
60–64
55–59
50–54
45–49   male ———— female
40–44
35–39
30–34
25–29
20–24
15–19
10–14
5–9
under 5

10 8 6 4 2 0 2 4 6 8 10   10 8 6 4 2 0 2 4 6 8 10   10 8 6 4 2 0 2 4 6 8 10

Biology

STUDENT HANDOUT–LESSON 38

Basic Principle   Stability in an ecosystem is a balance of competing effects.

Objective   Show how population size fluctuates due to birth rate, immigration, emigration, and death.

Materials   graph of *Human Population Age-Sex Distribution*

Procedure

1. Read the information about *Human Population Ecology*.

Human Population Ecology

Human populations are dynamic. Ecologists studying the density of human populations inhabiting different regions use their data to predict the future of each region in terms of the population's changing distribution and growth rate. Population density is influenced by natality (i.e., birth rate), immigration, emigration, and mortality (i.e., death rate). To the population ecologist, the most important attribute of a human population is its "age-sex structure." The ecologist contructs graphs showing the age distribution of males and females at five-year intervals living in a region, and uses the graph to draw simple conclusions about how the region's population will change.

---

2. Study the graph provided by your instructor and complete the *Observations & Analysis* section.

Student Handout–Lesson 38 *(Continued)*

Observations & Analysis

1. How is the population density of Mexico likely to change? Explain your reasoning according to the information presented in the graph.

_____

_____

_____

_____

_____

2. How is the population density of the United States likely to change? Explain your reasoning according to the information presented in the graph.

_____

_____

_____

_____

_____

3. How is the population density of Sweden likely to change? Explain your reasoning according to the information presented in the graph.

_____

_____

_____

_____

4. Assume that for the foreseeable future, the United States were to remain a more affluent society than Mexico. How might the population density of the United States change were the borders between the two countries open to the free migration of their populaces?

_____

_____

_____

_____

_____

Lesson 39: Teacher Preparation

Basic Principle   Stability in an ecosystem is a balance of competing effects.

Competency   Students will identify the chemical cycles of abiotic resources that affect organic matter.

Procedure

1. Draw the illustration shown below and review *The Recycling Process*. List the limited resources we recycle on a day-to-day basis (i.e., aluminum cans, plastics, paper, etc.).

2. Give students time to read the information on *Chemical Cycles in Nature* before completing the *Observations & Analysis* section.

Answer to Observations & Analysis

Diagrams will vary, but should look much like those shown. Allow students to add any terms they think appropriate and can defend.

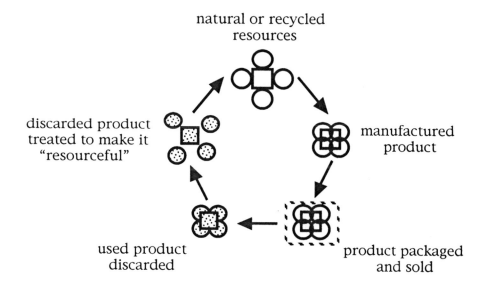

THE RECYCLING PROCESS

CHEMICAL CYCLES IN NATURE

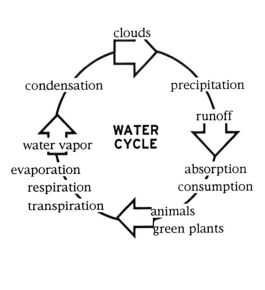

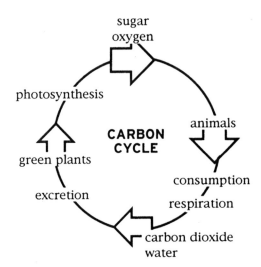

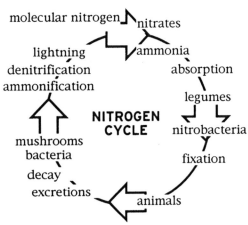

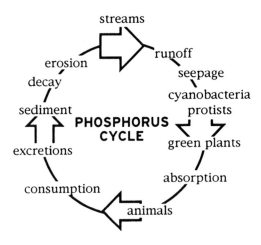

Biology

STUDENT HANDOUT–LESSON 39

Basic Principle   Stability in an ecosystem is a balance of competing effects.

Objective   Identify the chemical cycles of abiotic resources that affect organic matter.

Procedure

1. Read the information on *Chemical Cycles in Nature.*

Chemical Cycles in Nature

Because the Earth has limited chemical resources, natural chemical processes tend to be cyclical. A *cycle* is any set of events repeated over and over again. There are four basic chemical cycles in nature: the *water cycle*, the *carbon cycle*, the *nitrogen cycle*, and the *phosphorus cycle*. There are more than 2 billion trillion (2×10^{21}) liters of water in the oceans, lakes, rivers, streams, polar ice caps, and atmosphere covering the Earth, and all of it is recycled by physical means. Solar warming of the Earth's water causes it to evaporate into the atmosphere. Once in the atmosphere, the water vapor can cool and condense into rain, frost, or snow. It is pulled back to Earth by the force of gravity only to be evaporated again and again. In the process, water is cleansed of contaminating impurities. *Carbon* is recycled by chemical means. During photosynthesis, plants use the energy of the Sun to "fix" the carbon in carbon dioxide molecules into energy-rich sugar. Oxygen is given off in the process. All living organisms use sugar and oxygen during *respiration* to satisfy their energy needs. In the process, carbon dioxide is returned to the atmosphere. *Nitrogen* is also recycled by chemical means. About 79% of our atmosphere is composed of "free" *diatomic nitrogen* (N_2). During lightning storms, nitrogen is mixed with water vapor to form *nitrites* (NO^{2-}) and *nitric acid* (HNO_3). Rain brings this "fixed" nitrogen to the ground where it is absorbed by bacteria in the soil. *Nitrogen-fixing bacteria* provide plants with the nitrogen they need to make proteins and nucleic acids, two of the basic molecules of life. Other forms of bacteria called *decomposers* break down these macromolecules in decaying matter buried in the soil and return diatomic nitrogen, a light gas, to the atmosphere. Phosphorus, which does not normally exist in gaseous form, is recycled by more "terrestrial" means. Mostly found in eroded sedimentary rocks, phosphorus is dissolved in runoff water and combined with oxygen to form phosphates (PO_4). Phosphates are taken up by cyanobacteria and protists, incorporated into organic molecules (e.g., ATP, NADP, DNA, phospholipids), and absorbed by the roots of plants siding rivers, streams, and lakes. Animals consume the plants, and the phosphorus is returned to the waters when the animals die.

---

2. Study the handout illustrations. Then complete the *Observations & Analysis* section.

Observations & Analysis

Choose from the list of terms shown to diagram the events taking place during each natural chemical cycle. Write the terms along the curved lines or by the arrows to indicate the sequence in which these events occur. Some terms may be repeated more than once, while others are specific to a particular cycle. Add any terms you think are appropriate, but be prepared to defend your addition.

green plants	clouds	nitrobacteria
precipitation	photosynthesis	animals
streams	mushrooms	respiration
ammonification	bacteria	ammonia
evaporation	decay	upthrust
transpiration	runoff	seepage
consumption	nitrates	fixation
excretions	denitrification	legumes
absorption	oxygen	molecular nitrogen
carbon dioxide	volcanoes	oceans
cyanobacteria	protists	

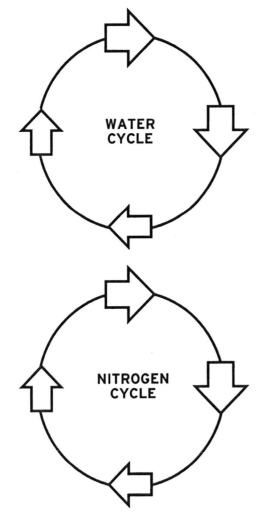

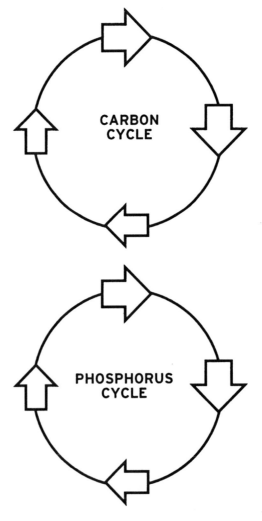

 **Biology**

Lesson 40: Teacher Preparation

Basic Principle   Stability in an ecosystem is a balance of competing effects.

Competency   Students will explain why producers and consumers are essential to the survival of an ecosystem.

Procedure   Give students time to read the information on *Producers and Consumers* before completing the *Observations & Analysis* section.

Answers to Observations & Analysis

1. Diagrams will vary, but should look much like the one shown.

2. Answers will vary, but should contain the following main point: The extinction of any species will force consumers of that species to alter their diet. The volume of different food resources will, therefore, change, causing a realignment of the delicate balance of the ecosystem.

3. Answers will vary, but should contain the following main point: The extinction of producers would drastically affect the ecosystem, since it is they that are the primary manufacturers of food for the planet through the process of photosynthesis.

A FOOD WEB

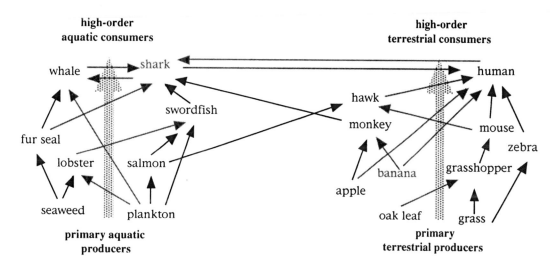

Biology

STUDENT HANDOUT—LESSON 40

Basic Principle   Stability in an ecosystem is a balance of competing effects.

Objective   Explain why producers and consumers are essential to the survival of an ecosystem.

Procedure

1. Read the information on *Producers and Consumers*.

Producers and Consumers

The biotic portion of an ecosystem is called a *community*. Each organism within a community interacts with the environment and affects the lives of other members of the community. Organisms in a community can be classified according to how they obtain food. Plants are the *primary producers* of food. Plants trap the energy of the Sun and make their own food by photosynthesis using water, nutrients from the soil, and carbon dioxide from the atmosphere. Animal *consumers* obtain the energy and nutrients stored in plants by eating plants or other animals that eat plants. *Decomposers* such as bacteria facilitate the decay of dead organisms and the excreted wastes of animals, putting nutrients back into the soil to be used again by plant producers.

---

2. Complete the *Observations & Analysis* section.

Observations & Analysis

1. Choose 10–20 organisms from the list of organisms to create a "food web" of organisms present in both an aquatic (ocean) and terrestrial (land) community. Remember that different predators may eat the same prey allowing more than one arrow to be directed at a single predator. It is also possible for two predators to consider each other as prey animals.

ladybug	shark	fur seal	whale
swordfish	tiger	monkey	banana
apple	oak leaf	shrimp	mouse
plankton	penguin	grasshopper	caterpillar
snake	wolf	hawk	bass
lobster	seaweed	starfish	salmon
sponge	squid	human	wild pig
zebra	grass	spider	woodpecker

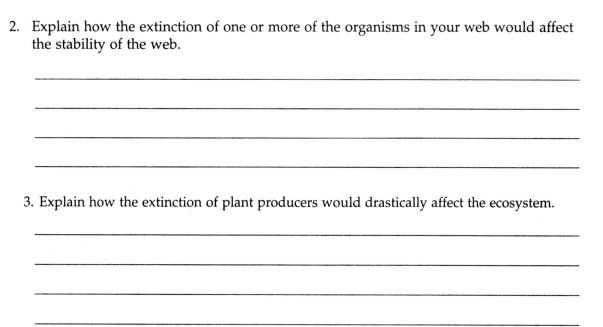

high-order aquatic consumers

primary aquatic producers

high-order terrestrial consumers

primary terrestrial producers

2. Explain how the extinction of one or more of the organisms in your web would affect the stability of the web.

_____

_____

_____

_____

3. Explain how the extinction of plant producers would drastically affect the ecosystem.

_____

_____

_____

_____

 **Biology**

Lesson 41: Teacher Preparation

Basic Principle   Stability in an ecosystem is a balance of competing effects.

Competency   Students will use a food pyramid to illustrate the flow of energy through an ecosystem.

Procedure

1. Write these two examples of food chains on the board and note that each chain begins with a producer.

EXAMPLES OF FOOD CHAINS

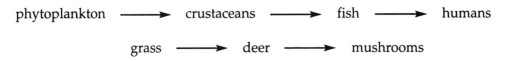

phytoplankton ⟶ crustaceans ⟶ fish ⟶ humans

grass ⟶ deer ⟶ mushrooms

2. Give students time to read the information on *Biomass and Food Pyramids*.
3. Draw the *Food Pyramid* and allow students to complete the *Observations & Analysis* section.

Answers to Observations & Analysis

1. Examples will vary, but should illustrate accurate relationships between predator and prey organisms.
2. Answers will vary, but should contain the following main points: Biomass measurements give ecologists hints about the stability of predator–prey relationships. If the biomass of a prey species is critically low, the ecologist can deduce that the predators of that species might have trouble finding food and might be forced to search for alternative sources of food. The stability of the ecosystem may be compromised, and interactions between organisms could be changed, resulting in the variability of community populations.

FOOD PYRAMID

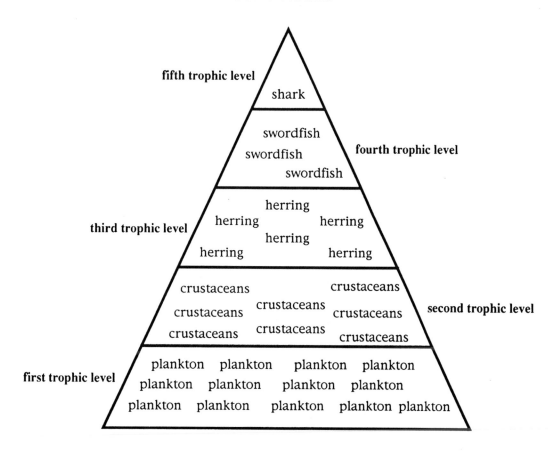

Biology

STUDENT HANDOUT–LESSON 41

Basic Principle   Stability in an ecosystem is a balance of competing effects.

Objective   Use a food pyramid to illustrate the flow of energy through an ecosystem.

Procedure

1. Read the information on *Biomass and Food Pyramids*.

Biomass and Food Pyramids

The successful survival of any given species is determined by the amount of food available to it. Producers, of course, have a nearly inexhaustible "food" supply in the Sun which will provide our planet with energy for another six billion years. Producers manufacture their own solid food (i.e., sugar) by performing photosynthesis. In every ecosystem, plants and animals are part of a *food chain* along which energy is transferred from one organism to another. The term *biomass* refers to the total mass of a particular species or group of species available for consumption in an ecosystem. The biomass of prey organisms must be greater than the biomass of predator organisms in order for predators to survive. This relationship can be summarized in a *food pyramid*, a diagram that describes how energy flows from one organism to another. Each level of the pyramid is called a *trophic level*, the base or *first trophic level* having the greatest amount of consumable energy. A food pyramid becomes more narrow from base to apex as energy in the form of heat is lost due to the physical contraints on the system. The Second Law of Thermodynamics (i.e., the law of entropy) is obeyed.

---

2. Complete the *Observations & Analysis* section.

Observations & Analysis

1. Give three examples of a food chain similar to the examples provided by your instructor. Add arrows as needed.

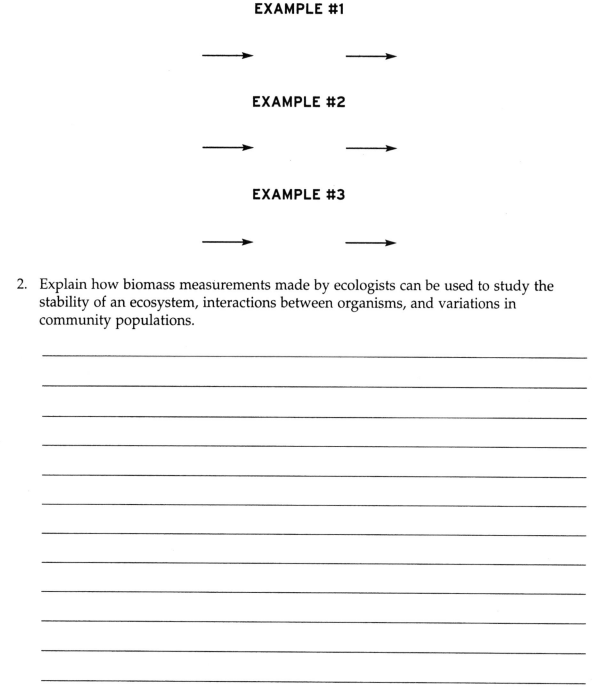

EXAMPLE #1

⟶   ⟶

EXAMPLE #2

⟶   ⟶

EXAMPLE #3

⟶   ⟶

2. Explain how biomass measurements made by ecologists can be used to study the stability of an ecosystem, interactions between organisms, and variations in community populations.

_____

_____

_____

_____

_____

_____

_____

_____

_____

_____

_____

Biology

Lesson 42: Teacher Preparation

Basic Principle   The frequency of alleles in a gene pool varies over time.

Competency   Students will show how lethal genes can be passed from generation to generation.

Procedure

1. Review the use of a Punnett Square by illustrating the results of a cross between two parents carrying alleles for tall (T) and short (t) as shown below. In the example, both parents are hybrid tall. Make sure students understand the distribution of offspring and the characteristics associated with them: 25% are purebred tall, 50% are hybrid tall, and 25% are purebred short.

2. Give students time to read the information on *Lethal Genes*.

3. Assist students in completing the *Observations & Analysis* section.

Answer to Observations & Analysis

See the Punnett Squares.

<table>
<tr><td></td><td></td><td colspan="2" align="center">hybrid female
(Tt)</td></tr>
<tr><td></td><td></td><td align="center">T</td><td align="center">t</td></tr>
<tr><td rowspan="2" align="center">hybrid male
(Tt)</td><td align="center">T</td><td align="center">TT</td><td align="center">Tt</td></tr>
<tr><td align="center">t</td><td align="center">Tt</td><td align="center">tt</td></tr>
</table>

1. Results of a cross between a hybrid male sufferer of Huntington's chorea and a healthy female: 50% of the offspring will develop Huntington's chorea.

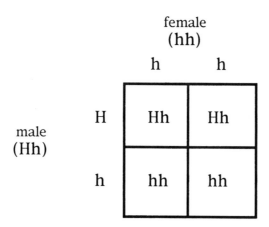

female
(hh)

	h	h
H	Hh	Hh
h	hh	hh

male
(Hh)

2. Results of a cross between a female carrier of hemophilia and a healthy male: 50% of the male offspring will have hemophilia; 50% of the female offspring will be carriers.

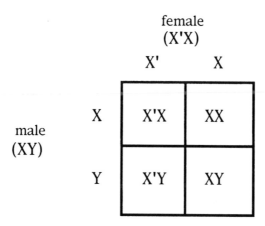

female
(X'X)

	X'	X
X	X'X	XX
Y	X'Y	XY

male
(XY)

3. Results of a cross between male and female carriers of sickle-cell anemia: 25% of the offspring will be normal; 50% will be carriers; 25% will have sickle-cell anemia.

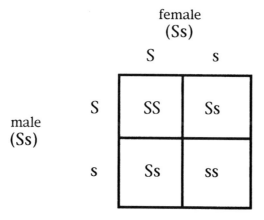

female
(Ss)

	S	s
S	SS	Ss
s	Ss	ss

male
(Ss)

Biology

STUDENT HANDOUT–LESSON 42

Basic Principle   The frequency of alleles in a gene pool varies over time.

Objective   Show how lethal genes can be passed from generation to generation.

Procedure

1. Read the information on *Lethal Genes*.

Lethal Genes

The alteration of alleles, called mutations, is the basis of evolution by means of natural selection; and while a small percentage of genetic mutations improve the adaptability of organisms to their environment, most are lethal. Lethal genes usually result in the termination of development before the affected organism reaches reproductive age. However, a few of these defective alleles are passed from generation to generation as either dominant or recessive alleles. Each of us carries several lethal genes; but unless they are dominant alleles, they will fail to be expressed throughout our life and we might never know we carry them. *Hemophilia* is an "X-linked" genetic disorder that is carried on the *X-chromosome* (i.e., sex chromosome). It is characterized by the affected individual's inability to form clotted blood following injury. A hemophiliac can bleed to death from the slightest cut. All male offspring of a female parent with this allele will have hemophilia, since the Y-chromosome that produces male offspring does not have a healthy allele to suppress the disease. Daughters of female "carriers" will carry the lethal gene but will not express the disease unless their male parent was a hemophiliac. *Huntington's chorea* is a dominant *autosomal* hereditary disorder that affects about 1 in 10,000 people. Autosomes are chromosomes other than sex chromosomes. The symptoms of Huntington's chorea—slurred speech and unsteady gait—develop slowly and appear at about middle age before more serious symptoms develop. As the disease worsens, there is a progressive deterioration of mental functioning resulting from brain damage to the cerebrum. The disease eventually results in the death of the individual after he or she has passed the lethal alleles onto offspring. *Sickle-cell anemia* is a recessive autosomal hereditary disorder. The disease is characterized by abnormal hemoglobin and the blood's failure to carry sufficient oxygen to the cells of the body. Offspring of parents who both carry the recessive allele form sickle-cell hemoglobin. Damaged red blood cells carrying defective hemoglobin can clog blood vessels and impede healthy blood flow. Pain attacks are the most common symptom leading to infections and lung damage that can result in death.

2. Complete the *Observations & Analysis* section.

Observations & Analysis

1. Use a Punnett Square to show how the allele for Huntington's chorea would be passed to the offspring of a hybrid male sufferer of the disease and a healthy female who does not carry the defective gene.

2. Use a Punnett Square to show how the allele for hemophilia would be passed to the offspring of a female carrier of the disease and a healthy male who does not carry the defective gene.

3. Use a Punnett Square to show how the allele for sickle-cell anemia would be passed to the offspring of male and female carriers of the defective gene.

Lesson 43: Teacher Preparation

Basic Principle   The frequency of alleles in a gene pool varies over time.

Competency   Students will explain how mutations are added to the gene pool.

Procedure   Give students time to read the information on *Natural Selection of a Chance Mutation* before completing the *Observations & Analysis* section.

Answer to Observations & Analysis

Answers will vary, but should contain the following main points: The mutation for dark coloration is inherited by offspring adapting them for survival in more shadowed areas of their ecosystem. As the forest grows more dense as the result of climatic change, these organisms increase in population due to their enhanced ability to camouflage themselves against predation. At the same time, their relatives containing the original gene for lighter color diminish in population due to their inability to protect themselves against predators.

Name _____ **Date** _____

Biology

STUDENT HANDOUT–LESSON 43

Basic Principle   The frequency of alleles in a gene pool varies over time.

Objective   Explain how mutations are added to the gene pool.

Procedure

1. Read the information on *Natural Selection of a Chance Mutation*.

Natural Selection of a Chance Mutation

Mutations can be caused by ultraviolet radiation from the Sun or toxic chemicals in the environment. They are the result of changes in the sequence of nitrogenous bases in strands of DNA that give instructions for the synthesis of structural and functional proteins. An organism that inherits a nonlethal mutation might, in the face of environmental change, become the beneficiary of a successful adaptation that increases its chances of survival.

---

2. Examine the illustration showing how a chance mutation spreads through the gene pool as the result of environmental change.

3. Complete the *Observations & Analysis* section.

SPREAD OF A CHANCE MUTATION THROUGH THE GENE POOL

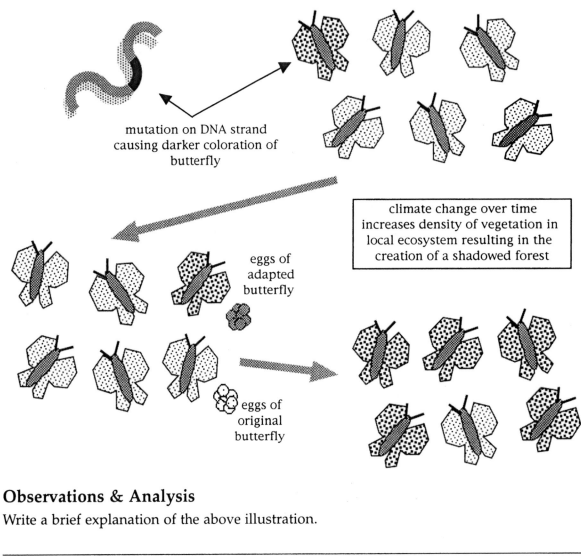

mutation on DNA strand
causing darker coloration of
butterfly

climate change over time
increases density of vegetation in
local ecosystem resulting in the
creation of a shadowed forest

eggs of
adapted
butterfly

eggs of
original
butterfly

Observations & Analysis

Write a brief explanation of the above illustration.

_____

_____

_____

_____

_____

_____

_____

_____

_____

_____

_____

_____

Lesson 44: Teacher Preparation

Basic Principle   The frequency of alleles in a gene pool varies over time.

Competency   Students will show how natural selection acts on phenotype rather than genotype.

Procedure   Give students time to read the information on *Genotype and Phenotype* before completing the *Observations & Analysis* section.

Answer to Observations & Analysis

Descriptions will vary and should clearly identify the mutations introduced into each generation (i.e., body spokes in second generation).

Biology

STUDENT HANDOUT–LESSON 44

Basic Principle   The frequency of alleles in a gene pool varies over time.

Objective   Show how natural selection acts on phenotype rather than genotype.

Procedure

1. Read the information on *Genotype and Phenotype*.

Genotype and Phenotype

Genotype refers to the particular set of alleles present in an organism. *Phenotype* refers to the physical traits displayed by an organism and is not necessarily a perfect manifestation of the organism's genotype. Since genes can be dominant, codominant, or recessive, not all genes will be expressed during the course of an organism's life. Environmental factors can also change how genes are expressed. Environmental factors can activate or suppress the expression of a gene or change the physical appearance of traits (i.e., malnutrition). Just as farmers artificially select and breed their livestock to produce strains of animals more useful to humans, nature selects those organisms best adapted for survival in a changing environment according to their physical traits.

---

2. Complete the *Observations & Analysis* section.

Observations & Analysis

Next to the illustration of each successive group of imaginative organisms, describe the environmental pressure that could have resulted in the natural selection of that generation.

_____

_____

_____

_____

_____

_____

_____

_____

_____

_____

_____

_____

_____

_____

_____

_____

_____

_____

_____

_____

_____

_____

Lesson 45: Teacher Preparation

Basic Principle   The frequency of alleles in a gene pool varies over time.

Competency   Students will explain how variations within a species increase the likelihood of species survival.

Procedure

1. Review the observations made by Charles Darwin that helped him to arrive at his theory of evolution be means of natural selection: (1) There are individual differences among the members of a species. (2) Species overreproduce. (3) There is limited food and space available to living things. (4) During competition for limited food and space, organisms least adaptible to change may fail to reproduce. The best adapted will survive to reproduce and pass their adaptations to their offspring.

2. Give students time to read the information on *Variability of Individual Traits* before completing the *Observations & Analysis* section.

Answer to Observations & Analysis

Answers will vary, but should include detailed descriptions of how given organisms are better adapted for survival than other members of their species in the face of specific environmental pressures.

Name _____ Date _____

Biology

STUDENT HANDOUT—LESSON 45

Basic Principle   The frequency of alleles in a gene pool varies over time.

Objective   Explain how variations within a species increase the likelihood of species survival.

Procedure

1. Read the information on *Variability of Individual Traits*.

Variability of Individual Traits

Multiple alleles for a given species trait give rise to phenotypic variability among the individuals of a species. A *species trait* is any physical characteristic shared by all members of a species (e.g., eye color). An *individual trait* is a variation of a species trait (e.g., the different eye colors: blue, brown, hazel, green, etc.). If all members of a species were exactly alike, all would suffer the detrimental effects of a changing environment that could result in the extinction of that species. Charles Darwin's observation of the existence of individual traits within a species, characteristics that set individuals apart from their relatives, served as the basis for his theory of evolution by means of natural selection. Without variability there would be no "selection."

---

2. Examine the handout illustration. Then complete the *Observations & Analysis* section.

VARIABILITY WITHIN A SPECIES

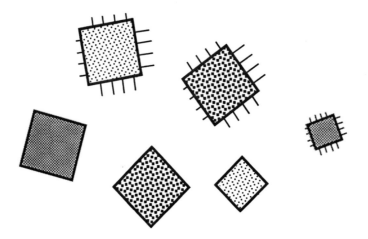

Observations & Analysis

Explain how the variations present in individuals within this imaginary species might help them to survive specific environmental pressures.

_____

_____

_____

_____

_____

_____

_____

 **Biology**

Lesson 46: Teacher Preparation

Basic Principle   Evolution is the result of genetic changes that occur in constantly changing environments.

Competency   Students will show how natural selection determines the differential survival of organisms.

Materials   coin

Procedure

1. Point out that the scientific notions of "organic mutability" and the "adaptive radiation of species" did not emerge as viable scientific ideas until the middle of the 18th century. The first widely accepted theory proposed to explain the then-hypothetical "transmutation" of species was suggested by the French naturalist Jean Baptiste Lamarck (1744–1829). According to his *theory of acquired characteristics*, organisms acquired adaptive traits during their lifetime that they passed to their offspring. In this manner, complex organisms evolved from simpler ones. Lamarck's most famous illustration of the theory was the evolution of a giraffe's long neck. He suggested that as the short-necked ancestors of modern giraffes reached higher and higher into the trees to find richer vegetation, their necks became longer—a trait that was inherited by their offspring. Lamarkian evolution has since been discredited for lack of evidence that traits acquired during a lifespan (e.g., strong muscles acquired from exercise) can be genetically transmitted to offspring. A man who loses an arm in an industrial accident does not pass on this trait to his son or daughter.

   From 1831 to 1836, the English naturalist Charles Robert Darwin (1809–1882) made his famous voyage aboard the *HMS Beagle*. On the trip, Darwin compiled volumes of information in which he described the enormous variety of plant and animal life off the west coast of South America. He was particularly intrigued by the comparative and contrasting physical characteristics of reptiles and birds inhabiting distant islands. Darwin explained the similarities and differences among the species by proposing that they had all evolved from a common ancestor after acquiring those traits that best adapted them for life on the islands they inhabited. He suggested that the struggle for survival—resulting from competition for limited resources within large populations of individuals—caused the elimination of those individuals least adapted for the struggle. After 20 years of further research—and after a meeting with the Welch naturalist Alfred Russel Wallace (1823–1913) who had come to the same conclusion based on his own voluminous study—Darwin published the *Origin of the Species by Means of Natural Selection*. Darwin likened "natural selection" to the "selective breeding" (e.g., artificial selection) of plants and animals that had been employed by farmers for centuries to create the most desirable domesticated vegetable grains and animal strains. However, Darwin could not explain the mechanism underlying the cause of individual differences that allowed one member of a species to become better adapted to its environment.

Ironically, the work of Darwin's unknown contemporary, the Austrian monk Gregor Mendel (1822–1884), had already elucidated the laws of inheritance which serve as the foundation of modern genetics. The relevance of Mendel's work went unrecognized until 1900. In support of Darwin's theory of evolution by means of natural selection, the German biologist August Friedrich Leopold Weismann (1834–1914) proposed that every organism contains an hereditary substance, which he called "germ plasm," within the confines of living cells. According to Weismann, germ plasm did not change with mere alterations to the body. Treatment of living cells with X-rays by American geneticists Thomas Hunt Morgan (1866–1945) and Hermann Joseph Muller (1890–1967), however, resulted in mutations of the physical structure of cells. Experimenting with X-rays, Morgan and Muller were able to alter the morphological structure of the organs of fruit flies (i.e., *Drosophila*). The gene was later located on the chromosomes (i.e., "colored bodies") residing in the nuclei of cells. In 1953, the American biologist James Watson (b. 1928) and his English associate Francis Crick (b. 1916) elucidated the structure of the macromolecule that comprises the gene: deoxyribonucleic acid (DNA).

2. Give students time to read the information on *The Theory of Evolution* before completing the activity and the *Observations & Analysis* section.

Answers to Observations & Analysis

1. Descriptions will vary, but should mention explicit differences between the organisms on these plates.

2. Answers will vary, but should contain the following main points: Natural selection, driven by competition for limited resources among organisms struggling to survive in a changing environment, forces the extinction of species least adapted to meet the needs of that competition while at the same time promoting the survival of those with successful adaptations. Mutations result in the creation of new phenotypes that enhance the adaptive capabilities of organisms.

Biology

STUDENT HANDOUT–LESSON 46

Basic Principle   Evolution is the result of genetic changes that occur in constantly changing environments.

Objective   Show how natural selection determines the differential survival of organisms.

Materials   coin

Procedure

1. Read the information on *The Theory of Evolution*.

The Theory of Evolution

Scientists have known for some time that many species alive during past ages are no longer alive today. Biologists are also aware that many species, like our own, did not exist long ago. For example, there is no evidence that human beings existed on Earth prior to five million years ago. Fossils are an important piece of evidence in the study of our planet's history, but they are not absolutely necessary to explain how living things have changed over the eons. The English naturalist Charles Robert Darwin (1809–1882) gathered information about the variety of plants and animals that inhabit the Galápagos Islands off the coast of South America. While there, he made several critical observations that helped him develop a *theory of evolution by means of natural selection*. He observed that: (1) there are individual differences among the members of a species, (2) species overreproduce to insure the survival of their kind, and (3) there is limited food and space available to living things. Darwin deduced that during competition for limited food and space, organisms least adapted to survive might not live to reproduce and, thereby, force their species closer to extinction. Those better adapted to survive and reproduce pass their favored traits on to their offspring.

---

2. In each of the four ovals in Plate A, draw a simple geometric shape (triangle, rectangle, etc.) to represent four identical creatures.

3. Add a single different mutation to each organism (straight lines, dots, squiggles, circles) so that you can tell the new "species" apart.

4. Choose two of the species to be "heads" and two to be "tails," before flipping a coin to see which species becomes extinct as a result of natural selection pressures. Choose one of the remaining two species to be "heads" and the other to be "tails," and flip again so that only one species remains.

5. Redraw four identical offspring of the surviving creature in the ovals on Plate B. Add a new mutation (e.g., limbs, eyes, etc.) to each member of the group to create four new species.

6. Repeat Steps 4 and 5 to complete Plates C and D.

7. Complete the *Observations & Analysis* section.

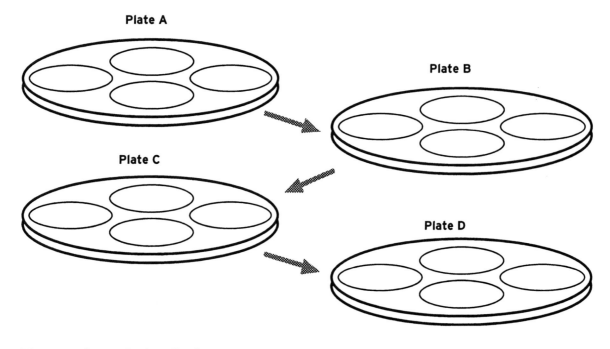

Plate A

Plate B

Plate C

Plate D

Observations & Analysis

1. How did the organisms in Plate D differ from those in Plate A?

   _____

   _____

   _____

   _____

   _____

2. Explain how mutation, natural selection (i.e., coin flipping), and extinction combined to give rise to the species on Plate D.

   _____

   _____

   _____

   _____

   _____

   _____

Lesson 47: Teacher Preparation

Basic Principle   Evolution is the result of genetic changes that occur in constantly changing environments.

Competency   Students will explain how reproductive and geographic isolation affect speciation.

Procedure   Give students time to read the information on *Allopatric and Sympatric Speciation* before completing the *Observations & Analysis* section.

Answer to Observations & Analysis

Answers will vary, but should include the following main points: Allopatric speciation refers to the creation of new species following genetic divergence among individuals separated by distance or geographic barriers. Sympatric speciation refers to the creation of new species resulting from the selection of variations within a species in the same region.

Name _____ Date _____

Biology

STUDENT HANDOUT–LESSON 47

Basic Principle   Evolution is the result of genetic changes that occur in constantly changing environments.

Objective   Explain how reproductive and geographic isolation affect speciation.

Procedure

1. Read the information on *Allopatric and Sympatric Speciation*.

Allopatric and Sympatric Speciation

A *species* is defined as an interbreeding population of individuals that share the same gene pool; the sum total of all alleles in the population. Different species do not interbreed and gene flow occurs only within a given species. *Speciation* refers to the mechanisms by which new species are produced, a process involving numerous genetic changes that lead to phenotypes that make mating between individuals impossible. Speciation normally results from the isolation of two populations that continue to diverge genetically. *Allopatric speciation* takes place when two populations become separated geographically by distance or natural barriers such as rivers or mountain ranges. *Sympatric speciation* refers to speciation among individuals in the same region that can no longer mate successfully as the result of cumulative genetic changes.

---

2. Examine the handout illustrations. Then complete the *Observations & Analysis* section.

ALLOPATRIC SPECIATION

SYMPATRIC SPECIATION

one species

emerging physical barrier

eroding physical barrier

two species

one species

passage of time accompanied by genetic divergence

two species

two species

Explain the difference between allopatric and sympatric speciations.

_____

_____

_____

_____

_____

_____

_____

Lesson 48: Teacher Preparation

Basic Principle   Evolution is the result of genetic changes that occur in constantly changing environments.

Competency   Students will analyze fossil evidence with regard to biological diversity, episodic speciation, and mass extinction.

Materials   information on dominant lifeforms of the geologic past

Procedure

1. Give students time to read the information on *Mass Extinction and Episodic Speciation.*

2. Point out that the idea that plants and animals have evolved, flourished, then ceased to exist was not fully accepted by biologists until the late 19th century. Earlier 17th- and 18th-century biologists suggested that creatures such as the giant sloth, *Megalonyx jeffersoni*, still roamed unexplored regions of North America. The fossilized bones of other creatures were believed to be the remains of existing animals that would one day be found alive in the farthest unexplored corners of the globe. The French anatomist Georges Cuvier (1769–1832) established the fact of extinction in his 1812 publication *Research on the Fossil Bones of Quadrupeds.* In that and other publications Cuvier reviewed the disposition and absence of fossils in many rock strata, most notably the sequence at Monmartre, Paris. The fossilized specimens of early sea creatures present in the Monmartre Sequence date back to the early Devonian Period of the Paleozoic Era. The Scottish geologist James Hutton (1726–1797) proposed that the land undergoes continual transformation by the same processes as those that occurred in the past. He suggested that studying the time it takes for these transformations to take place would provide clues to the actual age of the Earth. He deduced that the Earth was quite ancient and that rock strata buried deep in the Earth contained fossils that were many millions of years old. The geologist Charles Lyell (1797–1875) estimated the age of the Earth to be approximately 240,000,000 years old and gave a description of the Earth's geological history. Modern radioactive dating techniques estimate the age of our planet to be about 4.5 billion years.

3. Distribute copies of the information on dominant lifeforms and give students time to complete the *Observations & Analysis* section.

Answers to Observations & Analysis

1. Answers will vary, but should include the following main point: Mass extinctions due to climatic change, disease, or asteroid impacts with Earth can destroy whole species that might otherwise affect or control the populations of other species through predation. As a result, prey species would find themselves free to procreate, mutate, and evolve along any number of biological lineages.

2. Students should be able to identify the major groups associated with each geologic era.

DOMINANT LIFEFORMS OF THE GEOLOGIC PAST

	Beginning Years Ago (in millions)	Dominant Plant Life	Dominant Animal Life
CENOZOIC ERA			
Neogene	25	nonwoody herbs	wooly mammoths, saber-tooths, primates
Paleogene	65	grasslands, flowers	rise of placental and hoofed mammals
MESOZOIC ERA			
Cretaceous	145	first protected seeds	dinosaurs, first birds, small mammals
Jurassic	210	cycads and conifers	large dinosaurs, pouched mammals
Triassic	245	ferns and conifers	first dinosaurs, flying dinosaurs, egg-laying mammals
PALEOZOIC ERA			
Permian	280	conifers	modern insects, small reptiles
Pennsylvanian	320	cycads, conifers	amphibians, first reptiles
Mississippian	345	club mosses, cycads	ancient sharks, sea lilies
Devonian	405	first conifer forests	first amphibians, lungfish
Silurian	425	algae, first land plants	wingless insects, first fishes
Ordovician	500	marine algae	coral, trilobites, mollusks
Cambrian	600	marine algae	trilobites, brachiopods
PRECAMBRIAN ERA			
	4,500	algae, fungi	protists, worms, invertebrates

Biology

STUDENT HANDOUT–LESSON 48

Basic Principle   Evolution is the result of genetic changes that occur in constantly changing environments.

Objective   Analyze fossil evidence with regard to biological diversity, episodic speciation, and mass extinction.

Materials   information on dominant lifeforms of the geologic past

Procedure

1. Read the information on *Mass Extinction and Episodic Speciation*.

Mass Extinction and Episodic Speciation

Mutation and natural selection combine to produce the degree of speciation evident in biological communities. While mutations add variability to those communities, environmental forces cause the extinction of organisms least adapted for survival. Many more species have become extinct than are alive on the planet today. Extinction plays a primary role in the evolution of life, the geological evidence suggesting that there have been more than a dozen *mass extinctions* since life first evolved on the planet. During these global ecological calamities, whole populations of organisms, amounting to as much as 80% of the planet's lifeforms, perished within relatively short periods of geologic time (i.e., thousands of years). The dinosaurs that perished about sixty million years ago were probably the victims of one such event believed to have been caused by an asteroid collision with Earth. Mass extinctions can also be the result of sudden climatic change or disease. The fossil evidence shows that mass extinctions are typically followed by a population explosion, an increase in the rate of speciation within a group of organisms. Surviving species tend to flourish following a mass extinction as the result of reduced competition from demised predators. They may also benefit from climate changes favorable to their particular set of adaptations. The tiny warm-blooded insectivores that survived the mass extinction of the dinosaurs underwent a sudden *episodic speciation* that made the mammalian order one of the planet's most successful biological groups. These early mammals evolved into whole new families, genera, and species, giving rise to all modern mammals including humans. In recent geological times, the Earth's history is divided into three eras: the Paleozoic Era, the Mesozoic Era, and the Cenozoic Era. Each era is characterized by the most prominant group to dominate the fossil record of that era. They are the Age of the Fishes, the Age of the Reptiles, and the Age of the Mammals, respectively.

---

2. Examine the handout. Then complete the *Observations & Analysis* section.

Observations & Analysis

1. Explain how mass extinctions tend to result in the episodic speciation of existing biological communities.

   _____

   _____

   _____

   _____

   _____

2. Use the information handout provided by your instructor to list the dominating lifeforms of each geologic period.

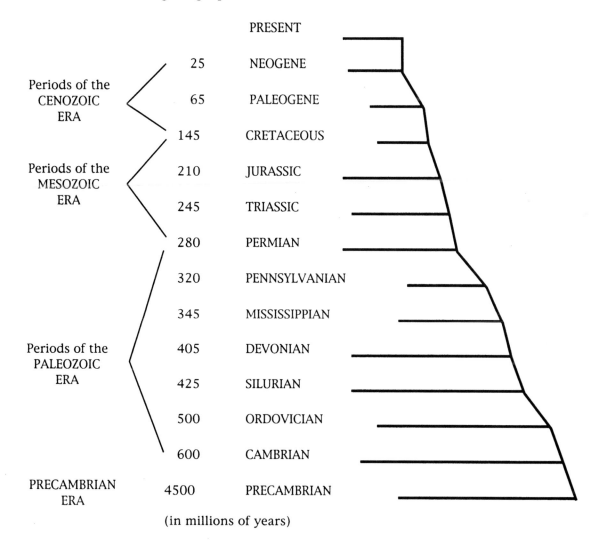

	PRESENT
	25 NEOGENE
Periods of the CENOZOIC ERA	65 PALEOGENE
	145 CRETACEOUS
Periods of the MESOZOIC ERA	210 JURASSIC
	245 TRIASSIC
	280 PERMIAN
	320 PENNSYLVANIAN
	345 MISSISSIPPIAN
Periods of the PALEOZOIC ERA	405 DEVONIAN
	425 SILURIAN
	500 ORDOVICIAN
	600 CAMBRIAN
PRECAMBRIAN ERA	4500 PRECAMBRIAN

(in millions of years)

Lesson 49: Teacher Preparation

Basic Principle   The internal environment of the human body remains relatively stable, or homeostatic, in the face of outside change due to the coordination of structures and functions among organ systems.

Competency   Students will explain how body systems provide cells with oxygen and nutrients.

Procedure   Give students time to read the information on *The Digestive, Respiratory, and Circulatory Systems* before completing the *Observations & Analysis* section.

Answers to Observations & Analysis

1. D	D	C	R
C	D	R	C
D	C	D	R
D	D	D	R
R	R	R	D

2. Answers will vary, but should include the following main point: Diseases of the digestive system impede the complete and proper assimilation of solid and liquid nutrients that supply the body's cells with energy and raw materials.

3. Answers will vary, but should include the following main point: Diseases of the respiratory system impede the complete and proper assimilation of gaseous oxygen needed by the body's cells for the production of energy through chemical respiration.

4. Answers will vary, but should include the following main point: Diseases of the circulatory system impede the complete and proper distribution of raw materials in the blood to the body's dependent cells.

Name _____ Date _____

Biology

STUDENT HANDOUT–LESSON 49

Basic Principle   The internal environment of the human body remains relatively stable, or homeostatic, in the face of outside change due to the coordination of structures and functions among organ systems.

Objective   Explain how body systems provide cells with oxygen and nutrients.

Procedure

1. Read the information on *The Digestive, Respiratory, and Circulatory Systems.*

The Digestive, Respiratory, and Circulatory Systems

All cells require oxygen and nutrients to survive. And since all body organs are comprised of tissues composed of cells, organ systems within the body must work together to provide each and every cell with these essentials. The process begins with the digestive and respiratory systems. The *digestive system* prepares liquid and solid nutrients for use by cells by breaking down the complex molecules that give living things the energy and raw materials (e.g., water, vitamins and minerals, proteins, carbohydrates, lipids, and nucleic acids) they require to establish and maintain their form and functional features. The *respiratory system* absorbs gases from the atmosphere and, through the tubular network of the *circulatory system*, provides cells with the molecular oxygen they need to release the energy content in food through the process of *chemical respiration*. The toxic product of chemical respiration, carbon dioxide, is then expelled from the body by mechanical respiration (i.e., breathing). The circulatory system also distributes the essential products of the digestive process to the cells of the body. The organs of the digestive system utilize a number of catalytic enzymes (i.e., ptyalin, pepsin, insulin, bile, etc.) to reduce complex proteins, carbohydrates, lipids, and nucleic acids to simpler biochemical units that can be used by individual cells: amino acids, saccharides (e.g., simple sugars such as glucose), fatty acids, and nucleotides, respectively. The healthy metabolic and catabolic activities of specialized cells throughout the body (i.e., muscle cells, bone cells, blood cells, nerve cells, etc.) is completely dependent upon the coordinated activities of these three body systems.

---

2. Complete the *Observations & Analysis* section.

Observations & Analysis

1. Use the list of structures below to identify the organs of the digestive (D), respiratory (R), and circulatory (C) systems.

____ tongue	____ large intestine	____ heart	____ alveoli
____ arteries	____ pancreas	____ lungs	____ capillaries
____ liver	____ veins	____ stomach	____ diaphragm
____ teeth	____ esophagus	____ small intestine	____ trachea
____ bronchi	____ epiglottis	____ larynx	____ villi

2. Explain how an infection affecting the digestive system would directly threaten a person's health.

_____

_____

_____

_____

_____

_____

3. Explain how an infection affecting the respiratory system would directly threaten a person's health.

_____

_____

_____

_____

_____

_____

4. Explain how an infection affecting the circulatory system would directly threaten a person's health.

_____

_____

_____

_____

_____

_____

 **Biology**

Lesson 50: Teacher Preparation

Basic Principle   The internal environment of the human body remains relatively stable, or homeostatic, in the face of outside change due to the coordination of structures and functions among organ systems.

Competency   Students will explain how organ systems remove toxic wastes from the body.

Procedure   Give students time to read the information on *The Excretory, Respiratory, and Circulatory Systems* before completing the *Observations & Analysis* section.

Answers to Observations & Analysis

1. E	E	C	E
C	E	R	C
E	C	E	R
R	R	R	R

2. Answers will vary, but should include the following main point: Diseases of the excretory system impede the complete and proper elimination from the body of the toxic products of cellular metabolism.

Biology

STUDENT HANDOUT–LESSON 50

Basic Principle   The internal environment of the human body remains relatively stable, or homeostatic, in the face of outside change due to the coordination of structures and functions among organ systems.

Objective   Explain how organ systems remove toxic wastes from the body.

Procedure

1. Read the information on *The Excretory, Respiratory, and Circulatory Systems*.

The Excretory, Respiratory, and Circulatory Systems

All cells produce toxic wastes as products of their many anabolic and catabolic chemical activities. *Urea* is one of the primary waste products formed in the liver from the breakdown of nitrogen compounds such as amino acids. The primary function of the *excretory system* is to filter and purify the blood passing through it and sequester harmful molecules for elimination from the body. The *respiratory system* facilitates the exchange of useful oxygen for toxic carbon dioxide, one of the products of chemical respiration. The *circulatory system* accommodates both these systems, serving as the route of transport through which all toxic substances reach their points of removal from the body.

---

2. Complete the *Observations & Analysis* section.

Observations & Analysis

1. Use the list of structures below to identify the organs of the excretory (E), respiratory (R), and circulatory (C) systems.

____ ureter	____ Bowman's capsule	____ heart	____ nephron
____ arteries	____ urinary bladder	____ lungs	____ capillaries
____ kidney	____ veins	____ urethra	____ diaphragm
____ alveoli	____ trachea	____ bronchi	____ epiglottis

2. Explain how an infection affecting the excretory system would directly threaten a person's health.

_____

_____

_____

_____

_____

_____

Lesson 51: Teacher Preparation

Basic Principle   The internal environment of the human body remains relatively stable, or homeostatic, in the face of outside change due to the coordination of structures and functions among organ systems.

Competency   Students will explain how nerve cells conduct electrochemical impulses and communicate with one another.

Procedure

1. Give students time to read the information on *Nerves and the Electrochemical Impulse* before completing the *Observations & Analysis* section.

2. Point out that the nerve theory of the nervous system, suggesting that the nervous system was composed of individual cells like all other organ systems, was first introduced by the Spanish cell biologist Santiago Ramón y Cajal (1852–1934). The theory was later used by the English neurophysiologist Charles Robert Sherrington (1857–1952) to develop the principles of reflex action. In 1963, the Australian physiologist Sir John Carew Eccles (b. 1903) shared the Nobel Prize with English physiologists Alan Lloyd Hodgkin (b. 1914) and Andrew Fielding Huxley (b. 1917) for describing the mechanism underlying the transmission of nerve impulses.

3. Draw the illustrations on this handout and review the difference between the resting potential and action potential of a neuron.

Answers to Observations & Analysis

1. Answers will vary, but should include the following main points: The semipermeable membrane of a neuron restricts the flow of positively and negatively charged ions to create a potential difference across the cell membrane. The separated chemical pastes of a chemical battery also store oppositely charged groups of ion to create a voltage.

2. Answers will vary, but should include the following main points: When a neuron is at rest, the inside of the cell has a negative charge relative to the outside (i.e., potential difference across the membrane about –70 mV). This is the resting potential. During the action potential, the potential difference becomes increasingly positive (i.e., to about +40 mV) as the membrane is altered to permit the flow of oppositely charged ions.

3. Answers will vary, but should include the following main points: As the action potential reaches the terminal branches of the neuron, neurotransmitters are released into the synapse against the dendrites of the other neurons. The neurotransmitters alter the cell membranes of the cells, stimulating action potentials in those cells.

SECTION OF AN AXON AT RESTING POTENTIAL

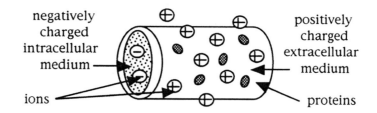

RECORDING OF AN ACTION POTENTIAL

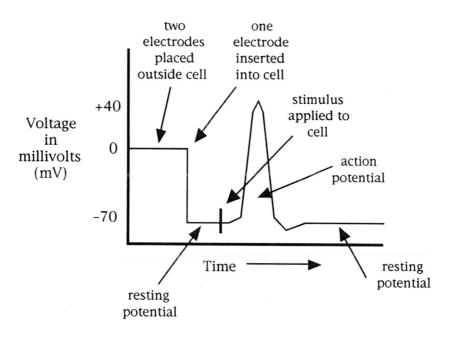

Biology

STUDENT HANDOUT–LESSON 51

Basic Principle   The internal environment of the human body remains relatively stable, or homeostatic, in the face of outside change due to the coordination of structures and functions among organ systems.

Objective   Explain how nerve cells conduct electrochemical impulses and communicate with one another.

Procedure

1. Read the information on *Nerves and the Electrochemical Impulse*.

Nerves and the Electrochemical Impulse

Nerve cells called *neurons* transmit messages to one another by sending *electrochemical signals*. As in all other cells, the cell membrane of a neuron is *semipermeable*, allowing the free flow of some molecules while restricting the flow of others. When a neuron is at rest, the intracellular medium of the cell is different from its extracellular medium. The intracellular medium contains a higher concentration of negatively charged ions, such as chlorine ions, than the extracellular medium. The extracellular medium contains a higher concentration of positively charged ions, such as sodium and potassium ions. The difference in concentration between the oppositely charged ions inside and outside the neuron creates a potential difference, or voltage, across the cell membrane. At rest, this potential difference is called the *resting potential*. The separation of ionic charges across the membrane of a neuron is similar to the separation of oppositely charged chemical pastes that give a chemical battery its voltage. When specialized proteins embedded in the cell membrane are activated, they alter the membrane slightly to permit the freer flow of ions across the membrane. As the ions flow across the membrane, the potential difference across the membrane drops. This electrochemical change in voltage, called the *action potential*, moves along the cell membrane from its *dendrites*, to its cell body, then along its *axon* to its *terminal branches*. At the terminal branches, chemical transmitters called *neurotransmitters* (e.g., acetylcholine, epinephrine) are released into the extracellular space, or *synapse*, against the dendrites of other neurons. The neurotransmitters stimulate the dendritic cell membranes of the other neurons to continue the transmission of the nerve impulse.

---

2. Examine the illustrations. Then complete the *Observations & Analysis* section.

NEURONS AND NERVE IMPULSES   **A SYNAPSE**

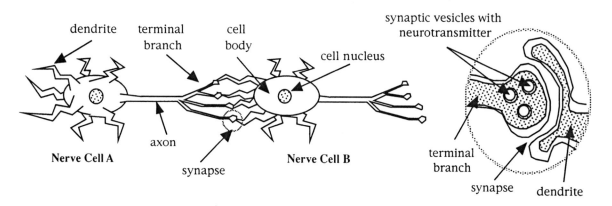

Observations & Analysis

1. Explain how a neuron is similar to a chemical battery.

    _____

    _____

    _____

    _____

2. Explain the difference between the resting potential and action potential of a neuron.

    _____

    _____

    _____

    _____

    _____

    _____

3. Explain how one neuron stimulates a second neuron to continue the transmission of nerve impulses.

    _____

    _____

    _____

    _____

    _____

    _____

Biology

Lesson 52: Teacher Preparation

Basic Principle   The internal environment of the human body remains relatively stable, or homeostatic, in the face of outside change due to the coordination of structures and functions among organ systems.

Competency   Students will explain how drugs interfere with communication between neurons.

Materials   handout of drug classification and action

Procedure

1. Display the list of drugs having general biological and behavioral effects.
2. Give students the time to read the information on *Drug Action at the Synapse* before completing the *Observations & Analysis* section.

Answers to Observations & Analysis

1. Answers will vary, but should contain the following main points: An action potential reaches the terminal branches of a neuron and stimulates the release of neurotransmitter molecules from synaptic vesicles into the synapse. The neurotransmitter molecules alter the neuronal membrane of cells across the synapse, stimulating an action potential in that membrane.
2. Answers will vary, but should contain the following main points: Drugs can prevent the release of neurotransmitters. Drugs can prevent the breakdown or reuptake of neurotransmitters acting at the synapse. Drugs can mimic the chemical action of neurotransmitters.

DRUG CLASSIFICATION AND ACTION

Drug Class	Group	Example	Addictive
sedative	barbiturate	alcohol	yes
		phenobarbitol	yes
stimulant	nicotine	nicotine	yes
	psychotogenics	LSD	no
	sympathomimetic	amphetamine	yes
	xanthines	caffeine	yes
anesthetics, analgesics, paralytics	analgesics	morphine	yes
		heroin	yes
	local anasthetic	novocaine	no
		cocaine	yes
	general anasthetic	nitrous oxide	no
		diethyl ether	no
		chloroform	no
	paralytic	curare	no
psychotogenics	*Cannabis sativa*	marijuana	yes
	ergot derivative	LSD	no
	Lophophora williamsii	mescaline	no

Biology

STUDENT HANDOUT–LESSON 52

Basic Principle   The internal environment of the human body remains relatively stable, or homeostatic, in the face of outside change due to the coordination of structures and functions among organ systems.

Objective   Explain how drugs interfere with communication between neurons.

Materials   handout of drug classification and action

Procedure

1. Read the information on *Drug Action at the Synapse*.

Drug Action at the Synapse

The transmission of nerve impulses from one neuron to another is dependent on the chemical action of a variety of neurotransmitters such as acetylcholine, serotonin, dopamine, gamma-aminobutyric acid, and norepinephrine. Neurotransmitter molecules released from the terminal branches of one neuron alter the integrity of neuronal membranes across the synapse, stimulating an action potential in those neurons. In order to return the cell membrane to its resting state, however, the action of the neurotransmitter must be neutralized. This can occur in a number of ways. Neurotransmitter molecules can be broken down chemically by substances present in the synapse. Or, they can be actively transported back into the terminal branches and returned to synaptic vesicles for further release. Drugs acting at the synapse can interfere with the communication between neurons by (1) blocking the release of neurotransmitters, (2) halting the breakdown of transmitters after release, or (3) preventing the "reuptake" of the neurotransmitter into synaptic vesicles. Some drugs inhibit the action of chemicals that break down neurotransmitters at the synapse, while others alter membrane proteins responsible for facilitating the return of neurotransmitters to their synaptic vesicles inside the terminal branches. Other drugs can mimic the chemical action of the neurotransmitters themselves. The action of drugs on the neurons of the peripheral and central nervous systems can lead to profound changes in behavior.

---

2. Examine the handout illustrations. Then complete the *Observations & Analysis* section.

Observations & Analysis

1. Describe the sequence of events that results in the continuation of a nerve impulse across a synapse.

    _____

    _____

    _____

    _____

    _____

    _____

    _____

2. Describe two ways that drugs can impede the flow of information between neurons.

    _____

    _____

    _____

    _____

    _____

    _____

    _____

    _____

    _____

    _____

    _____

    _____

    _____

    _____

    _____

    _____

    _____

Lesson 53: Teacher Preparation

Basic Principle   The internal environment of the human body remains relatively stable, or homeostatic, in the face of outside change due to the coordination of structures and functions among organ systems.

Competency   Students will explain the roles of sensory neurons, interneurons, and motor neurons in mediating communication between different parts of the body and the environment.

Procedure

1. Point out that the spinal cord, protected by bony vertebrae (i.e., bones of the back), relays information between the brain and the tissues of the body. The spinal cord controls reflexes like the "knee-jerk reflex" and "hot-iron reflex." Spinal reflexes cause muscles and organs of the body to react quickly to harmful stimuli, protecting the body from sustaining serious injury. The peripheral nerves branching out from the spinal cord attach directly to all of the organs of the body.

2. Give students time to read the information on *The Reflex Arc* before completing the *Observations & Analysis* section.

Answer to Observations & Analysis

Answers will vary, but should contain the following main points: The heat of a hot iron stimulates sensory receptors in the skin that relay information to the cell bodies of the dorsal root ganglion. Cell bodies of the dorsal root ganglion send their axons through the dorsal root of the spinal cord into the cord's gray matter. Interneurons in the gray matter relay the information to motor neurons located in the ventral region of the cord. Axons of motor neurons exit the spinal cord through the ventral roots of the cord and these efferent fibers cause muscles in the hand and arm to contract, pulling the hand away from the hot iron.

Biology

STUDENT HANDOUT–LESSON 53

Basic Principle   The internal environment of the human body remains relatively stable, or homeostatic, in the face of outside change due to the coordination of structures and functions among organ systems.

Objective   Explain the roles of sensory neurons, interneurons, and motor neurons in mediating communication between different parts of the body and the environment.

Procedure

1. Read the information on *The Reflex Arc*.

The Reflex Arc

A *reflex* is a rapid automatic response to a stimulus. Animal reflexes are mediated by the nervous system and may involve only a few neurons located in the gray matter of the spinal cord. A simple *reflex arc* is composed of three neurons: a *sensory* or *afferent* neuron, an *interneuron*, and a *motor* or *efferent* neuron. Afferent nerve fibers from sensory neurons distributed throughout the body transmit information to the spinal cord through the dorsal roots of the cord. Nerve impulses originating in sensory neurons are transmitted to interneurons that mediate the firing of motor neurons. The axons of motor neurons compose the efferent nerve fibers that activate muscles and organs throughout the body. Efferent nerve fibers exit the spinal cord through the ventral roots of the cord.

---

2. Examine the handout illustrations. Then complete the *Observations & Analysis* section.

THE SPINAL REFLEX

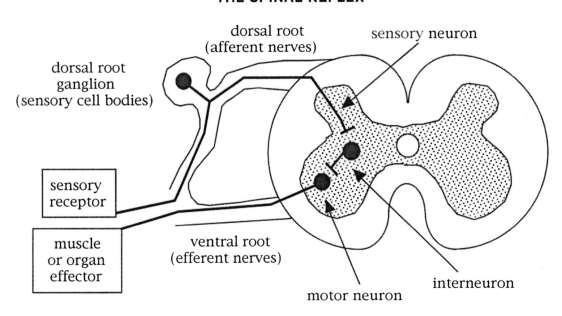

Observations & Analysis

Describe how touching a hot iron would elicit a reflex mediated by sensory neurons, interneurons, and motor neurons.

_____

_____

_____

_____

_____

_____

_____

_____

_____

_____

_____

Lesson 54: Teacher Preparation

Basic Principle   The internal environment of the human body remains relatively stable, or homeostatic, in the face of outside change due to the coordination of structures and functions among organ systems.

Objective   Students will identify the major structures of sensory organs.

Procedure   Give students time to read the information on *The Sense Organs* before completing the *Observations & Analysis* section.

Answers to Observations & Analysis

EY	EA	EA	EY
EA	EY	EY	EA
TO	EY	EA	EA
EY	NO	SK	EA
SK	SK	SK	EA
	NO		

Biology

STUDENT HANDOUT–LESSON 54

Basic Principle   The internal environment of the human body remains relatively stable, or homeostatic, in the face of outside change due to the coordination of structures and functions among organ systems.

Objective   Identify the major structures of sensory organs.

Procedure

1. Read the information on *The Sense Organs*.

The Sense Organs

The human body is equipped with *sense organs* that detect environmental changes. Human beings can recognize a variety of stimuli such as light and sound, odor and flavor, pressure, heat, and cold. The sense organs that detect this information are the *eyes, ears, nose, tongue,* and *skin*. Light is detected by the eyes. Visible light energy given off by a light source in the form of *photons* pass through the transparent front of the eye called the *cornea* into the eye through the *pupil*. The amount of light that passes into the eye is controlled by a ring of colored muscles called the *iris*. A *lens* behind the iris focuses light toward the back of the eye onto a layer of cells called the *retina*. Cells of the retina send signals to the brain through the *optic nerve*. The brain translates the nerve signals into visual images. A healthy eye cannot see without the brain. The brain, however, is able to form visual images such as those that appear to us in dreams.

Mechanical sound vibrations are detected by the *ears*. The vibrations enter the *external ear* or *pinna* and move into the *auditory canal*. At the end of the auditory canal, sound waves vibrate a thin wall of tissue called the *tympanic membrane* (i.e., ear drum), causing three small bones located in the *middle ear*—called the *malleus, incus,* and *stapes*—to oscillate. The shaking stapes vibrates a liquid inside a "snail-shaped" organ in the *internal ear* called the *cochlea*. The inner walls of the cochlea are lined with microscopic hairs that vibrate with the vibrating fluid. The hairs are connected to nerve fibers that send signals through the auditory nerve to the brain.

Odors are detected by *olfactory cells* located in the *nasal mucous membrane* inside the nose. Chemicals in the air excite these cells to send messages to the *olfactory bulbs* inside the front of the skull on the underside of the brain.

The sense of taste is largely a matter of telling the difference between different odors. The *taste buds* of the tongue can detect chemicals that are sweet, salty, bitter, or sour. That is the reason why a person with a "stuffy" cold can hardly taste the food he or she eats.

> Pressure, heat, and cold are detected by specialized cells in the skin. Two types of nerve endings called *Meisner* and *Pacinian corpuscles* are sensitive to light or heavy pressure exerted against the skin. *Ruffini's end organs* are sensitive to the presence of heat, while *Krause bulbs* are sensitive to the loss of heat (i.e., cold). Free nerve endings in the skin and tissues of the internal organs relay sensation of pain.

2. Complete the *Observations & Analysis* section.

Observations & Analysis

Identify the structures belonging to each major sense organ: eyes (EY), ears (EA), nose (NO), tongue (TO), and skin (SK).

_____ cornea	_____ auditory canal	_____ auditory nerve	_____ lens
_____ malleus	_____ pupil	_____ iris	_____ cochlea
_____ taste bud	_____ optic nerve	_____ incus	_____ tympanum
_____ retina	_____ olfactory bulb	_____ Krause bulb	_____ stapes
_____ Meisner corpuscle	_____ Ruffini ending	_____ Pacinian corpuscle	_____ pinna
	_____ olfactory cell		

Lesson 55: Teacher Preparation

Basic Principle   The internal environment of the human body remains relatively stable, or homeostatic, in the face of outside change due to the coordination of structures and functions among organ systems.

Competency   Students will explain how feedback loops in the nervous and endocrine systems regulate conditions within the body.

Materials   handout of major hormones of the endocrine system

Procedure

1. Give students time to read the information on *Regulation of the Endocrine System* before completing the *Observations & Analysis* section.

2. Review the chart listing the *Major Hormones of the Endocrine System.*

3. Point out that endocrinologists of the 19th century correlated a variety of diseases with abnormalities of the endocrine organs. The Irish physician Robert James Graves (1796–1853) described symptoms resulting from the overactivity of the thyroid: a condition resulting in the swelling of the gland, called goiter. English physician Thomas Addison (1793–1860) recognized symptoms resulting from deficiency of adrenal cortical function resulting in weakness, abnormal skin secretions, weight loss, and low blood pressure. The English physiologist Edward Albert Sharpey-Schafer (1850–1935) and his co-worker George Oliver (1841–1915) discovered the functions of the adrenal medulla in the production of the "flight or fight" hormone, adrenaline. The American neurophysiologist Walter Bradford Cannon (1871-1945) is best known for his clear description of the "flight or fight" response. When confronted with a threatening or anxiety-producing situation, the adrenal medulla secretes adrenaline (also called epinephrine) directly into the bloodstream. Adrenaline initiates a variety of responses in different body cells. The hormone: (1) causes the liver to release its reserves of carbohydrate for quick energy, (2) dilates blood vessels supplying blood to the heart, lungs, and skeletal muscles, (3) constricts blood vessels of the intestinal tract to slow down energy-consuming digestive functions, and (4) promotes quick blood-clotting in the event an injury should occur to the body. Prolonged stress and anxiety can have disasterous effects on a person's overall health. Preparing the body for action when no action can be taken can have serious side effects.

Answer to Observations & Analysis

Answers will vary, but should contain the following main point: The sight of a mountain lion would activate the sympathetic nerves to stimulate the adrenal medulla to release adrenaline into the bloodstream. The adrenaline would ready the body for flight or fight by causing the liver to release its reserves of carbohydrate for quick energy; dilating blood vessels supplying blood to the heart, lungs, and skeletal muscles; constricting blood vessels of the intestinal tract to slow down energy-consuming digestive functions; and promoting quick blood-clotting in the event an injury should occur to the body.

MAJOR HORMONES OF THE ENDOCRINE SYSTEM

Gland	Hormone	Controlled by
anterior pituitary	growth hormone (GH)	GH-releasing factors
	thyroid-stimulating hormone (TSH)	TSH-releasing factors
posterior pituitary	oxytocin	hypothalamic neurons
	vasopressin	hypothalamic neurons
thyroid	thyroxin	TSH
parathyroids	parathromone	plasma calcium concentration
adrenal cortex	cortisol	adrenocorticotrophic hormone
	aldosterone	angiotensin
adrenal medulla	epinephrine	sympathetic nerves
pancreas	insulin and glucogon	plasma glucose concentration
gonads		
ovaries	estrogen	follicle-stimulating hormone
		lutenizing hormone
testes	testosterone	lutenizing hormone

Biology

STUDENT HANDOUT–LESSON 55

Basic Principle   The internal environment of the human body remains relatively stable, or homeostatic, in the face of outside change due to the coordination of structures and functions among organ systems.

Objective   Explain how feedback loops in the nervous and endocrine systems regulate conditions within the body.

Materials   handout of major hormones of the endocrine system

Procedure

1. Read the information on *Regulation of the Endocrine System.*

Regulation of the Endocrine System

Much of the metabolism of mammals is regulated by *hormones* produced by organs under the control of the nervous system. The organs that produce hormones are called *endocrine glands*. An endocrine gland is an organ that secretes hormones into the extracellular environment or directly into the bloodstream. Hormones influence the body's ability to (1) regulate essential nutrients, (2) respond to danger, (3) produce healthy offspring, and (4) grow. The major glands of the endocrine system are the *pituitary*, the *pineal*, the *thyroid*, the *parathyroid*, the *thymus*, the *adrenals*, and the glands of the male and female reproductive organs, the *testes* and *ovaries*. The nervous system can control endocrine glands by sending nerve signals directly to a particular gland. Or, it can send signals to the "master" endocrine gland: the pituitary. The pituitary gland is located at the base of the brain beneath a nucleus of specialized neurons called the hypothalamus. Neurons in the hypothalamus send signals to the pituitary gland which, in turn, produces hormones that influence the secretions of other endocrine glands. The pituitary is surrounded by capillaries that transport its hormonal secretions throughout the body. The endocrine glands are sensitive to the presence of excess hormone. When the amount of a particular hormone rises to high levels, the gland that produces that hormone will "shut down" to prevent the cells it controls from "overreacting." This type of control is called *negative feedback*. Too little hormone of a specific kind can cause the pituitary to send hormonal commands to a particular endocrine gland to begin producing more of the needed hormone. This is a *positive feedback loop*. The ability of the nervous system to regulate the activity of endocrine glands allows the body to achieve *homeostasis*, the maintenance of a constant internal environment.

---

2. Study the diagram on *Feedback Loops* and the chart of *Major Hormones of the Endocrine System* before completing the *Observations & Analysis* section.

Copyright © 2005 by John Wiley & Sons, Inc.

FEEDBACK LOOPS

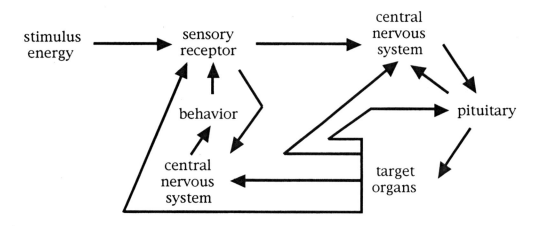

Observations & Analysis

Explain how the sight of a mountain lion in the wild would cause the nervous system and endocrine organs of a hiker to react in a "flight or fight" reaction.

_____

_____

_____

_____

_____

_____

_____

_____

_____

_____

_____

_____

_____

_____

_____

_____

_____

 **Biology**

Lesson 56: Teacher Preparation

Basic Principle   Organisms have a variety of mechanisms to combat disease.

Competency   Students will explain the role of the skin in providing nonspecific defenses against disease.

Procedure

1. Give students time to read the information on *Germs and the Body's Defenses* before completing the *Observations & Analysis* section.

2. Point out that the "father of medicine," Hippocrates (460 B.C.E.–377 B.C.E.), believed that epidemic outbreaks of infectious diseases were rooted in the disruption of the Earth's atmosphere. He noted that epidemics were usually associated with poor weather conditions and local disasters (e.g., earthquakes and volcanic eruptions) that produced sickening "exhalations" from poisoned or stagnating pools of water that accelerated putrification of plant and animal matter. Hippocrates's *miasmatic theory* remained the most widely accepted theory of disease until the late 19th century. The observation of the Dutch microscopist Anton van Leeuwenhoek (1632–1723) led to the belief by many epidemiologists that microbes were the cause of disease, although there was little direct evidence to support that view. The English physician Edward Jenner (1749–1823) succeeded in finding an effective vaccine against smallpox in 1796, but could not explain how his treatment worked. In the middle of the 19th century, the English physician John Snow (1813–1858) published *On the Mode of Communication of Cholera* in which he proposed that the agent of transmission that had spread cholera to epidemic proportions throughout London was in the contaminated water of a local well. He could not, however, isolate the agent. In 1840, the German anatomist and histologist Jacob Henle (1809–1885) published *Pathological Investigations* in which he argued that living organisms were responsible for diseases in humans, animals, and plants. He noted that living things alone were capable of reproduction and that progressively morbid infectious diseases must have a similar organic cause. He proposed a series of "filtration" methods to isolate the microbes responsible for ill health. The German bacteriologist Heinrich Hermann Koch (1843–1910) fulfilled that dream less than forty years later. Koch and his associates developed techniques for the isolation and culturing of bacteria so that they could be used to replicate diseases in laboratory animals. In 1860, the French chemist and microbiologist Louis Pasteur (1822–1895) discovered that fermentation of sugars was dependent upon the action of microorganisms (e.g., anaerobic bacteria and yeasts) and that these "germs" could be killed by heat. Pasteurization—a method of heating the fermenting mixture—is used today as the primary method of killing yeasts used in the manufacture of beers, wines, and dairy products. Pasteur published his *germ theory* in 1865, inspiring the English surgeon Joseph Lister (1827–1912) to perform the first antiseptic operation in 1867. In 1891, the German bacteriologist Paul Ehrlich (1854–1915) developed the first techniques in chemotherapy using synthetic drugs to kill infectious organisms.

Answer to Observations & Analysis

Answers will vary, but should contain the following main point: The skin serves as a physical barrier preventing the invasion of disease-producing microorganisms.

Name _____ Date _____

Biology

STUDENT HANDOUT–LESSON 56

Basic Principle   Organisms have a variety of mechanisms to combat disease.

Objective   Explain the role of the skin in providing nonspecific defenses against disease.

Procedure

1. Read the information about *Germs and the Body's Defenses*.

Germs and the Body's Defenses

The human body is vulnerable to attack by the variety of foreign organisms we call *germs*. The term refers to any number of microscopic organisms such as *bacteria*, *viruses*, *protists*, and *fungi*. Germs can be spread from one person to another by touching, sneezing, coughing, or coming into contact with another person's bodily fluids (e.g., saliva on a shared drinking glass). Earlier surgeons did not recognize the importance of sterilizing their surgical equipment or washing their hands before performing an operation until the *germ theory* was proposed by the French microbiologist and chemist Louis Pasteur (1822–1895). Pasteur's student Joseph Lister (1827–1912) performed the first *antiseptic* surgery in 1867. The German bacteriologist Robert Koch (1843–1910) devised methods for isolating, culturing, and studying germs that cause infectious diseases. The body's first lines of defense against infection are (1) the *mucous membranes* of the respiratory tract, (2) the *skin*, and (3) the *inflammatory response*. The mucous membranes of the nose and respiratory tract trap dust and dirt that carry microscopic germs. "Hairlike" cilia embedded in the membranes gently "sweep" the foreign material out of the nose and mouth. The skin serves as a barrier that protects the internal organs from invasion by foreign substances called *antigens*. When the skin is broken, the body's defenses go into action. The inflammatory response begins when invading microorganisms attack body cells by increasing blood supply to the affected area. Blood platelets clot the blood and seal the injury. Specialized white blood cells produced by the *immune system* then attack the antigens and destroy them. The protein *interferon* present in the bloodstream and extracellular fluid "interferes" with the reproduction of viruses that get into the wound.

---

2. Complete the *Observations & Analysis* section.

Observations & Analysis

Explain how the skin provides the first line of defense against germs capable of entering the body.

_____

_____

_____

_____

_____

_____

_____

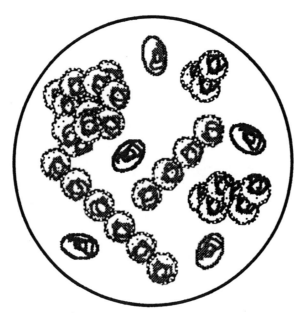

Bacillus, streptococcus, and staphylococcus
(x100,000)

 **Biology**

Lesson 57: Teacher Preparation

Basic Principle   Organisms have a variety of mechanisms to combat disease.

Competency   Students will explain the role of antibodies in the body's response to infection.

Procedure

1. Give students time to read the information on *Immunity Against Disease*.

2. Point out that the science of immunology is fairly new, having progressed since the middle of the 20th century with the science of molecular biology. In 1938, the Swedish chemist Arne Wilhelm Kaurin Tiselius (1902–1971) used his newly invented electrophoresis technique to isolate a number of animal proteins, among them a variety of alph-, beta-, and gammaglobulin antibodies. Of increasing interest to modern immunologists are the autoimmune diseases (e.g., rheumatoid arthritis and AIDS) that defy easy analysis. The immune system gone awry, attacking its own body tissues as it would a foreign invader, is the most challenging group of diseases to face the medical research laboratories of the world.

3. Complete the *Observations & Analysis* section.

Answer to Observations & Analysis

Answers will vary, but should contain the following main points: The lymphatic system filters disease-producing viruses and bacteria from the blood. Specialized lymphocytes called T-cells and helper T-cells alert other special lymphocytes called B-cells to produce antibodies. Antibodies surround and bind to viruses and bacteria in the blood, marking them for further destruction by more lymphocytes.

Biology

STUDENT HANDOUT–LESSON 57

Basic Principle   Organisms have a variety of mechanisms to combat disease.

Objective   Explain the role of antibodies in the body's response to infection.

Procedure

1. Read the information on *Immunity Against Disease*.

Immunity Against Disease

The next line of defense following the invasion of the body by germs is the *immune response*. The immune response is controlled by two systems: the *lymphatic* and *immune systems*. The lymphatic system is a system of interconnected lymph nodes and accessory organs including the *spleen*, *thymus*, *tonsils*, and *adenoids*. The vessels and nodes of the lymphatic system filter foreign substances and cell wastes from blood and extracellular fluids. Lymph nodes also store *lymphocytes*, the most plentiful type of white blood cell produced in the bones. Specialized lymphocytes, white blood cells called *T-cells*, alert other special lymphocytes called *B-cells* to produce *antibodies*. Antibody molecules are large macromolecular proteins that surround and bind to viruses, bacteria, and other foreign invaders. When a specific group of invaders is immobilized, white blood cells can gather, attack, and destroy them. Antibodies can remain in the bloodstream for a long time, making the body resistant to future invasion by the same germs. This resistance is called *immunity*. Immunity is the resistance to a disease-producing organism or other harmful substance. Natural immunity, called *passive immunity*, results from the direct transfer of antibodies from one source to another. For example, a pregnant woman can transfer her antibodies to her developing offspring.

---

2. Study the handout illustrations. Then complete the *Observations & Analysis* section.

THE IMMUNE RESPONSE   THE LYMPHATIC SYSTEM

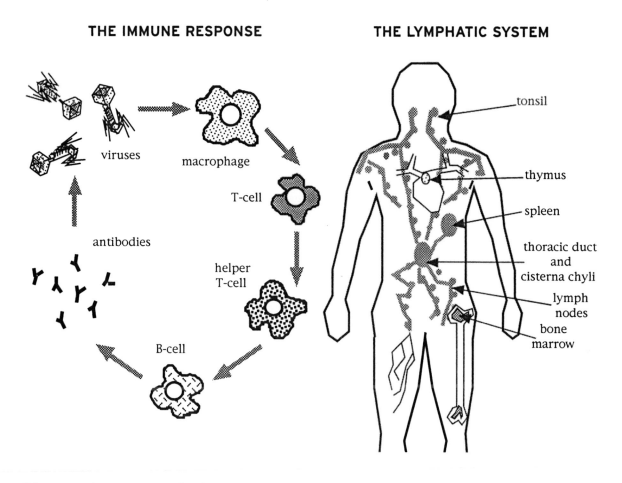

Observations & Analysis

Describe the sequence of events that leads to the production of antibodies and how these macromolecular proteins destroy disease-producing viruses and bacteria.

_____

_____

_____

_____

_____

_____

_____

_____

_____

_____

_____

Lesson 58: Teacher Preparation

Basic Principle   Organisms have a variety of mechanisms to combat disease.

Competency   Students will explain how vaccinations protect an individual from infectious disease.

Procedure   Give students time to read the information on *Vaccinations and Active Immunity* before completing the *Observations & Analysis* section.

Answer to Observations & Analysis

Answers will vary, but should contain the following main points: A vaccine is a modified form of an infectious virus that elicits an antibody reaction in the inoculated individual. The lymphatic system filters the modified virus from the blood so that specialized lymphocytes called T-cells and helper T-cells can alert other special lymphocytes called B-cells to produce antibodies. The manufactured antibodies will then be present to mark the disease-producing agent for destruction should the active form of the virus enter the person's body.

Biology

STUDENT HANDOUT–LESSON 58

Basic Principle   Organisms have a variety of mechanisms to combat disease.

Objective   Explain how vaccinations protect an individual from infectious disease.

Procedure

1. Read the information on *Vaccinations and Active Immunity*.

Vaccinations and Active Immunity

A *vaccine* is a laboratory-prepared form of a virus that is modified to elicit a specific antibody reaction that produces immunity to a specific disease. This form of immunity is called *active immunity*. A vaccine is usually made of the "dead" or "inactivated" form of the germ. A *vaccination* is an inoculation that introduces the modified antigen into the body of a person. The procedure was first used in 1796 by the English physician Edward Jenner (1749–1823) who treated milkmaids infected with cowpox. Jenner's procedure enabled the infected individuals to fight off subsequent infections, their bodies having been "primed" to fight off the disease-producing agents. The development of a cowpox vaccine against smallpox later led to the production of vaccines against many other infectious diseases.

---

2. Complete the *Observations & Analysis* section.

Observations & Analysis

Give a detailed description of how vaccinations prepare a person to fight off an infectious virus.

_____

_____

_____

_____

_____

_____

_____

_____

_____

_____

_____

_____

_____

_____

_____

_____

_____

_____

_____

_____

_____

_____

_____

Lesson 59: Teacher Preparation

Basic Principle   Organisms have a variety of mechanisms to combat disease.

Competency   Students will explain the important difference between bacteria and viruses, and their relationship to infectious disease.

Procedure

1. Point out that 20th-century advances in the art and science of electron microscopy have led to the elucidation of structure and function of thousands of microorganisms including viruses and bacteria. Since the first genetic engineering experiments performed on the plasmids of the bacterium *Eschericia coli* in the early 1970s, by American biochemists Stanley Cohen (b. 1922) and Har Gobind Khorana (b. 1922), the positive role of bacteria in the future of medical research cannot be underestimated.

2. Give students time to read the information on *Viruses and Bacteria* before completing the *Observations & Analysis* section.

Answers to Observations & Analysis

1. Answers will vary, but should contain the following main points: Viruses are smaller in size than bacteria (see handout illustrations). A virus is nothing more than a strand of hereditary RNA or DNA surrounded by a sugar-protein coat. Bacteria are self-sufficient unicellular organisms that contain many of the organelles common to other cells.

2. Answers will vary, but should contain the following main points: Viruses act by commandeering the metabolic apparatus of the cell for the sole purpose of reproduction and the translation of its own proteins. Infectious bacteria develop a parasitic relationship with the host organism and deplete the host's nutrient resources, resulting in its illness and death.

Name _____ Date _____

Biology

STUDENT HANDOUT–LESSON 59

Basic Principle   Organisms have a variety of mechanisms to combat disease.

Objective   Explain the important difference between bacteria and viruses, and their relationship to infectious disease.

Procedure

1. Read the information on *Viruses and Bacteria*.

Viruses and Bacteria

A *virus* is a tiny noncellular particle that can infect living cells. A virus is hardly more than a strand of hereditary material (e.g., RNA) protected by a sugar-protein coat that commandeers the host cell's biochemical machinery in order to reproduce itself. The common cold, chickenpox, rabies, polio, and AIDS are caused by viruses. With the advances in our knowledge of how genes work, viruses have been modified to create useful vaccines and to kill pests that can infect plants and livestock. Viruses have also been used in the field of genetic engineering in the development of therapies for a number of diseases. Unlike viruses, bacteria belong to the *Kingdom Monera*. Monerans are living unicellular organisms that lack a cell nucleus to protect their chromosomes. There are four major groups of bacteria: autotrophs, heterotrophs, parasites, and decomposers. Bacteria may develop a symbiotic relationship with their host. This means that both the bacteria and the host benefit from the presence of the bacteria. All animals—even humans—have bacteria in their digestive tracts that help them digest certain foods (e.g., dairy products). In a parasitic relationship, the bacteria use up too much of the host's resources and the host always suffers and may die.

---

2. Study the illustrations before completing the *Observations & Analysis* section.

VIRUSES	BACTERIA

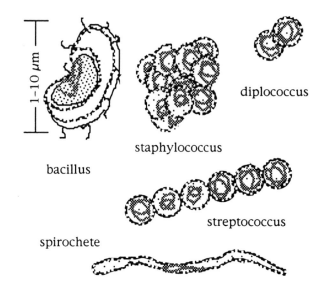

helical   icosahedral

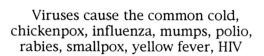

bacteriophage

diplococcus

staphylococcus

bacillus

streptococcus

spirochete

Viruses cause the common cold, chickenpox, influenza, mumps, polio, rabies, smallpox, yellow fever, HIV

Bacteria cause cholera, pneumonia, scarlet fever, tentanus, tuberculosis, typhoid fever

Observations & Analysis

1. Compare and contrast the structural characteristics of viruses and bacteria.

_____

_____

_____

_____

_____

_____

2. Contrast the action of viruses with those of bacteria in producing infectious disease.

_____

_____

_____

_____

_____

_____

_____

 **Biology**

Lesson 60: Teacher Preparation

Basic Principle   Organisms have a variety of mechanisms to combat disease.

Competency   Students will explain why a compromised immune system (as in the case of AIDS) may be unable to survive infection by microorganisms that might otherwise be benign.

Procedure

1. Give students time to read the information on *Autoimmune and Immunodeficiency Disease*.

2. Point out that since the first AIDS cases were reported in the early 1980s, more than 500,000 AIDS cases and more than 300,000 deaths have been reported in the United States. It is estimated that more than 1,000,000 Americans will be infected with the virus by the early part of the 21st century. AIDS cases have been reported in nearly every country on the globe, the disease affecting an estimated 25 million adults and children. No cure exists for this deadly disease, although a few drugs have been developed to slow the pace at which HIV is able to replicate itself in infected host T4 cells. The threat of HIV infection and AIDS continues to represent one of the most troubling challenges to public-health organizations around the world.

3. Have students complete the *Observations & Analysis* section.

Answer to Observations & Analysis

Answers will vary, but should contain the following main points: The human immunodeficiency virus (HIV) infects T4 cells and commandeers those cells' metabolic apparati. Since T4 cells are essential to the production of antibodies that protect the human body against infectious disease, the resulting HIV infection eventually limits the body's immune response. HIV uses the T4 cell's own nutrient and metabolic resources in making more HIV that is released from infected cells to further infect the body.

Name _____ Date _____

Biology

STUDENT HANDOUT–LESSON 60

Basic Principle   Organisms have a variety of mechanisms to combat disease.

Objective   Explain why a compromised immune system (as in the case of AIDS) may be unable to survive infection by microorganisms that might otherwise be benign.

Procedure

1.   Read the information on *Autoimmune and Immunodeficiency Disease*.

Autoimmune and Immunodeficiency Disease

In normal cases, the immune system can recognize and destroy invaders without hurting the body's healthy cells. Sometimes, however, the body's own defenses behave abnormally and start attacking the body's own tissues. Physicians call this condition an *autoimmune disease*. *Rheumatoid arthritis* and *lupus* are autoimmune diseases. In other cases, the immune system becomes so debilitated that its normal response to invading organisms becomes severely limited. The *human immunodeficiency virus (HIV)* has such an effect on the body's immune response. *Acquired immune deficiency syndrome*, known as *AIDS*, is caused by infection with HIV, a virus that attacks specific cells of the immune system: T4 lymphocytes. The attack reduces the efficiency of these critical cells by impeding their ability to elicit the production of antibodies in healthy B-cells. With the suppression of the immune system, the body is left exposed to invasion by any number of microorganisms that might otherwise have been easily destroyed by the immune response. Even normally benign organisms such as *Eschericia coli* are free to reproduce in a person with AIDS and use up vital nutrient resources necessary for the survival of the patient.

---

2.   Complete the *Observations & Analysis* section.

THE ACTION OF HIV

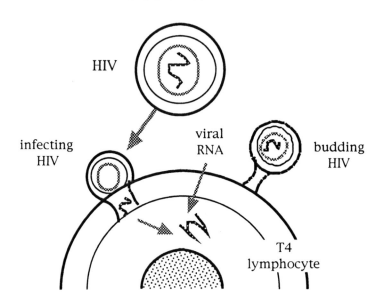

Observations & Analysis

Describe the sequence of events that leads to the weakening of the body's normal immune response following infection with HIV.

_____

_____

_____

_____

_____

_____

_____

_____

_____

_____

_____

_____

_____

_____

_____

TENTH-GRADE LEVEL

Biology

PRACTICE TEST

Biology

PRACTICE TEST

Directions: Use the Answer Sheet to darken the letter of the choice that best answers each question.

1. Which cell organelle regulates the flow of nutrients in and out of a cell?

   (A) cell membrane

   (B) nucleus

   (C) mitochondrion

   (D) ribosomes

2. Which cell organelle is the site of protein synthesis?

   (A) cell membrane

   (B) nucleus

   (C) mitochondrion

   (D) ribosomes

3. Which cell organelle provides the cell with energy?

   (A) cell membrane

   (B) nucleus

   (C) mitochondrion

   (D) ribosomes

4. Which cell organelle directs the chemical activities of the cell?

   (A) cell membrane

   (B) nucleus

   (C) mitocondrion

   (D) ribosomes

5. Which phrase best describes an enzyme?

   (A) primary energy source

   (B) secondary energy source

   (C) protein catalyst

   (D) hereditary material

6. Which organelle contains molecules that can "trap" the energy of the Sun?

   (A) chloroplasts

   (B) vacuoles

   (C) mitochondria

   (D) ribosomes

7. How is a virus different from a prokaryotic or eukaryotic cell?

   (A) A virus has no well-defined nucleus.

   (B) A virus needs a host to supply it with nutrients.

   (C) A virus contains strands of hereditary macromolecules.

   (D) A virus has no protective covering.

8. Which phrase best summarizes the term "transcription"?

   (A) mRNA made from DNA

   (B) DNA made from mRNA

   (C) tRNA made from mRNA

   (D) proteins made on ribosome

9. Which phrase best summarizes the term "translation"?

   (A) mRNA made from DNA

   (B) DNA made from mRNA

   (C) tRNA made from mRNA

   (D) proteins made on ribosomes

10. Which phrase best describes the function of endoplasmic reticulum?

    (A) energy factory

    (B) transports nutrients around cell

    (C) prepares nutrients for transport out of cell

    (D) site of transcription

11. Which phrase best describes the function of Golgi apparatus?

    (A) energy factory

    (B) transports nutrients around cell

    (C) prepares nutrients for transport out of cell

    (D) site of translation

12. Which phrase best describes the function of mitochondria?

    (A) traps the energy of the Sun

    (B) completes the breakdown of glucose to form carbon dioxide

    (C) translates the genetic code

    (D) regulates the flow of nutrients between cell organelles

13. Which of the following molecular subunits combine to form polysaccharides?

    (A) amino acids

    (B) simple sugars

    (C) nucleotides

    (D) fatty acids

14. Which of the following molecular subunits combine to form lipids?

    (A) amino acids

    (B) simple sugars

    (C) nucleotides

    (D) fatty acids

15. Which of the following molecular subunits combine to form proteins?

    (A) amino acids

    (B) simple sugars

    (C) nucleotides

    (D) fatty acids

16. Which of the following molecular subunits combine to form nucleic acids?

    (A) amino acids

    (B) simple sugars

    (C) nucleotides

    (D) fatty acids

17. Which of the following lists the stages of mitosis in their proper order?

    (A) interphase, metaphase, anaphase, telophase, prophase

    (B) interphase, prophase, metaphase, anaphase, telophase

    (C) telophase, anaphase, interphase, metaphase, prophase

    (D) anaphase, telophase, metaphase, prophase, interphase

Directions: Use the diagrams illustrating different types of chromosomal alterations to answer questions 18, 19, 20, and 21.

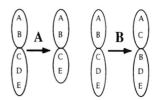

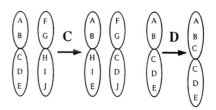

18. Which diagram illustrates a chromosomal alteration by translocation: A, B, C, or D?

19. Which diagram illustrates a chromosomal alteration by inversion: A, B, C, or D?

20. Which diagram illustrates a chromosomal alteration by duplication: A, B, C, or D?

21. Which diagram illustrates a chromosomal alteration by deletion: A, B, C, or D?

22. Which of the following terms best describes gamete formation?

    (A) disjunction

    (B) mitosis

    (C) meiosis

    (D) transcription

23. Which term best describes the process of fertilization?

    (A) fusion of male and female gametes

    (B) germ cell undergoes reduction division

    (C) crossing over of chromosomes

    (D) inversion of chromosomes

24. Which sequence of terms best summarizes the stages of human embryonic development?

    (A) zygote, fetus, embryo, embryonic disc, morula, blastocyst, fertilization

    (B) fetus, embryo, zygote, embryonic disc, blastocyst, morula, fertilization

    (C) fertilization, zygote, morula, blastocyst, embryo, embryonic disc, fetus

    (D) fertilization, morula, blastocyst, embryo, embryonic disc, zygote, fetus

25. Which embryonic germ layer contains cells that differentiate to form skin and nervous tissue?

    (A) ectoderm

    (B) endoderm

    (C) mesoderm

26. Which embryonic germ layer contains cells that differentiate to form the alimentary canal?

    (A) ectoderm

    (B) endoderm

    (C) mesoderm

27. Which embryonic germ layer contains cells that differentiate to form skeletal bones and muscles?

    (A) ectoderm

    (B) endoderm

    (C) mesoderm

28. Which of the following pair of genes will result in the production of a normal male offspring?

    (A) XXY

    (B) YY

    (C) XY

    (D) XX

Directions: Use the Punnett Squares to answer questions 29, 30, and 31.

29. Which Punnett Square illustrates the crossing of a hybrid tall pea plant and a purebred short pea plant: A, B, or C?

30. What percent of the offspring from the crossing illustrated in Punnett Square A will be short pea plants?

    (A) 0%

    (B) 25%

    (C) 50%

    (D) 75%

31. What percent of the offspring from the crossing illustrated in Punnett Square C will be hybrid tall pea plants?

    (A) 0%

    (B) 25%

    (C) 50%

    (D) 75%

32. Which of the following causes sex-linked genetic disorders?

    (A) an abnormal gene on the Y-chromosome

    (B) an abnormal gene on the X-chromosome

    (C) crossing over on autosomal chromosomes

    (D) chromosomal deletions

33. Which of the following is NOT a biochemical subunit of a DNA or RNA macromolecule?

    (A) ribose sugar

    (B) phosphate

    (C) amino acid

    (D) nitrogenous base

34. Which of the following makes the duplication of a strand of DNA possible?

    (A) hydrogen bonding between purines and pyrimidines

    (B) ionic bonding between purines and pyrimidines

    (C) covalent bonding between purines and pyrimidines

    (D) hydrophyllic bonding between purines and pyrimidines

35. Which best summarizes the function of mRNA molecules?

    (A) transports the genetic code from the nucleus to the cytoplasm

    (B) transports amino acids to ribosomes

    (C) makes DNA duplication possible

    (D) prevents the catalysis of tRNA

36. Which best summarizes the function of tRNA molecules?

    (A) transports the genetic code from the nucleus to the cytoplasm

    (B) transports amino acids to ribosomes

    (C) makes DNA duplication possible

    (D) prevents the catalysis of mRNA

37. Which best describes how genetic mutations occur?

    (A) The sequence of deoxyribose-sugars and phosphates is altered.

    (B) The sequence of nitrogenous bases is altered.

    (C) The sequence of amino acids is altered.

    (D) Ribosomes become inoperative.

38. Which of the following is crucial to the production of recombinant DNA?

    (A) viral RNA

    (B) bacterial plasmids

    (C) eukaryotic nucleoplasm

    (D) mitochondrial DNA

39. Which of the following is used by criminal investigators to identify the DNA of suspected criminals?

    (A) electroplating

    (B) incubation

    (C) titration

    (D) gel electrophoresis

40. Which of the following summarizes the function of a retrovirus in gene therapy?

    (A) regulates the production of new tRNA

    (B) promotes the translation of viral proteins

    (C) employs reverse transcription to manufacture new DNA

    (D) catalyses mutated DNA

41. Which term best describes an organism's habitat?

    (A) home

    (B) diet

    (C) occupation

    (D) neighborhood

42. Which term best describes an organism's niche?

    (A) home

    (B) diet

    (C) occupation

    (D) neighborhood

43. Which term best describes an ecosystem?

    (A) home

    (B) diet

    (C) occupation

    (D) neighborhood

44. Which of the following is NOT a basic tenet of the theory of evolution?

    (A) Organisms within a species tend to overpopulate.

    (B) An ecosystem has limited natural resources.

    (C) Amphibians evolve into reptiles.

    (D) There are individual differences among the members of a species.

Directions: Use the graph to answer questions 45, 46, and 47.

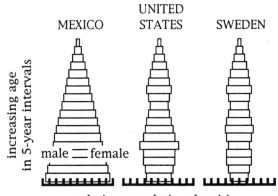

relative population densities

45. How is the population density of Mexico likely to change in the next 15 years?

    (A) It will probably increase.

    (B) It will probably decrease.

    (C) It will probably remain stable.

    (D) There is not enough data to make a prediction.

46. How is the population density of Sweden likely to change in the next 15 years?

    (A) It will probably increase.

    (B) It will probably decrease.

    (C) It will probably remain stable.

    (D) There is not enough data to make a prediction.

47. Which country will most likely have a relatively stable population density for the foreseeable future?

    (A) Mexico

    (B) United States

    (C) Sweden

    (D) The populations of all of these countries are unstable.

48. Which of the following is NOT a natural chemical cycle?

    (A) nitrogen cycle

    (B) water cycle

    (C) carbon cycle

    (D) sulfur cycle

49. Which of the following organisms is a producer?

    (A) beetle

    (B) fern

    (C) earthworm

    (D) sparrow

50. Which of the following organisms is a consumer?

    (A) bumblebee

    (B) apple tree

    (C) grass

    (D) phytoplankton

51. Which sequence describes the arrangement of organisms from top to bottom in a food pyramid?

    (A) plankton, krill, fish, dolphin

    (B) dolphin, fish, krill, plankton

    (C) krill, fish, plankton, dolphin

    (D) fish, plankton, krill, dolphin

52. Which of the following can cause a genetic mutation?

    (A) radiation

    (B) toxic chemicals

    (C) crossing over

    (D) all of the above

53. Which of the following best describes how evolution occurs by means of natural selection?

    (A) Genotype is favored by environmental change.

    (B) Phenotype is favored by environmental change.

    (C) Mutations always produce more adaptable organisms.

    (D) The environment causes specific mutations that make organisms more resistant to environmental change.

54. How does increased variation within a species affect the species' chances of survival?

    (A) It ensures the species' survival.

    (B) It dooms the species to extinction.

    (C) It has no effect on the species' chances of survival.

    (D) It increases the species' chances of survival.

55. Which of the following best summarizes the concept of allopatric speciation?

    (A) Populations separated by geographic barriers evolve in different ways.

    (B) Populations within a community evolve different reproductive strategies.

    (C) Populations merge to form symbiotic relationships.

    (D) Predator–prey relationships accelerate changes in survival strategies.

56. Which of the following best summarizes the concept of sympatric speciation?

    (A) Populations separated by geographic barriers evolve in different ways.

    (B) Populations within a community evolve different reproductive strategies.

    (C) Populations merge to form symbiotic relationships.

    (D) Predator–prey relationships accelerate changes in survival strategies.

57. Which of the following is NOT evident in the fossil record?

    (A) biological diversity

    (B) episodic speciation

    (C) mass extinction

    (D) clearly identifiable transitions between all old and new living forms

58. Which of the following organs is of primary importance in filtering toxic wastes from the blood?

    (A) lungs

    (B) heart

    (C) liver

    (D) kidneys

59. Which of the following best describes the action potential of a neuron?

    (A) Membrane permeability to specific intracellular and extracellular ions is altered.

    (B) Osmosis is reduced.

    (C) Ionization of protein-bound intracellular metals (e.g., Fe) produces a voltage along the axon.

    (D) Electrons are transferred along the axon.

60. Which of the following best describes action taking place at the terminal ending of a neuron?

    (A) action potential

    (B) saltatory conduction

    (C) transmitter reuptake

    (D) protein translation

61. How do most drugs interfere with communication between neurons?

    (A) They prevent the development of an action potential.

    (B) They prevent axonal membrane proteins from facilitating repolarization.

    (C) They block the binding of neurotransmitters to dendrite receptor proteins.

    (D) They reduce the concentration of intracellular chloride ions.

Directions: Use the diagram to answer questions 62, 63, and 64.

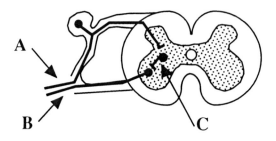

62. Which structure is part of a sensory neuron: A, B, or C?

63. Which structure is part of an interneuron: A, B, or C?

64. Which structure is part of a motor neuron: A, B, or C?

Biology Practice Test *(Continued)*

Directions: Choose the letter of the sense organ to which each structure belongs.

(A) eye

(B) ear

(C) skin

(D) nose

65. pupil

66. malleus

67. cochlea

68. iris

69. tympanic membrane

70. Ruffini ending

71. cornea

72. olfactory bulb

73. Pacinian corpuscle

74. Which of the following illustrates the principle of homeostasis?

(A) piloerection resulting from a decrease in ambient temperature

(B) dilation of extremity blood vessels during a long-distance run

(C) constriction of smooth muscle arterioles during a long-distance run

(D) all of the above

75. Which of the following best describes a negative feedback loop?

(A) nervous system stimulates an increase in sensitivity to a hormone

(B) endocrine gland produces less hormone in response to a rise in blood hormonal levels

(C) adrenal glands release adrenaline to initiate "flight or fight" response

(D) hypothalamus increases production of ACTH in response to injections of growth hormone

76. What is the body's last line of defense against infection?

(A) skin and mucous membranes

(B) inflammatory response

(C) immune response

(D) antiseptic sterilization

77. Which of the following best describes the function of antibodies?

(A) mark germs for destruction by leucocytes

(B) alert B-cells to activate T-cells

(C) reduce the action of lymphocytes against healthy body tissues

(D) control the production of vaccines

78. Which of the following is an example of passive immunity?

(A) vaccination against polio

(B) contracting measles as a child

(C) transfer of antibodies from pregnant mother to child

(D) all of the above

79. Which of the following differentiates a bacteria from a virus?

    (A) absence of a well-defined nucleus

    (B) must invade a host to reproduce

    (C) protective outer covering

    (D) contains nucleic acids

80. Which of the following makes AIDS a potentially lethal disease?

    (A) HIV attacks cardiac tissue.

    (B) HIV sensitizes the immune system to the body's own healthy tissues.

    (C) HIV interferes with the immune system's ability to fight infection.

    (D) HIV is a sexually transmitted disease.

Biology

PRACTICE TEST: ANSWER SHEET

Name _____ **Date** _____ **Period** _____

Darken the circle above the letter that best answers the question.

#	A B C D	#	A B C D	#	A B C D	#	A B C D
1.	O O O O	21.	O O O O	41.	O O O O	61.	O O O O
2.	O O O O	22.	O O O O	42.	O O O O	62.	O O O O
3.	O O O O	23.	O O O O	43.	O O O O	63.	O O O O
4.	O O O O	24.	O O O O	44.	O O O O	64.	O O O O
5.	O O O O	25.	O O O O	45.	O O O O	65.	O O O O
6.	O O O O	26.	O O O O	46.	O O O O	66.	O O O O
7.	O O O O	27.	O O O O	47.	O O O O	67.	O O O O
8.	O O O O	28.	O O O O	48.	O O O O	68.	O O O O
9.	O O O O	29.	O O O O	49.	O O O O	69.	O O O O
10.	O O O O	30.	O O O O	50.	O O O O	70.	O O O O
11.	O O O O	31.	O O O O	51.	O O O O	71.	O O O O
12.	O O O O	32.	O O O O	52.	O O O O	72.	O O O O
13.	O O O O	33.	O O O O	53.	O O O O	73.	O O O O
14.	O O O O	34.	O O O O	54.	O O O O	74.	O O O O
15.	O O O O	35.	O O O O	55.	O O O O	75.	O O O O
16.	O O O O	36.	O O O O	56.	O O O O	76.	O O O O
17.	O O O O	37.	O O O O	57.	O O O O	77.	O O O O
18.	O O O O	38.	O O O O	58.	O O O O	78.	O O O O
19.	O O O O	39.	O O O O	59.	O O O O	79.	O O O O
20.	O O O O	40.	O O O O	60.	O O O O	80.	O O O O

Each group of circles is labeled A B C D.

Biology

KEY TO PRACTICE TEST

#	Answer		#	Answer		#	Answer		#	Answer
1.	A		21.	A		41.	A		61.	C
2.	D		22.	C		42.	C		62.	A
3.	C		23.	A		43.	D		63.	C
4.	B		24.	C		44.	C		64.	B
5.	C		25.	A		45.	A		65.	A
6.	A		26.	B		46.	B		66.	B
7.	B		27.	C		47.	B		67.	B
8.	A		28.	C		48.	D		68.	A
9.	D		29.	B		49.	B		69.	B
10.	B		30.	A		50.	A		70.	C
11.	C		31.	C		51.	B		71.	A
12.	B		32.	B		52.	D		72.	D
13.	B		33.	C		53.	B		73.	C
14.	D		34.	A		54.	D		74.	D
15.	A		35.	A		55.	A		75.	B
16.	C		36.	B		56.	B		76.	C
17.	B		37.	B		57.	D		77.	A
18.	C		38.	B		58.	D		78.	C
19.	B		39.	D		59.	A		79.	B
20.	D		40.	C		60.	C		80.	C

Section II: Chemistry

LESSONS AND ACTIVITIES

Lesson 61 Students will relate the position of an element in the Periodic Table to its atomic number and mass.

Lesson 62 Students will relate the position of an element in the Periodic Table to its quantum electron configuration and reactivity with other elements in the table.

Lesson 63 Students will use the Periodic Table to identify metals, metalloids, nonmetals, halogens, and noble gases.

Lesson 64 Students will use the Periodic Table to identify alkali metals, alkaline earth metals, and transition metals.

Lesson 65 Students will use the Periodic Table to identify trends in ionization energy, electronegativity, and the relative sizes of atoms.

Lesson 66 Students will explain the experimental evidence demonstrating the much smaller size and large mass of the nucleus relative to the atom as a whole.

Lesson 67 Students will show how atoms form ions and how atoms combine to form ionically bonded molecules.

Lesson 68 Students will show how atoms form covalently bonded molecules.

Lesson 69 Students will show how covalently bonded atoms can form large biological molecules.

Lesson 70 Students will show how salt crystals such as NaCl are repeating patterns of positive and negative ions held together by electrostatic attraction.

Lesson 71 Students will use the Atomic-Molecular Theory of Matter to explain how solids differ from liquids and liquids differ from gas.

Lesson 72 Students will draw Lewis dot (i.e., electron-dot) structures or atoms and ions.

Lesson 73 Students will show that matter is conserved in a chemical reaction.

Lesson 74 Students will describe chemical reactions by writing balanced chemical equations.

Lesson 75 Students will explain the concept of a "mole."

Lesson 76 Students will determine the molar masses of a molecule from its chemical formula using a table of atomic masses.

Lesson 77 Students will convert the mass of a molecular substance to moles.

Chemistry-Contents *(Continued)*

CHEMISTRY PRACTICE TEST

Lesson 61: Teacher Preparation

Basic Principle   The Periodic Table displays the elements in increasing atomic number, and shows how periodicity of the physical and chemical properties of the elements relates to atomic structure.

Competency   Students will relate the position of an element in the Periodic Table (see page 365) to its atomic number and mass.

Procedure

1. Give students time to read the information on *Atomic Number and Mass*.

2. In 1753, the Swedish naturalist Carolus Linnaeus (1707–1778) simplified the classification of living species by introducing his binomial classification system for organizing plants and animals in the living kingdoms. Chemists saw the practical and theoretical benefits of having an organized system of classification for the natural elements. With the development of newer methods of chemical analysis, more elements were discovered in the following decades; and the French chemist Antoine Laurent Lavoisier (1743–1794) was one of the first to publish a complete list of the chemical elements of his time. In his 1789 work entitled *Traité Élémentaire de Chimie (The Thirty Chemical Elements)*, Lavoisier listed and described the chemical and physical properties of the thirty known elements.

   Advances in electrochemistry, led by the English chemist Humphry Davy (1778–1829), demonstrated the electrochemical affinities between the elements and gave John Newlands (1837–1898) a rationale for his speculative periodic law. Newlands was the first to propose the idea of a periodic law publicly; and, despite ridicule by the members of the Chemical Society of London, Newlands's Law of Octaves was given firm and lasting confirmation in 1869 by the work of Dmitri Mendeleev (1766–1844) and the German chemist Lothar Meyer (1830–1895). In 1870, Meyer published a graph that clearly showed a periodic relationship between the relative atomic volumes and atomic weights of the known elements; but his work was overshadowed by the uncanny intuition of Mendeleev. The power of Mendeleev's arguments centered on his predictions of the precise characteristics of the undiscovered elements gallium, scandium, and germanium.

3. Give students time to complete the *Observations & Analysis* section.

Answers to Observations & Analysis

1. The lightest elements are found in the upper left-hand corner of the periodic table. The heaviest elements are found in the lower right-hand corner.

2. Answers will vary, but should include the following main points: Newlands's periodic law suggested that elements with similar chemical affinities for other elements could be placed in the same group or family. Mendeleev used the law to arrange the known elements in rows and columns, suggesting that gaps in the table represented as yet undiscovered elements.

3. Answers will vary, but should include the following main points: The elucidation of the structure of the atom by Ernst Rutherford allowed his student Henry Moseley to show that listing the elements by their atomic number—and not atomic mass—caused the elements to fall into line in agreement with laboratory data.

Name _____ Date _____

Chemistry

STUDENT HANDOUT–LESSON 61

Basic Principle   The Periodic Table displays the elements in increasing atomic number, and shows how periodicity of the physical and chemical properties of the elements relates to atomic structure.

Objective   Relate the position of an element in the Periodic Table to its atomic number and mass.

Procedure

1. Read the information on *Atomic Number and Mass*.

Atomic Number and Mass

The atomic theory of John Dalton (1766–1844) led to the classification system that compared atoms according to their relative weights. It was not until 1807, however, that the English chemist Humphry Davy (1778–1829) showed that elements had varying degrees of electrical affinity for one another which determined their chemical reactivity. Using electrolysis, Davy discovered the elements barium, boron, magnesium, potassium, sodium, and strontium within a period of two short years. His experiments prompted chemists to list the known elements in an *electrochemical series*, a scale of relative chemical affinities. In the 1860s, several chemists stumbled upon the idea that the chemical and physical properties of the elements were *periodic* and that it was possible to group the elements in families that shared similar chemical affinities and characteristics. The English chemist John Newlands (1837–1898) was the first to propose the idea of a *periodic law* that would organize the elements according to their mass and chemical properties. Newlands's periodic law was given firm and lasting confirmation in 1869 by Dmitri Mendeleev (1766–1844) who with Newlands's ideas had predicted the discoveries of the elements gallium, scandium, and germanium. Versions of Mendeleev's *periodic table*, with elements arranged in vertical families and horizontal periods, listed elements in order of increasing atomic mass from the upper left of the chart to the lower right. The elucidation of the structure of the atom by the physicist Enrst Rutherford (1871–1937) allowed his student Henry Moseley (1887–1915) to show that *atomic number*, and not *atomic mass*, was the determinant factor in making sense of the periodic law. When atoms were placed in order of their atomic number (i.e., a measure of the number of positively charged protons in the nucleus of the atom), all of the elements fell into line in agreement with laboratory data. The electron-shell model of the atom, proposed by the Danish physicist Niels Bohr (1885–1962), allowed chemists to explain the absolute reactivities of the elements.

---

2. Study the illustration. Then complete the *Observations & Analysis* section.

GENERAL ORGANIZATION OF THE PERIODIC TABLE OF ELEMENTS

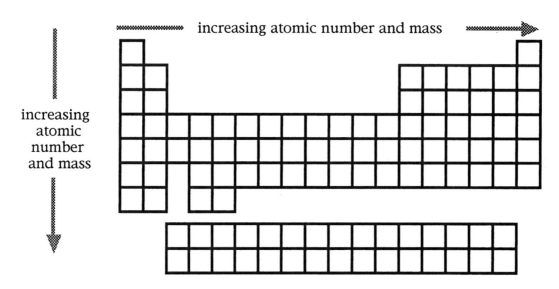

increasing atomic number and mass

increasing atomic number and mass

Observations & Analysis

1. Where are the lightest elements placed on the Periodic Table? The heaviest elements?

_____

_____

_____

_____

2. How did Newlands's periodic law persuade Mendeleev to arrange the known elements of their time in vertical columns and horizontal rows?

_____

_____

_____

_____

3. Why are the elements of the modern Periodic Table arranged according to increasing atomic number?

_____

_____

_____

_____

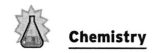 **Chemistry**

Lesson 62: Teacher Preparation

Basic Principle   The Periodic Table displays the elements in increasing atomic number, and shows how periodicity of the physical and chemical properties of the elements relates to atomic structure.

Competency   Students will relate the position of an element in the Periodic Table to its quantum electron configuration and reactivity with other elements in the table.

Procedure

1. Explain that Max Planck's (1858–1947) experiments on "black body radiation" demonstrated that the electromagnetic radiation (e.g., photons) given off by objects traverse space in discrete packets of energy. The electromagnetic spectrum is not, therefore, a continuous spectrum. Following the work of Planck and Niels Bohr (1885–1962), other scientists closely evaluated the series of spectral lines created by the hydrogen atom.

2. Draw the illustration showing how physicists quantify the "quantum leaps" made by the hydrogen electron as it goes from one energy level to another, absorbing energy as it leaps to higher levels and emitting energy as it falls to lower levels.

3. In this illustration, the horizontal lines depict the principal energy levels (e.g., K=1, L=2, M=3, N=4, O=5, etc.). The *Lyman series* represents electron jumps that radiate photons in the ultraviolet frequencies. The *Balmer series* represents electron jumps that radiate photons in the visible light frequencies (e.g., red, orange, yellow, green, blue, indigo, and violet). The *Paschen series* represents electron jumps that radiate photons in the infrared frequencies. The hydrogen electron requires about 218×10^{-18} ergs of energy to expel it completely from the atom.

4. Draw the illustrations showing the axial orientations of the *s* and *p* orbitals. Point out that the quantum electron orbitals are not all spherical. The *s* orbitals are spherical and increase in size as electrons move farther from the nucleus. The *p* and *d* orbitals are "dumbbell-shaped" clouds of energy aligned with the *x*, *y*, and *z* axes surrounding the nucleus.

5. Give students time to complete the *Observations & Analysis section.*

Answer to Observations & Analysis

Element	1s	2s	2p	2p	2p	3s	3p	3p	3p	4s
hydrogen	(.)	( )	( )	( )	( )	( )	( )	( )	( )	( )
helium	(..)	( )	( )	( )	( )	( )	( )	( )	( )	( )
lithium	(..)	(.)	( )	( )	( )	( )	( )	( )	( )	( )
beryllium	(..)	(..)	( )	( )	( )	( )	( )	( )	( )	( )
boron	(..)	(..)	(.)	( )	( )	( )	( )	( )	( )	( )
carbon	(..)	(..)	(.)	(.)	( )	( )	( )	( )	( )	( )
nitrogen	(..)	(..)	(.)	(.)	(.)	( )	( )	( )	( )	( )
oxygen	(..)	(..)	(..)	(.)	(.)	( )	( )	( )	( )	( )
fluorine	(..)	(..)	(..)	(..)	(.)	( )	( )	( )	( )	( )
neon	(..)	(..)	(..)	(..)	(..)	( )	( )	( )	( )	( )
sodium	(..)	(..)	(..)	(..)	(..)	(.)	( )	( )	( )	( )
magnesium	(..)	(..)	(..)	(..)	(..)	(..)	( )	( )	( )	( )
aluminum	(..)	(..)	(..)	(..)	(..)	(..)	(.)	( )	( )	( )
silicon	(..)	(..)	(..)	(..)	(..)	(..)	(.)	(.)	( )	( )
phosphorus	(..)	(..)	(..)	(..)	(..)	(..)	(.)	(.)	(.)	( )
sulfur	(..)	(..)	(..)	(..)	(..)	(..)	(..)	(.)	(.)	( )
chlorine	(..)	(..)	(..)	(..)	(..)	(..)	(..)	(..)	(.)	( )
argon	(..)	(..)	(..)	(..)	(..)	(..)	(..)	(..)	(..)	( )
potassium	(..)	(..)	(..)	(..)	(..)	(..)	(..)	(..)	(..)	(.)
calcium	(..)	(..)	(..)	(..)	(..)	(..)	(..)	(..)	(..)	(..)

SPECTRAL LINES FOR HYDROGEN

infinity

n=7
n=6
n=5

n=4

n=3

n=2

energy needed to expel the electron
$(218 \times 10^{-18}$ ergs$)$

Paschen series

Balmer series

n=1

Lyman series

ORIENTATION OF ORBITALS

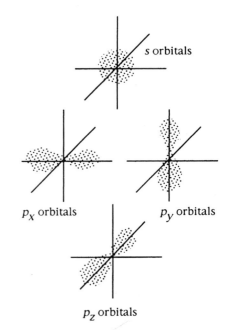

s orbitals

p_x orbitals

p_y orbitals

p_z orbitals

Chemistry

STUDENT HANDOUT–LESSON 62

Basic Principle   The Periodic Table displays the elements in increasing atomic number, and shows how periodicity of the physical and chemical properties of the elements relates to atomic structure.

Objective   Relate the position of an element in the Periodic Table to its quantum electron configuration and reactivity with other elements in the table.

Procedure

1. Read the information about Quantum Electron Configurations.

Quantum Electron Configurations

The experiments of Max Planck (1858–1947) confirmed that energy released from a heated body is emitted in discrete packets of energy called *quanta*. The Danish physicist Niels Bohr (1885–1962), working as a student of Ernst Rutherford (1871–1937) who demonstrated that electrons orbit an atom at vast distances from its nucleus, suggested that electrons were confined to specific *energy levels* around the nucleus. He suggested that electrons absorbing quanta (e.g., photons) of specific energies "leap" to more distant energy levels. Electrons that "fall" to lower energy levels release photons (e.g., electromagnetic radiation at specific frequencies). The energy levels occupied by electrons comprise the *quantum electron configuration* of that atom. The Bohr Model of the atom gives the chemist a way of explaining the relative chemical reactivities of the elements, since it requires less energy to remove an electron that is already far from the nucleus than it does to remove one close to the nucleus. According to Bohr's model, electrons farthest from the nucleus of an atom, the valence electrons, are the only electrons involved in chemical reactions with other atoms. The elements arranged on the Periodic Table, according to vertical families and horizontal periods, are placed in groups with similar *electrochemical affinities* that determine chemical reactivities. The elements hydrogen, lithium, and sodium, for example, have similar electrochemical affinities and chemical reactivities. They are all placed in Family 1 (IA), the first vertical column on the table. Based on Bohr's model, the quantum electron configurations of the elements in Family 1 (IA) show that the atoms of elements in Family 1 have a single electron in their outer shell. The elements beryllium, magnesium, and calcium in Family 2 (IIA) have two valence electrons. The quantum electron configuration can be used to explain the chemical reactivity with an element.

---

2. Study the illustrations. Then complete the *Observations & Analysis* section.

ELECTRON ORBITALS

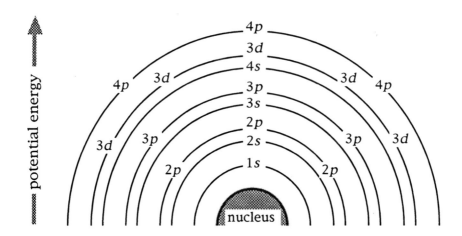

The potential energies of orbiting electrons are determined by their distance from the nucleus. The orbitals are called *s*, *p*, *d*, and *f* orbitals, each orbital specifying the energies of the electrons in that orbital. Each orbital can hold one or two electrons, the orbital with the least potential energies filling first. Only the first three principal energy levels (i.e., 1, 2, 3) and part of the 4th principal energy level are shown. The 1*s*, 2*s*, 3*s*, and 4*s* orbitals each hold a maximum of two electrons. The 2*p*, 3*p*, and 4*p* orbitals each hold a maximum of three pairs of electrons. The 3*d* orbital like other *d* orbitals farther from the nucleus can hold a maximum of five pairs of electrons.

Observations & Analysis

In each set of parentheses, place one or two dots to indicate the number of electrons present in the electron orbitals of each element. Hydrogen, helium, and lithium are given as examples.

Element	1s	2s	2p	2p	2p	3s	3p	3p	3p	4s
hydrogen	(.)	( )	( )	( )	( )	( )	( )	( )	( )	( )
helium	(..)	( )	( )	( )	( )	( )	( )	( )	( )	( )
lithium	(..)	(.)	( )	( )	( )	( )	( )	( )	( )	( )
beryllium	( )	( )	( )	( )	( )	( )	( )	( )	( )	( )
boron	( )	( )	( )	( )	( )	( )	( )	( )	( )	( )
carbon	( )	( )	( )	( )	( )	( )	( )	( )	( )	( )
nitrogen	( )	( )	( )	( )	( )	( )	( )	( )	( )	( )
oxygen	( )	( )	( )	( )	( )	( )	( )	( )	( )	( )
fluorine	( )	( )	( )	( )	( )	( )	( )	( )	( )	( )
neon	( )	( )	( )	( )	( )	( )	( )	( )	( )	( )
sodium	( )	( )	( )	( )	( )	( )	( )	( )	( )	( )
magnesium	( )	( )	( )	( )	( )	( )	( )	( )	( )	( )
aluminum	( )	( )	( )	( )	( )	( )	( )	( )	( )	( )
silicon	( )	( )	( )	( )	( )	( )	( )	( )	( )	( )
phosphorus	( )	( )	( )	( )	( )	( )	( )	( )	( )	( )
sulfur	( )	( )	( )	( )	( )	( )	( )	( )	( )	( )
chlorine	( )	( )	( )	( )	( )	( )	( )	( )	( )	( )
argon	( )	( )	( )	( )	( )	( )	( )	( )	( )	( )
potassium	( )	( )	( )	( )	( )	( )	( )	( )	( )	( )
calcium	( )	( )	( )	( )	( )	( )	( )	( )	( )	( )

Lesson 63: Teacher Preparation

Basic Principle   The Periodic Table displays the elements in increasing atomic number, and shows how periodicity of the physical and chemical properties of the elements relates to atomic structure.

Competency   Students will use the Periodic Table to identify metals, metalloids, nonmetals, halogens, and noble gases.

Procedure   Give students time to read the information on *Metals, Metalloids, Nonmetals, Halogens, and Noble Gases* before completing the *Observations & Analysis* section.

Answers to Observations & Analysis

1.
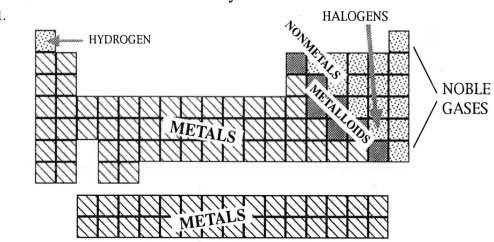

2. Answers will vary, but should include the following main points: All metals readily conduct heat and electricity in varying degrees.

3. Answers will vary, but should include the following main points: Metalloids can be made to conduct heat and electricity under certain circumstances, making them ideal for the fabrication of computer chips that require elements able to "switch on" or "switch off" when subjected to an electric current.

4. Answers will vary, but should include the following main points: Nonmetals resist the flow of heat and electricity and, therefore, serve as ideal insulators.

5. Answers will vary, but should include the following main points: Halogens react violently with most other elements on the table, especially the alkali and alkaline metals of Families 1 and 2.

6. Answers will vary, but should include the following main points: Noble gases are characteristically unreactive gaseous substances.

7. Answers will vary, but should include the following main points: Alkali and alkaline metals react violently with other elements, especially those in Family 17.

Chemistry

STUDENT HANDOUT–LESSON 63

Basic Principle   The Periodic Table displays the elements in increasing atomic number, and shows how periodicity of the physical and chemical properties of the elements relates to atomic structure.

Objective   Use the Periodic Table to identify metals, metalloids, nonmetals, halogens, and noble gases.

Procedure

1. Read the information on *Metals, Metalloids, Nonmetals, Halogens, and Noble Gases*.

Metals, Metalloids, Nonmetals, Halogens, and Noble Gases

The Periodic Table allows the quick identification of elements according to their most obvious physical and chemical properties. With the exception of hydrogen, which is a gas at room temperature, the elements in Families 1–2 tend to be *light metals* that react violently with the members of many other chemical families. The elements in Families 3–7 are *brittle metals*, while the elements in Families 8–11 are *ductile metals*. The metals of Family 12 tend to have *low boiling points*. Families 13–16 also include metals such as aluminum, gallium, indium, thallium, tin, lead, bismuth, and polonium. All metals readily conduct heat and electricity in varying degrees. The same families include the *metalloids* boron, silicon, germanium, arsenic, antimony, tellurium, and astatine. Metalloids can be made to conduct heat and electricity under certain circumstances, making them ideal for the fabrication of computer chips that require elements able to "switch on" or "switch off" when subjected to an electric current. The other members of Families 14–16 are *nonmetals* that resist the flow of heat and electricity and, therefore, serve as ideal insulators. With the exception of astatine, the other elements in Family 17, called *halogens*, react violently with most other elements on the table, especially the alkali and alkaline metals of Families 1 and 2. The *noble gases* of Family 18 are characteristically unreactive gaseous substances.

---

2. Examine the handout illustrations. Then complete the *Observations & Analysis* section.

GENERAL ORGANIZATION OF THE PERIODIC TABLE OF ELEMENTS

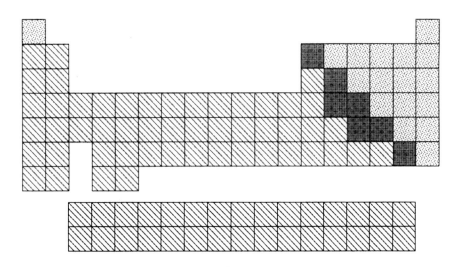

Observations & Analysis

1. In bold lettering, identify the elements of the Periodic Table as metals, metalloids, nonmetals, halogens, and noble gases.

2. What are the characteristic properties of metals? _____

_____

3. What are the characteristic properties of metalloids? _____

_____

4. What are the characteristic properties of nonmetals? _____

_____

5. What are the characteristic properties of halogens? _____

_____

6. What are the characteristic properties of noble gases? _____

_____

7. What chemical property is shared by alkali and alkaline metals?

_____

_____

Lesson 64: Teacher Preparation

Basic Principle   The Periodic Table displays the elements in increasing atomic number and shows how periodicity of the physical and chemical properties of the elements relates to atomic structure.

Competency   Students will use the Periodic Table to identify alkali metals, alkaline earth metals, and transition metals.

Procedure

1. Give students time to read the information on *Alkali Metals, Alkaline Metals, and Transition Metals* before completing the *Observations & Analysis* section.

2. Explain that unlike the atoms of the alkali and alkaline earth metals, having one or two easily ionizable valence electrons, the electronic configurations of the atoms of transitions elements make them more difficult to classify. In the elements of Families 1, 2, 13, 14, 15, 16, and 17, valence electrons occupy the *s* and *p* orbitals of principal energy levels. The valence electrons of transition elements, however, can be drawn from *s* orbitals into *d* orbitals that contain a single electron in any one of five *d* orbitals.

3. Draw the "outer" quantum electron configuration of iron (Fe) to illustrate how the electrons of its outermost electron shells are distributed. Electrons from its 4*s* orbital can be drawn into lower energy states to affect the production of a number of positively charged iron ions.

Outer Electron Configuration of Iron (atomic number = 26)					
(All lower electron energy levels are filled.)					
3*d*	3*d*	3*d*	3*d*	3*d*	4*s*
(..)	(.)	(.)	(.)	(.)	(..)

Answers to Observations & Analysis

1. Answers will vary, but should include the following main points: The alkali metals exhibit highly reactive chemical properties, reacting readily with oxygen to produce water-soluble hydroxides. The alkaline earth metals react with oxygen to form sparingly soluble oxides that can react with water to form acid-neutralizing hydroxides.

2. Answers will vary, but should include the following main points: The transition elements exhibit multiple valencies, forming +1 or +2 ions. The alkali metals can form only +1 ions. The alkaline metals can form only +2 ions.

3. Answers will vary, but should include the following main points: The transition elements are the best electrical conductors because they have more unpaired valence electrons that are free to conduct electrical current.

Name _____   **Date** _____

Chemistry

STUDENT HANDOUT–LESSON 64

Basic Principle   The Periodic Table displays the elements in increasing atomic number and shows how periodicity of the physical and chemical properties of the elements relates to atomic structure.

Objective   Use the Periodic Table to identify alkali metals, alkaline earth metals, and transition metals.

Procedure

1. Read the information on *Alkali Metals, Alkaline Earth Metals, and Transition Metals.*

Alkali Metals, Alkaline Earth Metals, and Transition Metals

The *alkali metals* of Family 1 exhibit highly reactive chemical properties. The atoms of these elements form ions with a +1 charge only due to their loosely held single valence electron. They react with oxygen to produce water-soluble hydroxides. The *alkaline earth metals* of Family 2 form ions with a +2 charge only due to their pair of loosely held valence electrons. They react with oxygen to form sparingly soluble oxides that can react with water to form acid-neutralizing hydroxides. The *transition elements* of Families 3–12 all contain *d* orbitals that cause them to exhibit multiple valences. Multiple valences give these atoms a variability of ionic possibilities. They can become +1 or +2 ions. For this reason, transition elements form a number of complex ions and that can bond with negatively charged atoms to form conductive metallic compounds.

---

2. Complete the *Observations & Analysis* section.

Observations & Analysis

1. How do the chemical properties of alkali metals differ from those of alkaline earth metals?

   _____

   _____

   _____

   _____

2. How do the chemical properties of transition elements differ from those of the alkali metals and alkaline earth metals?

   _____

   _____

   _____

   _____

3. Although alkali metals, alkaline earth metals, and transition metals are all metals, which of these would be the best electrical conductor? Explain your reasoning.

   _____

   _____

   _____

   _____

   _____

   _____

   _____

Chemistry

Lesson 65: Teacher Preparation

Basic Principle   The Periodic Table displays the elements in increasing atomic number, and shows how periodicity of the physical and chemical properties of the elements relates to atomic structure.

Competency   Students will use the Periodic Table to identify trends in ionization energy, electronegativity, and the relative sizes of atoms.

Procedure

1. Give students time to read the information on *Ionization Energy, Electronegativity, and Atomic Radius.*

2. Point out that the electronegativity of an atom is a measure of its ability to attract electrons to itself. The American chemist Linus Pauling (1901–1994) created an arbitrary scale based on bond-energy calculations in which fluorine is the most electronegative element. The alkali metals are the least electronegative. Other scales based on a variety of atomic properties have been proposed. However, in every case the relative arrangements of the elements remains the same. The difference in electronegativities between the atoms of two elements determines the kind of chemical bond between them. The electrons of a covalently bonded molecule tend to remain close to the atom of the element with the greater electronegativity, creating a dipole molecule having distinctly positive and negative poles.

3. Give students time to complete the *Observations & Analysis* section.

Answers to Observations & Analysis

1. Answers will vary, but should include the following main points: Ionization energy is the amount of energy needed to expel an electron from an atom. Electronegativity refers to an atom's ability to attract the electrons of other atoms.

2. Answers will vary, but should include the following main point: As the atomic radius of the atoms in a given family increases, the electronegativity of the elements decreases.

3. The electrons of a CO_2 molecule would be found closer to the oxygen atoms. The electrons of a NH_3 molecule would be found closer to the nitrogen atom. The electrons of a CI_4 molecule would be found equidistant between the carbon and iodine atoms.

Chemistry

STUDENT HANDOUT–LESSON 65

Basic Principle   The Periodic Table displays the elements in increasing atomic number, and shows how periodicity of the physical and chemical properties of the elements relates to atomic structure.

Objective   Use the Periodic Table to identify trends in ionization energy, electronegativity, and the relative sizes of atoms.

Procedure

1. Read the information on *Ionization Energy, Electronegativity, and Atomic Radius*.

Ionization Energy, Electronegativity, and Atomic Radius

All chemical reactions are the result of the transfer or sharing of valence electrons. The amount of energy required to completely remove an electron from an electron orbital is called *ionization energy*. Because all elements but hydrogen have more than one electron, all elements have two or more ionization energies. The ionization energy of a single hydrogen electron, for example, is 210×10^{-18} ergs. A hydrogen atom that absorbs this amount of energy will lose its electron. The alkali metals have the lowest ionization energies, largely due to their relatively small atomic radius compared to the other elements on the Periodic Table. The overall radius of atoms increases from left to right across the periods of the Periodic Table. The elements helium, neon, and fluorine have the highest ionization potentials, holding electrons close to their nuclei with their outermost electron orbitals either full or nearly full. The term *electronegativity* refers to the ability of atoms to attract the electrons of other atoms. Elements on the right side of the Periodic Table, such as the halogens or elements of the oxygen family, are the most electronegative. Electronegativity increases from left to right across the Periodic Table and decreases down the table as the radii of atoms increase. The electrons shared in a covalent bond between two atoms will be found closer to the atom with the higher electronegativity. Such a molecule will exhibit the properties of a dipole.

---

2. Study the information *Electronegativity of Common Elements* before completing the *Observations & Analysis* section.

ELECTRONEGATIVITY OF COMMON ELEMENTS

H					
2.1					

Li	Be	C	N	O	F
1.0	1.5	2.5	3.0	3.5	4.0

Na	Mg	Si	P	S	Cl
0.9	1.2	1.8	2.1	2.5	3.0

K	Ca	Ge	As	Se	Br
0.8	1.0	1.7	2.0	2.4	2.8

Cs	Ba			Te	I
0.7	0.9			2.2	2.5

Observations & Analysis

1. Explain the difference between ionization energy of an element and electronegativity.

   _____

   _____

2. How is the electronegativity of the elements in a family related to the atomic radius of the elements in that family?

   _____

   _____

3. Where are the electrons of a covalently bonded CO_2 molecule likely to be found? The electrons of a NH_3 molecule? The electrons of a CI_4 molecule?

   _____

   _____

Lesson 66: Teacher Preparation

Basic Principle   The Periodic Table displays the elements in increasing atomic number, and shows how periodicity of the physical and chemical properties of the elements relates to atomic structure.

Competency   Students will explain the experimental evidence demonstrating the much smaller size and large mass of the nucleus relative to the atom as a whole.

Procedure

1. Draw the illustration showing how scientists estimated the mass of electrons relative to the mass of the atomic nucleus. Explain that negatively charged electrons directed through an electric field and directed at a photographic plate were deflected to a much higher degree than heavier atomic nuclei. The degree of deflection of the negatively and positively charged particles gives an approximation of the masses of these particles required to create such deflections.

2. Give students time to read the information on *The Rutherford Atom* before completing the *Observations & Analysis* section.

Answers to Observations & Analysis

1. Answers will vary, but should include the following main points: Thomson's model depicted the atom as a large positively charged object with negatively charged electrons embedded within it. According to that model, positively charged alpha particles (e.g., helium nuclei) directed at a foil made of such atoms would be deflected back as they approached the foil.

2. Answers will vary, but should include the following main points: The results of Rutherford's experiments showed that the helium nuclei directed at the gold foil passed neatly through the foil. This could only be true if the size of the atomic nucleus was much smaller than that supposed by J. J. Thomson. The atom must, according to these results, be made mostly of empty space, the electrons circling the nucleus at vast distances from the center of the atom.

ESTIMATING THE MASS OF AN ELECTRON
RELATIVE TO THE MASS OF THE ATOMIC NUCLEUS

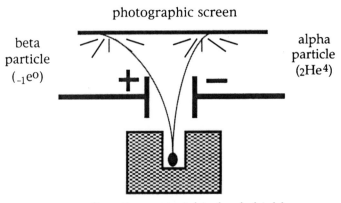

radioactive material in lead shield

Name _____ Date _____

Chemistry

STUDENT HANDOUT–LESSON 66

Basic Principle   The Periodic Table displays the elements in increasing atomic number, and shows how periodicity of the physical and chemical properties of the elements relates to atomic structure.

Objective   Explain the experimental evidence demonstrating the much smaller size and large mass of the nucleus relative to the atom as a whole.

Procedure

1. Read the information on *The Rutherford Atom*.

The Rutherford Atom

The New Zealand-born English physicist Ernst Rutherford (1871–1937) demonstrated that the nucleus of an atom was extremely compact compared to the atom as a whole. He bombarded a sheet of gold foil with alpha radiation composed of positively charged helium nuclei emitted from a shielded source. According to the model of the atom proposed by J. J. Thomson (1856–1940), the "large" positively charged centers of the gold atoms, embedded with electrons like "plums in a pudding," would deflect the similarly charged alpha particles. Instead, the majority of alpha particles passed easily through the foil producing visible flashes of light on a zinc sulfide screen. Rutherford concluded that the nuclei of the gold atoms had to be very small and compact in order for the alpha particles to pass neatly through the foil without deflection. In 1913, Rutherford's gifted student, Henry Moseley (1887–1915), used X-ray spectroscopy to determine the number of positively charged protons occupying the massive nuclei of atoms. Moseley's new atomic numbers (e.g., the number of protons in the nucleus) were used to revise The Periodic Table of Elements put forth by Dmitri Mendeleev (1834–1907). Working with Rutherford in England, the Danish physicist Niels Bohr (1885–1962) explained the variety of light spectra emitted by the atoms of different elements using his electron-shell model of the atom. He placed the electrons, measuring 0.0005 times the mass of a proton, at vast distances from the nucleus. According to the Bohr model, electrons jumped from one electron-shell or "energy level" to another by absorbing or emitting electromagnetic energy. Electrons jumped to higher levels by absorbing discrete quantities of energy, and fell to lower levels by emitting discrete quantities of energy.

---

2. Examine the handout illustrations before completing the *Observations & Analysis* section.

RUTHERFORD'S GOLD-FOIL EXPERIMENT

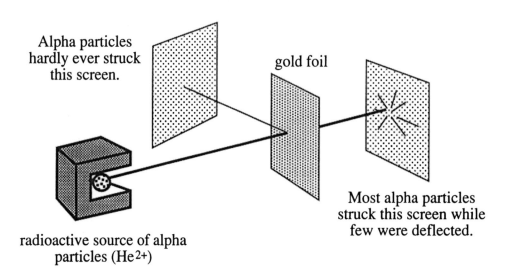

Alpha particles
hardly ever struck
this screen.

gold foil

Most alpha particles
struck this screen while
few were deflected.

radioactive source of alpha
particles (He²⁺)

Observations & Analysis

1. Explain why the Thomson model of the atom predicted that alpha particles bombarding a sheet of gold foil would be deflected back from the foil.

_____

_____

_____

_____

_____

2. Explain why the results of Rutherford's experiments caused him to reject the Thomson model of the atom.

_____

_____

_____

_____

_____

_____

_____

_____

_____

_____

Lesson 67: Teacher Preparation

Basic Principle   The biochemical, chemical, and physical properties of matter result from the ability of atoms to form bonds based on electrostatic forces between electrons and protons and between atoms and molecules.

Competency   Students will show how atoms form ions and how atoms combine to form ionically bonded molecules.

Procedure

1. Give students time to read the information on *Ions and Ionic Bonds*.

2. Point out that ionic compounds have no net charge. They are neutral. This means that cations combine with anions in sufficient numbers to cancel their opposing charges. For example, two positively charged sodium ions ($2Na^{+1}$), each with a +1 charge, combine with a single oxygen ion (O^{-2}) that has a –2 charge. The resulting ionic compound is sodium oxide: Na_2O [i.e., $(2 \times +1) + (1 \times -2) = 0$].

3. Give students time to examine the handout and complete the *Observations & Analysis* section.

Answers to Observations & Analysis

element	cation formation	ionic compound	anion formation	element
Li	Li • $\longrightarrow$ Li^+ + e-	LiF	:F: + e- $\longrightarrow$ F^-	F
K	K • $\longrightarrow$ K^+ + e-	KBr	:Br: + e- $\longrightarrow$ Br^-	Br
Mg	Mg: $\longrightarrow$ Mg^{+2} + 2e-	$MgCl_2$	:Cl: + e- $\longrightarrow$ Cl^-	Cl
Ca	Ca: $\longrightarrow$ Ca^{+2} + 2e-	CaI_2	:I: + e- $\longrightarrow$ I^-	I
Rb	Rb• $\longrightarrow$ Rb^+ + e-	Rb_2O	:O: + 2e- $\longrightarrow$ O^{-2}	O
Cs	Cs • $\longrightarrow$ Cs^+ + e-	Cs_2S	:S: + 2e- $\longrightarrow$ S^{-2}	S

Chemistry

STUDENT HANDOUT–LESSON 67

Basic Principle   The biochemical, chemical, and physical properties of matter result from the ability of atoms to form bonds based on electrostatic forces between electrons and protons and between atoms and molecules.

Objective   Show how atoms form ions and how atoms combine to form ionically bonded molecules.

Procedure

1. Read the information on *Ions and Ionic Bonds*.

Ions and Ionic Bonds

The Bohr model of the atom proposed by Danish physicist Niels Bohr (1885–1962) served to explain the chemical reactivity of the elements. According to the model, the nucleus of every atom, comprised of positively charged protons and neutral neutrons, is circled by negatively charged electrons moving in specific electron orbitals. The orbitals close to the atomic nucleus contain fewer electrons than shells that are farther away, the specific number of electrons in each orbital determined by the laws of electromagnetism and quantum mechanics. Refer to the chart showing the number of electrons accommodated by the four principal energy levels. According to the Bohr model, atoms are most stable when their outermost electron-shell is filled with electrons. Atoms achieve this goal by losing, gaining, or sharing electrons with other atoms. Electrons that are lost, gained, or shared by atoms are called *valence electrons*. Atoms that lose electrons become positively charged as they are left with a greater number of protons than electrons. Atoms that gain electrons become negatively charged as they are left with a fewer number of protons than electrons. An atom with a net positive or negative charge is called an *ion*. Positively charged ions are called *cations*, and are normally formed by elements in Families I (1), IIA (2), IIIB (13). Negatively charged ions are called *anions*, and are normally formed by elements in Families VB (15), VIB (16), and VIIB (17). The electrostatic charges of cations and anions attract one another to form compounds held together by *ionic bonds*.

---

2. Examine the handout illustrations. Then complete the *Observations & Analysis* section.

ELECTRON CAPACITY OF THE FIRST FOUR PRINCIPAL ENERGY LEVELS

Principal Energy Level	Electron Capacity	Suborbital	Maximum Electron Pairs
1	2	$1s$	1
2	8	$2s$	1
		$2p$	3
3	18	$3s$	1
		$3p$	3
		$3d$	5
4	32	$4s$	1
		$4p$	3
		$4d$	5
		$4f$	7

ION FORMATION

The electron-dot formula for sodium illustrates its single valence electron. When this electron is lost, the ion becomes a cation (i.e., a positively charged ion). The electron-dot formula for chlorine illustrates the seven valence electrons found in its $2s$ and three $2p$ orbitals. When chlorine gains an eighth electron to fill its last $2p$ orbital, it becomes an anion (i.e., a negatively charged ion).

$$Na\cdot \longrightarrow Na^+ + e^- \qquad \ddot{\underset{..}{:Cl}}: + e^- \longrightarrow Cl^-$$

IONIC BOND FORMATION

The sodium cation with a charge of +1 is attracted by the chlorine anion with a charge of –1. The two atoms combine in a ratio of 1 : 1 to form an ionic compound called NaCl.

$$Na^+Cl^-$$

Observations & Analysis

Use electron-dot formulas to show how the atoms in these elements form ionic bonds.

element	cation formation	ionic compound	anion formation	element
Li	_____	_____	_____	F
K	_____	_____	_____	Br
Mg	_____	_____	_____	Cl
Ca	_____	_____	_____	I
Rb	_____	_____	_____	O
Cs	_____	_____	_____	S

Lesson 68: Teacher Preparation

Basic Principle   The biochemical, chemical, and physical properties of matter result from the ability of atoms to form bonds based on electrostatic forces between electrons and protons and between atoms and molecules.

Competency   Students will show how atoms form covalently bonded molecules.

Procedure

1. Review the concepts of *ionization* and *electronegativity*.
2. Give students time to read the information on *Covalent Bonds*.
3. Assist students in completing the activity and the *Observations & Analysis* section. Have them note that in every molecule there are eight valence electrons—shared in single, double, or triple bonds—in the proximity of each atom with the exception of hydrogen which requires only two electrons to fill its 1*s* orbital.

Answers to Observations & Analysis

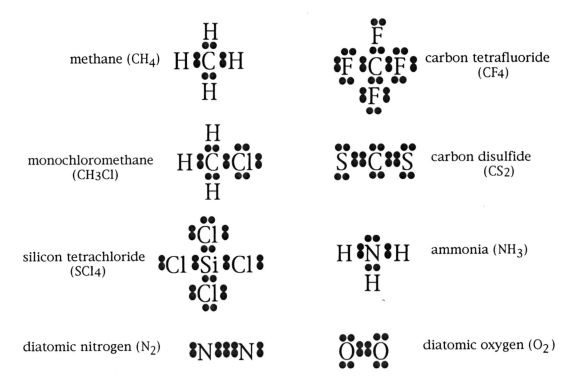

Chemistry

STUDENT HANDOUT–LESSON 68

Basic Principle   The biochemical, chemical, and physical properties of matter result from the ability of atoms to form bonds based on electrostatic forces between electrons and protons and between atoms and molecules.

Objective   Show how atoms form covalently bonded molecules.

Procedure

1. Read the information on *Covalent Bonds*.

Covalent Bonds

The moderately electronegative elements in Families IV (14), V (15), and VI (16) attract electrons from similarly electronegative elements that would otherwise form anions and ionic bonds with alkali and alkaline earth metals. Elements in the carbon, nitrogen, and oxygen families readily share their outer-shell electrons with other atoms. They form *covalent bonds* with other atoms so that all atoms in the resulting compound have full outer electron orbitals. In the illustration, a single carbon atom forms covalent bonds with two oxygen atoms to create a compound called carbon dioxide. All three atoms in the molecule have full outer shells, making the molecule stable. The four pairs of valance electrons shared by the carbon and two oxygen atoms are found in the 2s and three 2p orbitals of each atom.

---

2. Examine the handout illustrations. Then complete the *Observations & Analysis* section.

carbon (C): $1s(2)$, $2s(2)$, $2p(1)$, $2p(1)$ oxygen (O): $1s(2)$, $2s(2)$, $2p(2)$, $2p(1)$, $2p(1)$

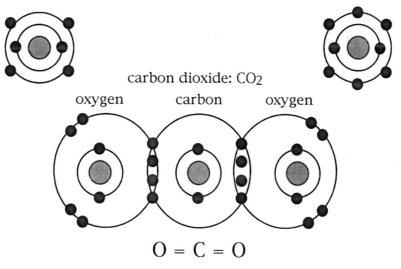

carbon dioxide: CO_2

oxygen   carbon   oxygen

$$O = C = O$$

Observations & Analysis

Draw electron-dot diagrams of the following covalent compounds: methane, CH_4; carbon tetrafluoride, CF_4; monochloromethane, CH_3Cl; carbon disulfide, CS_2; silicon tetrachloride, $SiCl_4$; ammonia, NH_3; diatomic nitrogen, N_2; and diatomic oxygen, O_2.

Lesson 69: Teacher Preparation

Basic Principle   The biochemical, chemical, and physical properties of matter result from the ability of atoms to form bonds based on electrostatic forces between electrons and protons and between atoms and molecules.

Competency   Students will show how covalently bonded atoms can form large biological molecules.

Procedure   Give students time to read the information on *Covalently Bonded Atoms of Macromolecules* before completing the *Observations & Analysis* section.

Answer to Observations & Analysis

Answers will vary, but should include the following main points: Because of their moderate electronegativity, atoms of carbon, nitrogen, and oxygen will share electrons rather than give them up completely to form ions. The highly electronegative atoms of the halogen group, like the highly electropositive atoms of the alkali metal family, form ions incapable of forming long nonpolar atomic chains.

Chemistry

STUDENT HANDOUT–LESSON 69

Basic Principle   The biochemical, chemical, and physical properties of matter result from the ability of atoms to form bonds based on electrostatic forces between electrons and protons and between atoms and molecules.

Objective   Show how covalently bonded atoms can form large biological molecules.

Procedure

1. Read the information on *Covalently Bonded Atoms of Macromolecules.*

Covalently Bonded Atoms of Macromolecules

The large macromolecules that serve as the basic molecules of life (e.g., carbohydrates, lipids, proteins, and nucleic acids) are the result of carbon's ability to form covalent bonds with other atoms such as hydrogen, oxygen, and nitrogen. The illustration shows the chemical formula and structural formulas of a simple carbohydrate (i.e., glucose) molecule. More complex carbohydrates such as plant cellulose are formed by covalently linking simple carbohydrate units together. Lipids, proteins, and nucleic acids are synthesized in similar fashion.

---

2. Examine the handout illustrations. Then complete the *Observations & Analysis* section.

CHEMICAL FORMULA OF GLUCOSE: $C_6H_{12}O_6$

Electron-dot formula of glucose:

Structural formula of glucose:

Shorthand structural formula of glucose:

Observations & Analysis

Explain why the atoms of covalently bonded molecules can form long chain macromolecular structures, while highly electronegative and electropositive atoms such as the halogens and alkali metals, respectively, cannot.

_____

_____

_____

_____

_____

_____

_____

_____

 **Chemistry**

Lesson 70: Teacher Preparation

Basic Principle   The biochemical, chemical, and physical properties of matter result from the ability of atoms to form bonds based on electrostatic forces between electrons and protons and between atoms and molecules.

Competency   Students will show how salt crystals such as NaCl are repeating patterns of positive and negative ions held together by electrostatic attraction.

Procedure

1. Give students time to read the information on *Ionic Salts*.

2. Point out that pure water is not an effective electrical conductor unless it is "contaminated" with ions that can transfer differential electric charges from one place to another. The electronegative properties of the oxygen atom present in the covalently stable water molecule can attract the cations of such compounds. This provokes the ions in the salt to become "dissociated" in water solution. Evaporating the water of a salt solution allows the cations and anions to "reassociate," forming a repeating pattern of ions: a crystalline salt.

3. Assist students in completing the *Observations & Analysis* section.

Answers to Observations & Analysis

1. Answers will vary, but should include the following main points: As a water solution dissolves, the cations and anions dissolved in the salt solution are attracted to one another. As a result, they form a repeating pattern of positive and negative ions held together by electrostatic attraction.

2. Answers will vary, but should include the following main points: In water solution, the cations and anions that comprise a salt are separated. The presence of these mobile electrostatic charges allows the passage of electrical current across a potential difference or voltage.

3. Answers will vary, but should include the following main points: The atoms of Families I (1) and II (2) form cations that are attracted to the anions derived from acids.

Chemistry

STUDENT HANDOUT–LESSON 70

Basic Principle   The biochemical, chemical, and physical properties of matter result from the ability of atoms to form bonds based on electrostatic forces between electrons and protons and between atoms and molecules.

Objective   Show how salt crystals such as NaCl are repeating patterns of positive and negative ions held together by electrostatic attraction.

Procedure

1.   Read the information on *Ionic Salts*.

Ionic Salts

A *salt* is any member of a group of compounds comprised of cations derived from a metal or an ammonia-containing compound and an anion derived from a non-metal or acid. Normal salts include common table salt, sodium chloride (NaCl), or any number of other salts such as magnesium fluoride (MgF_2), or $Ca(NO_3)_2$. *Acid salts* contain additional hydrogen such as in the acid salts sodium carbonate ($NaHCO_3$), sodium hydrogen-sulfate ($NaHSO_4$), or potassium phosphonate (KH_2PO_4). All salts are ionic compounds that are soluble in water and can conduct electricity in solution.

---

2.   Examine the handout illustrations. Then complete the *Observations & Analysis* section.

FORMATION OF CRYSTALLINE SALTS

| cations and anions in an evaporating solution | cations and anions attracted by electrostatic charges | cations and anions in a crystal |

Observations & Analysis

1. Explain how a salt crystal is formed.

   _____

   _____

   _____

   _____

   _____

   _____

2. Explain why an ionic salt will conduct electricity in solution.

   _____

   _____

   _____

   _____

3. Explain why ionic salts are formed between atoms of elements in Families I (1) and II (2) and the anions derived from acids.

   _____

   _____

   _____

   _____

   _____

   _____

Lesson 71: Teacher Preparation

Basic Principle   The biochemical, chemical, and physical properties of matter result from the ability of atoms to form bonds based on electrostatic forces between electrons and protons and between atoms and molecules.

Competency   Students will use the Atomic-Molecular Theory of Matter to explain how solids differ from liquids and liquids differ from gas.

Procedure

1. Draw the illustration to show how atoms behave as they are subjected to an increase in temperature (i.e., the absorption of heat radiation). Explain that atoms in a solid will move faster as they absorb heat (e.g., low frequency electromagnetic radiation) and move farther apart as they gain angular momentum. In this manner, solids are transformed to liquids, liquids to gas, and gases to plasma, the latter comprising a chemical change that involves the ionization of atoms that lose electrons to become charged particles.

2. Give students time to read the information on *Solids, Liquids, and Gases*.

3. Assist students in completing the *Observations & Analysis* section.

Answer to Observations & Analysis

Diagrams will vary, but should show how the individual atoms become separated from an organized arrangement to become a more random arrangement of particles.

THE ATOMIC-MOLECULAR THEORY EXPLANATION OF PHASE CHANGE

   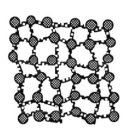   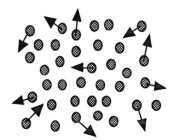

| orderly arrangement of atoms in a solid | disorderly arrangement of atoms in a liquid | separated and randomly moving atoms in a vapor |

 increasing temperature from the absorption of radiant energy ⟶

Name _____ **Date** _____

Chemistry

STUDENT HANDOUT–LESSON 71

Basic Principle   The biochemical, chemical, and physical properties of matter result from the ability of atoms to form bonds based on electrostatic forces between electrons and protons and between atoms and molecules.

Objective   Use the Atomic-Molecular Theory of Matter to explain how solids differ from liquids and liquids differ from gas.

Procedure

1. Read the information on *Solids, Liquids, and Gases*.

Solids, Liquids, and Gases

Matter exists in four states or *phases:* solid, liquid, gas, or plasma. *Solids*, like rock and glass, have definite shape and definite volume at room temperature. *Liquids*, like water and mercury, can change shape at room temperature while retaining the same volume. *Gases*, like oxygen and carbon dioxide, change both shape and volume at room temperature. A *plasma* is a highly energized gas made of electrically charged particles such as the particles radiating toward Earth from the Sun or the fire at the tip of a burning match. Matter can change from one form or phase to another. The *Atomic-Molecular Theory of Matter* suggests that all material objects are composed of rudimentary particles called *atoms* that are always in motion. Heating a solid causes the atoms that make up the solid to absorb heat energy and move faster. As the atoms absorb heat energy, they move more freely, move farther apart, and take on the characteristics of a liquid and, eventually, a gas. The transformation from a solid to a liquid is called *melting*. The transformation from a liquid to a gas is called *vaporization*. Some solids (like frozen carbon dioxide—commonly called dry ice) change directly into a gas when warmed. This process is called *sublimation*. Cooling a gas to form a liquid is called *condensation*. Cooling a liquid to form a solid is called *freezing*. Heating a gas to extreme temperatures can cause electrons to leave their orbits around the atomic nucleus. The "gas" produced is an electrically charged *plasma*. With the exception of the formation of a plasma, all of these changes are physical changes. In a physical change, the shape or form of the matter may change, but it remains the same kind of matter. Ice, water, and steam (i.e., solid, liquid, and vapor) are all different chemical forms of water.

---

2. Examine the handout illustrations. Then complete the *Observations & Analysis* section.

Observations & Analysis

Draw a diagram to illustrate what happens to the particles that comprise a solid as it is heated to extreme temperatures. Label your diagram to show how the particles comprising the solid behave according to the Atomic-Molecular Theory of Matter.

 **Chemistry**

Lesson 72: Teacher Preparation

Basic Principle   The biochemical, chemical, and physical properties of matter result from the ability of atoms to form bonds based on electrostatic forces between electrons and protons and between atoms and molecules.

Competency   Students will draw Lewis-dot (i.e., electron-dot) structures of atoms and ions.

Procedure

1. Give students time to read the information on *Electron-dot Formulas*.
2. Assist students in completing the *Observations & Analysis* section.

Answer to Observations & Analysis

See the diagrams.

Na•   Cs •   Ca⦂   Sr⦂

Al⦂   Ga⦂   ⦂Si⦂   ⦂Ge⦂

⦂P⦂   ⦂Sb⦂   ⦂Se⦂   ⦂Po⦂

⦂Br⦂   ⦂At⦂   ⦂Ne⦂   ⦂Rn⦂

Name _____ **Date** _____

Chemistry

STUDENT HANDOUT–LESSON 72

Basic Principle The biochemical, chemical, and physical properties of matter result from the ability of atoms to form bonds based on electrostatic forces between electrons and protons and between atoms and molecules.

Objective Draw Lewis-dot (i.e., electron-dot) structures of atoms and ions.

Procedure

1. Read the information on *Electron-dot Formulas*.

Electron-dot Formulas

The American chemist Gilbert Newton Lewis (1875–1946) contributed to the study of atomic structure and bonding. Lewis's work led him to an atomic model known as the *Lewis–Langmuir octet* which explained the distinction between ionic and covalent bonding in the formation of chemical bonds. The theory assumed that atoms' outermost electron shell were most stable when they contained a full complement of eight (i.e., an octet) electrons. Lewis's publication in 1943 on the *Valence and the Structure of Atoms and Molecules* created a model of atoms whose chemical behavior was dependent upon the affinity of valence electrons for their electronegative atomic nucleus. His electron-dot formulas provide chemists with a shorthand method of illustrating the bonding characteristics of atoms.

---

2. Examine the handout illustrations. Then complete the *Observations & Analysis* section.

LEWIS ELECTRON-DOT FORMULAS

Lewis electron-dot formulas show the number of electrons present in the outermost electron orbitals of the principle energy levels indicated by the family number (e.g., I, II, III, IV, etc.) of elements in a given chemical family.

Observations & Analysis

Draw Lewis electron-dot formulas for the following atoms: sodium, cesium, calcium, strontium, aluminum, gallium, silicon, germanium, phosphorus, antimony, selenium, polonium, bromine, astatine, neon, and radon.

Lesson 73: Teacher Preparation

Basic Principle   The conservation of atoms in chemical reactions leads to the principle of conservation of matter and the ability to calculate the masses of products and reactants.

Competency   Students will show that matter is conserved in a chemical reaction.

Materials   balance, small Ehrlenmeyer flask, balloon, baking soda, vinegar

Procedure

1. Point out that chemists of the 17th century fabricated glassware that made it possible to capture escaping gases produced by chemical reactions. This allowed them to measure the masses of all the products produced. The discovery that the mass of the products was always equal to the mass of the reactants in these experiments served as the basis for the Law of Conservation of Matter.

2. Give students time to perform the activity before completing the *Observations & Analysis* section.

Answers to Observations & Analysis

1. Drawings should illustrate that the balance remains zero as the gas produced by the reaction inflates the balloon.

2. Yes.

3. Answers will vary, but should include the following main points: The results demonstrate that matter was neither created nor destroyed by this chemical reaction. The particles comprising the reactants were simply rearranged to form new chemical products.

4. Answers will vary, but should include the following main points: Chemical reactions are balanced to show that the same kind and number of atoms present in the reactants of a chemical reaction are still present in the products.

5. Answers will vary, but should include the following main points: Allow the gas to escape and measure the mass of the remaining products. The difference between the mass of the reactants and the remaining products is equal to the mass of the gas that escaped.

Chemistry

STUDENT HANDOUT–LESSON 73

Basic Principle   The conservation of atoms in chemical reactions leads to the principle of conservation of matter and the ability to calculate the masses of products and reactants.

Objective   Show that matter is conserved in a chemical reaction.

Materials   balance, small Ehrlenmeyer flask, balloon, baking soda, vinegar

Procedure

1. According to the *Law of Conservation of Matter*, the mass of the products of a chemical reaction is the same as the mass of the reactants. Matter is neither created nor destroyed in a chemical reaction. The atoms comprising the reactants are merely rearranged to produce new products. Perform the demonstration below to illustrate this point.

2. Pour a tablespoon of vinegar into a small Ehrlenmeyer flask.

3. Scoop a teaspoon of baking soda into a balloon and stretch the opening of the balloon over the mouth of the flask. Do not spill the baking soda into the liquid-filled flask.

4. Place the flask on a balance. Zero the balance to record the mass of the setup.

5. Lift the balloon and pour its contents into the flask. Observe the chemical reaction and record the mass of the setup again.

6. Complete the *Observations & Analysis* section.

DEMONSTRATING THE LAW OF CONSERVATION OF MATTER

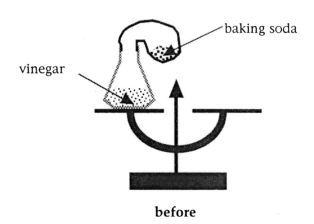

baking soda

vinegar

before   **after**

Mass of reactants, flask, and balloon: _____   Mass of products, flask, and balloon: _____

Observations & Analysis

1. Draw your observations of the reaction in the space above the word "after."

2. Is the mass of the products the same as the mass of the reactants? _____

3. How do these results confirm the Law of Conservation of Matter?

_____

_____

_____

4. Use your results to explain why chemical equations are balanced.

_____

_____

_____

_____

5. Suggest a simple procedure you could use to measure the mass of the gas produced in this chemical reaction.

_____

_____

_____

_____

_____

Chemistry

Lesson 74: Teacher Preparation

Basic Principle   The conservation of atoms in chemical reactions leads to the principle of conservation of matter and the ability to calculate the masses of products and reactants.

Competency   Students will describe chemical reactions by writing balanced chemical equations.

Procedure

1. Give students time to read the information on *Balancing Chemical Equations.*
2. Make sure students understand the uses of subscripts and coefficients before completing the *Observations & Analysis* section.

Answers to Observations & Analysis

1. $NaOH + HCl \longrightarrow H_2O + NaCl$ (already balanced)
2. $Mg(OH)_2 + H_2SO_4 \longrightarrow 2H_2O + MgSO_4$
3. $2HgO \longrightarrow 2Hg + O_2$
4. $2Fe_2O_3 + 3C \longrightarrow 4Fe + 3CO_2$
5. $CH_4 + 2O_2 \longrightarrow CO_2 + 2H_2O$
6. $MgCl_2 + K_2S \longrightarrow MgS + 2KCl$
7. $2KBr + Pb(NO_3)_2 \longrightarrow 2KNO_3 + PbBr_2$
8. $2SO_2 + O_2 + 2H_2O \longrightarrow 2H_2SO_4$
9. $2Ca + O_2 \longrightarrow 2CaO$
10. $6CO_2 + 6H_2O \longrightarrow C_6H_{12}O_6 + 6O_2$

Name _____   Date _____

Chemistry

STUDENT HANDOUT–LESSON 74

Basic Principle   The conservation of atoms in chemical reactions leads to the principle of conservation of matter and the ability to calculate the masses of products and reactants.

Objective   Describe chemical reactions by writing balanced chemical equations.

Procedure

1. Read the information on *Balancing Chemical Equations.*

> ### Balancing Chemical Equations
>
> A *chemical equation* is a "sentence" that describes a chemical reaction. Like the syntax of a grammatically correct sentence, a chemical equation uses letters, words, and rules of grammar to communicate an idea. The "letters" of a chemical equation are the *symbols* of the *chemical elements*. The "words" are the *formulas* for individual molecules and compounds. Each formula contains *subscripts* that give the number of atoms for each element in reacting molecules and compounds. The basic "rule of grammar" in chemistry is the *Law of Conservation of Matter* which states that the mass of the products produced in a chemical reaction is the same as the mass of the reactants. The atoms taking part in the reaction are neither created nor destroyed but simply rearranged. *Coefficients* are used to "keep count" of the number of atoms rearranged in such reactions. They show the proportion of reactants necessary to produce given products.

2. Examine the handout illustrations. Then complete the *Observations & Analysis* section.

BALANCING A SIMPLE CHEMICAL EQUATION

The chemical equation for the synthesis of water reads as follows:
"Two molecules of hydrogen combine with one molecule
of oxygen to produce 2 molecules of water."

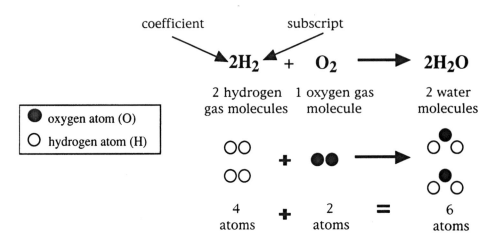

Observations & Analysis

Add coefficients to balance the following chemical equations.

1. ____ NaOH + ____ HCl ⟶ ____ H_2O + ____ NaCl

2. ____ $Mg(OH)_2$ + ____ H_2SO_4 ⟶ ____ H_2O + ____ $MgSO_4$

3. ____ HgO ⟶ ____ Hg + ____ O_2

4. ____ Fe_2O_3 + ____ C ⟶ ____ Fe + ____ CO_2

5. ____ CH_4 + ____ O_2 ⟶ ____ CO_2 + ____ H_2O

6. ____ $MgCl_2$ + ____ K_2S ⟶ ____ MgS + ____ KCl

7. ____ KBr + ____ $Pb(NO_3)_2$ ⟶ ____ KNO_3 + ____ $PbBr_2$

8. ____ SO_2 + ____ O_2 + ____ H_2O ⟶ ____ H_2SO_4

9. ____ Ca + ____ O_2 ⟶ ____ CaO

10. ____ CO_2 + ____ H_2O ⟶ ____ $C_6H_{12}O_6$ + ____ O_2

Lesson 75: Teacher Preparation

Basic Principle   The conservation of atoms in chemical reactions leads to the principle of conservation of matter and the ability to calculate the masses of products and reactants.

Competency   Students will explain the concept of a "mole."

Procedure

1. Give students time to read the information on *The Concept of the Mole.*

2. Point out that Avogadro's Law was not quickly accepted by other chemists, who failed to carefully quantify the amounts of reactants used in their experiments. But, the law, and therefore the concept of a mole, was finally vindicated by the Italian scientist Stanislao Cannizzaro (1826–1910). Cannizzaro laid the foundations of modern chemistry with his experimental determinations of atomic weights. In 1858, he showed that once the molecular weight of a volatile compound was found from measuring its vapor density, one could estimate, within limits, the atomic weight of its elemental components using the known weights of other elemental components. Cannizzaro showed that the application of Avogadro's law yielded a comprehensible system of atomic weights.

3. Give students time to complete the *Observations & Analysis* section.

Answers to Observations & Analysis

By subtracting the mass of the molecular oxygen from the mass of the two moles of mercuric oxide, one can determine the mass of two moles of reactant mercury. If the mass of two moles of mercury is 402 grams (i.e., $434 - 32 = 402$), then one mole of mercury must have a mass of 201 grams. Since one mole of any substance is the same as 6.02×10^{23} atoms or molecules of that substance, then 3.01×10^{23} atoms of mercury (i.e., 0.5 mole) must have a mass of 100.5 grams.

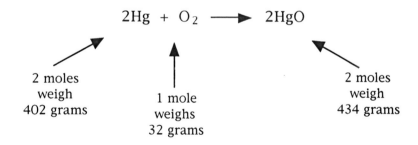

$$2Hg \ + \ O_2 \longrightarrow \ 2HgO$$

2 moles
weigh
402 grams

1 mole
weighs
32 grams

2 moles
weigh
434 grams

Chemistry

STUDENT HANDOUT–LESSON 75

Basic Principle   The conservation of atoms in chemical reactions leads to the principle of conservation of matter and the ability to calculate the masses of products and reactants.

Objective   Explain the concept of a "mole."

Procedure

1. Read the information on *The Concept of the Mole*.

The Concept of the Mole

The Italian chemist Amadeo Avogadro (1776–1856) determined that equal volumes of any two gases, at the same temperature and pressure, contain the same number of molecules. The number of molecules, called *Avogadro's number*, present in a liter of gas is about 6.02×10^{23} molecules. A liter of carbon dioxide gas (CO_2), therefore, contains the same number of molecules as a liter of molecular oxygen (O_2). This observation became known as *Avogadro's Law* and allowed chemists to determine the relative masses of the elements and the number of molecules in a given mass of substance. Since a liter of molecular oxygen has a mass of 32 grams, and an equal volume of carbon dioxide gas has a mass of 44 grams, the mass of Avogadro's number of carbon atoms must be 12 grams. The mass of Avogadro's number of atoms of a given substance is called *one mole* of that substance. A *mole* of any substance is the quantity of the substance that has a mass (in grams) that is the same as its relative molecular weight. Using the concept of the mole, chemists can weigh out a given number of molecules of a substance by weighing out an equal number of moles. The coefficients used in balancing chemical equations refer to the number of moles of reactants that will react to produce a specific quantity of products.

---

2. Examine the handout illustrations. Then complete the *Observations & Analysis* section.

Observations & Analysis

Given the observation below that two moles of mercury react with one mole of molecular oxygen to produce two moles of mercuric oxide, use Avogadro's Law to determine the mass of about 3.01×10^{23} atoms of mercury.

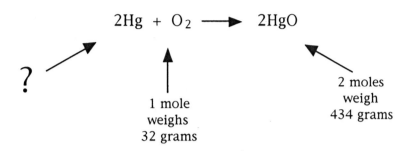

$$2Hg \ + \ O_2 \longrightarrow \ 2HgO$$

?

1 mole
weighs
32 grams

2 moles
weigh
434 grams

Lesson 76: Teacher Preparation

Basic Principle   The conservation of atoms in chemical reactions leads to the principle of conservation of matter and the ability to calculate the masses of products and reactants.

Competency   Students will determine the molar masses of a molecule from its chemical formula using a table of atomic masses.

Procedure

1. Give students time to read the information on *Chemical Formulas and Molar Mass*.
2. Give students time to complete the *Observations & Analysis* section.

Answers to Observations & Analysis

1. 28
2. 58
3. 98
4. 16
5. 17
6. 180
7. 110
8. 147
9. 160
10. 46

Chemistry

STUDENT HANDOUT–LESSON 76

Basic Principle   The conservation of atoms in chemical reactions leads to the principle of conservation of matter and the ability to calculate the masses of products and reactants.

Objective   Determine the molar masses of a molecule from its chemical formula using a table of atomic masses.

Procedure

1. Read the information on *Chemical Formulas and Molar Mass*.

Chemical Formulas and Molar Mass

The *molar mass* of an element is the mass in grams of Avogadro's number of atoms of that element (i.e., 6.02×10^{23} atoms). The molar mass of carbon, for example, is approximately 12 grams. There are 6.02×10^{23} atoms of carbon in one mole of carbon. The molar mass of a molecule is the total mass of the mass of Avogadro's number of atoms in that molecule. The molar mass of water, H_2O, is 18 grams, since there are 6.02×10^{23} molecules of water in a mole of water weighing 18 grams. One mole of molecular hydrogen, H_2, has a mass of 2 grams while one mole of atomic oxygen has a mass of 16 grams. To find the molar mass of any molecule, the chemist adds the total molar mass of the individual atoms in that molecule.

---

2. Complete the *Observations & Analysis* section.

Observations & Analysis

Show all work in finding the molar masses of the following compounds:

1. N_2: _____ grams

2. NaCl: _____ grams

3. H_2SO_4: _____ grams

4. CH_4: _____ grams

5. NH_3: _____ grams

6. $C_6H_{12}O_6$: _____ grams

7. $CaCl_2$: _____ grams

8. $RbNO_3$: _____ grams

9. Fe_2O_3: _____ grams

10. C_2H_5OH: _____ grams

Lesson 77: Teacher Preparation

Basic Principle The conservation of atoms in chemical reactions leads to the principle of conservation of matter and the ability to calculate the masses of products and reactants.

Competency Students will convert the mass of a molecular substance to moles.

Procedure

1. Give students time to read the information on *Number of Moles of a Substance*.
2. Give students time to complete the *Observations & Analysis* section.

Answers to Observations & Analysis

1. 2
2. 3
3. 0.5
4. 6.5
5. 0.1
6. 0.66
7. 5
8. 0.2
9. 0.125
10. 1.33

Chemistry

STUDENT HANDOUT–LESSON 77

Basic Principle   The conservation of atoms in chemical reactions leads to the principle of conservation of matter and the ability to calculate the masses of products and reactants.

Objective   Convert the mass of a molecular substance to moles.

Procedure

1. Read the information about *Number of Moles of a Substance.*

Number of Moles of a Substance

The number of moles of a given substance is the mass of the substance divided by its molar molecular mass. The number of moles in 174 grams of sodium chloride, NaCl, is 3 moles, since there are 58 grams of sodium chloride in one mole of that substance (i.e., $174 \div 58 = 3$).

---

2. Complete the *Observations & Analysis* section.

Observations & Analysis

Show all work in finding the number of moles in the given masses of each substance.

1. There are _____ moles of N_2 in 56 grams of that substance.

2. There are _____ moles of NaCl in 174 grams of that substance.

3. There are _____ moles of H_2SO_4 in 49 grams of that substance.

4. There are _____ moles of CH_4 in 104 grams of that substance.

5. There are _____ moles of NH_3 in 1.7 grams of that substance.

6. There are _____ moles of $C_6H_{12}O_6$ in 120 grams of that substance.

7. There are _____ moles of $CaCl_2$ in 550 grams of that substance.

8. There are _____ moles of $RbNO_3$ in 29.4 grams of that substance.

9. There are _____ moles of Fe_2O_3 in 20 grams of that substance.

10. There are _____ moles of C_2H_5OH in 69 grams of that substance.

Chemistry

Lesson 78: Teacher Preparation

Basic Principle   The conservation of atoms in chemical reactions leads to the principle of conservation of matter and the ability to calculate the masses of products and reactants.

Competency   Students will calculate the masses of reactants and products in a chemical reaction from the mass of one of the reactants or products.

Procedure

1. Give students time to read the information on *Moles and Balanced Equations*.

2. Point out that the *mole* is the standard of mass used by chemists to measure the quantities of reactants and products. It is derived from Avogadro's law which states that gases combine in simple integral volumes (i.e., 6.02×10^{23} atoms or molecules of gas per liter of gas). The Italian chemist Stanislao Cannizzaro (1826–1910), who revived the work of Amedeo Avogadro (1776–1856), defined the relative density of a gas as the weight of the gas divided by the weight of an equal volume of hydrogen gas at the same temperature and pressure. Since molecular hydrogen contains two atoms of hydrogen, it follows that the molecular weight of a gas is twice its density relative to hydrogen.

3. Give students time to complete the *Observations & Analysis* section.

Answers to Observations & Analysis

1. *Balanced Equation:* $2Li$ + $2H_2O$ $\longrightarrow$ $2LiOH$ + H_2

   Masses in grams: $2(7)$ + $2(1+1+16)$ = $2(7+16+1)$ + $(1+1)$

   14   +   36   =   48   +   2

   Final answer: 14 grams of lithium and 36 grams of water

2. *Balanced Equation:* HCl + $NaOH$ $\longrightarrow$ $NaCl$ + H_2O

   Masses in grams: $(1+35)$ + $(23+16+1)$ = $(23+35)$ + $(1+1+16)$

   36   +   40   =   58   +   18

   Final answer: 108 grams of hydrochloric acid and 120 grams of sodium hydroxide

3. *Balanced Equation:* CH_4 + $2O_2$ $\longrightarrow$ CO_2 + $2H_2O$

   Masses in grams: $(12+4)$ + $2(16+16)$ = $(12+16+16)$ + $2(1+1+16)$

   16   +   64   =   44   +   36

   Final answer: 24 grams of methane

4. *Balanced Equation:* $6CO_2$ + $6H_2O$ $\longrightarrow$ $C_6H_{12}O_6$ + $6O_2$

   Masses in grams: $6(12+16+16)$ + $6(1+1+16)$ = $[(6 \times 12)+(12 \times 1)+(6 \times 16)]$ + $6(2 \times 16)$

   264   +   108   =   180   +   192

   Final answer: 45 grams of glucose (*NOTE:* Only 66 grams of carbon dioxide will react with 27 grams of water.)

Name _____ **Date** _____

Chemistry

STUDENT HANDOUT–LESSON 78

Basic Principle   The conservation of atoms in chemical reactions leads to the principle of conservation of matter and the ability to calculate the masses of products and reactants.

Objective   Calculate the masses of reactants and products in a chemical reaction from the mass of one of the reactants or products.

Procedure

1. Read the information on *Moles and Balanced Equations.*

Moles and Balanced Equations

The coefficients of a balanced chemical reaction tell a chemist the number of moles of each reactant necessary to produce the products of that reaction. In the simple equation describing the decomposition of water, two moles of water will decompose to produce two moles of diatomic hydrogen and one mole of diatomic oxygen:

$$2H_2O \longrightarrow 2H_2 + O_2$$

Two moles of water, each mole having a molecular mass of 18 grams (i.e., for a total of 36 grams of water), produces two moles of diatomic hydrogen, each mole having a molecular mass of 2 grams (i.e., for a total mass of 4 grams of diatomic hydrogen), and one mole of diatomic oxygen, each mole having a mass of 32 grams. To calculate the mass of one reactant or product in a chemical reaction, the chemist relies upon the Law of Conservation of Matter which states that the mass of the products of all chemical reactions is the same as the mass of the reactants. The total mass of the products and reactants in the decomposition of water are the same: 36 grams [i.e., $(2 \times 18) = (2 \times 2) + (2 \times 16)$]. The Periodic Table, which gives the masses of each element (i.e., Avogadro's number of atoms of a given element), is used to calculate the molecular masses of reactants and products.

---

2. Examine the handout illustrations. Then complete the *Observations & Analysis* section.

Observations & Analysis

1. Write a balanced chemical equation describing how the element lithium reacts with water to produce lithium hydroxide and diatomic hydrogen. How many grams of lithium and water are required to produce 48 grams of lithium hydroxide?

2. Write a balanced chemical equation describing how hydrochloric acid reacts with sodium hydroxide to produce sodium chloride and water. How many grams of hydrochloric acid and sodium hydroxide are required to produce 174 grams of sodium chloride?

3. Write a balanced chemical equation describing how the methane is oxidized to form carbon dioxide and water. How many grams of methane are required to produce 66 grams of carbon dioxide?

4. Write a balanced chemical equation describing how plants synthesize glucose and oxygen from carbon dioxide and water. How many grams of glucose will be produced from 88 grams of carbon dioxide combined with 27 grams of water?

Chemistry

Lesson 79: Teacher Preparation

Basic Principle   The Kinetic-Molecular Theory describes the motion of atoms and molecules, and explains the properties of gases.

Competency   Students will illustrate the random motion of molecules in a gas and their collisions to explain the observable pressure on that surface.

Procedure

1. Give students time to read the information on *Boyle's Law*.

2. Point out that German physicist Rudolf Clausius (1822–1888) imagined heat as a form of mechanical energy arising from the motions of molecules. He proposed a kinetic theory of matter in 1857 that joined the physicist's thermodynamic models to the chemist's atomic–molecular model. His ideas led to the work of James Clerk Maxwell (1831–1879) and Ludwig Boltzmann (1844–1906) who developed a statistical interpretation of thermodynamics and molecular physics by portioning out the total energy of a system among the translational, vibrational, and rotational motion of molecules.

3. Give students time to complete the *Observations & Analysis* section.

Answers to Observations & Analysis

1. According to Boyle's Law, the product PV remains constant. Therefore, $P_1V_1 = P_2V_2$, where P_1 is initial pressure, V_1 is initial volume, P_2 is final pressure, and V_2 is final volume.

$$P_1V_1 = P_2V_2 \qquad \frac{P_1V_1}{P_2} = V_2 \qquad \frac{(76)(200)}{152} = 100 \text{ ml}$$

2. Reducing the volume of 400 ml of gas by 75% leaves 100 ml of gas.

$$P_1V_1 = P_2V_2 \qquad \frac{P_1V_1}{V_2} = P_2 \qquad \frac{(152)(400)}{100} = 608 \text{ cm Hg}$$

Chemistry

STUDENT HANDOUT–LESSON 79

Basic Principle   The Kinetic-Molecular Theory describes the motion of atoms and molecules, and explains the properties of gases.

Objective   Illustrate the random motion of molecules in a gas and their collisions to explain the observable pressure on that surface.

Procedure

1. Read the information on *Boyle's Law*.

Boyle's Law

In 1660, the English chemist Robert Boyle (1627–1691) made the first quantitative measurements decribing the behavior of gases under pressure. He found that the pressure (P) of an enclosed mass of gas doubles when it is compressed at constant temperature to half its original volume (V). Boyle discovered that while the product PV is constant (PV=k), it depends on the temperature and amount of gas present. The relationship, known as *Boyle's Law*, states that for a given mass of gas at constant temperature, the volume of the gas is inversely proportional to the pressure exerted by the gas. The behavior of gases at varying volumes, pressures, and temperatures can be explained according to the *Kinetic-Molecular Theory* which postulates the existence of submicroscopic-material particles (i.e., atoms) whose motion is determined by the energy they absorb and the perfectly elastic collisions they make with other particles.

---

2. Examine the handout illustrations. Then complete the *Observations & Analysis* section.

THE EFFECTS OF CHANGING VOLUME
ON GAS PRESSURE AT CONSTANT TEMPERATURE

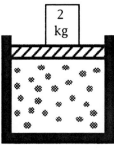

20 grams of gas
occupying 16 liters
at 25°C

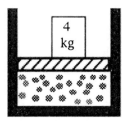

20 grams of gas
occupying 8 liters
at 25°C

20 grams of gas
occupying 4 liters
at 25°C

In the illustration, the pressure exerted by the gas doubles
as the volume of the gas is halved.

Observations & Analysis

1. A mass of gas occupies 200 milliliters of volume at 76 centimeters of mercury (i.e., standard atmospheric pressure at sea level) at 20°C. What is the volume of the gas at 152 centimeters of mercury?

2. A mass of gas occupies 400 milliliters of volume at 152 centimeters of mercury at 20°C. What is the pressure exerted by the gas when its volume is reduced by 75%?

Lesson 80: Teacher Preparation

Basic Principle   The Kinetic-Molecular Theory describes the motion of atoms and molecules, and explains the properties of gases.

Competency   Students will illustrate the random motion of molecules to explain the phenomenon of diffusion.

Procedure

1. Give students time to read the information on *Diffusion*.

2. Point out that the Scottish chemist Thomas Graham (1805–1869) was the first to state a fundamental law of gaseous diffusion in 1829. He discovered that the rate of diffusion of a gas is inversely proportional to the square root of the gas's density. This relationship is known as *Graham's Law*. In 1850, Graham published his studies on diffusion in liquids. James Clerk Maxwell, later in 1859, used his statistical kinetic theory of heat to explain the phenomenon of diffusion.

3. Explain the following relationship:

$$\frac{\text{rate of diffusion of gas X}}{\text{rate of diffusion of gas Y}} = \sqrt{\frac{\text{density of gas Y}}{\text{density of gas X}}}$$

   If gas X is 9 times denser than gas Y, then gas Y will diffuse 3 times as rapidly as gas X.

4. Give students time to complete the *Observations & Analysis* section.

Answers to Observations & Analysis

1. Drawings will differ, but should show that the molecules of ammonia spread out until evenly distributed throughout the box.

2. Drawings will differ, but should show that the molecules of salt spread out until evenly distributed throughout the beaker as the cube of salt gets smaller and smaller.

Chemistry

STUDENT HANDOUT–LESSON 80

Basic Principle   The Kinetic-Molecular Theory describes the motion of atoms and molecules, and explains the properties of gases.

Objective   Illustrate the random motion of molecules to explain the phenomenon of diffusion.

Procedure

1. Read the information on *Diffusion*.

Diffusion

Diffusion is the process by which molecules move spontaneously from regions of higher concentration to regions of lower concentration without the aid of stirring or other mechanical interference. According to the Kinetic-Molecular Theory of Matter, molecules at ordinary temperatures are in random, constant motion. Therefore, the number of molecules spreading away from a region of higher concentration will be greater than the number of molecules moving into it. The process will continue until the concentrations between the two regions become uniform. A simple example of diffusion is the diffusion of perfume throughout a room after opening a small bottle of the concentrated fragrance. Diffusion occurs in liquids as well as in gases. A dissolving solute will diffuse evenly throughout a given solvent across similar concentration gradients.

---

2. Complete the *Observations & Analysis* section.

Observations & Analysis

1. Illustrate the diffusion of gas particles from an opened bottle of ammonia after several minutes, then two and four hours.

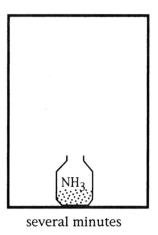 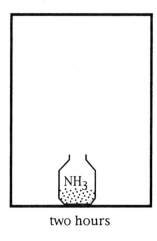 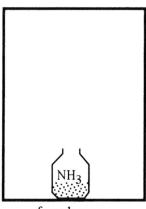

several minutes   two hours   four hours

2. Illustrate the diffusion of solute particles from a cube of salt throughout a warm water solvent after several minutes, then one and two hours.

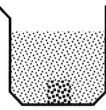 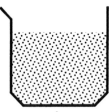

several minutes   one hour   two hours

Chemistry

Lesson 81: Teacher Preparation

Basic Principle   The Kinetic-Molecular Theory describes the motion of atoms and molecules, and explains the properties of gases.

Competency   Students will apply the gas laws relating to pressure, temperature, and volume of ideal gases and mixtures of ideal gases.

Procedure

1. Give students time to read the information on *The Gas Laws* before completing the *Observations & Analysis* section.

2. Review the basic formulas describing the three gas laws:

Boyle's Law	Charles's Law	Gay-Lussac's Law
$PV = k$	$\dfrac{V}{T} = k$	$\dfrac{P}{T} = k$

Answer to Observations & Analysis

The formula used is Gay-Lussac's Law since the volume of the gas is held constant inside the strong container: $P/T = K$. Since $P_1/T_1 = P_2/T_2$, then, $P_2T_1/P_1 = T_2$. Students need to convert degrees Celsius to Kelvin ($40°C = 313K$).

$$\frac{(190)(313K)}{(114)} = (521.7K) = (248.7°C)$$

Chemistry

STUDENT HANDOUT–LESSON 81

Basic Principle The Kinetic-Molecular Theory describes the motion of atoms and molecules, and explains the properties of gases.

Objective Apply the gas laws relating to pressure, temperature, and volume of ideal gases and mixtures of ideal gases.

Procedure

1. Read the information on *The Gas Laws*.

The Gas Laws

In chemistry and physics, the behavior of gases under different conditions of temperature, pressure, and volume can be predicted using a set of equations called *Gas Laws: Boyle's Law, Charles's Law,* and *Gay-Lussac's Law.* All three laws were determined empirically by experiment with a variety of gases and are valid for all substances in the gaseous state. *Boyle's Law* states that for a given mass of gas at constant temperature, the volume of the gas is inversely proportional to the pressure exerted by the gas. In 1787, the French chemist Jacques Charles (1746–1823) noted that gases such as hydrogen, oxygen, and nitrogen all expanded by 1/273 of their volume with a single degree Celsius increase in temperature. The volume of these gases were reduced by the same fraction with a single degree decrease in temperature. The Irish chemist William T. Kelvin (a.k.a., Lord Kelvin, 1824–1907) used this empirical fact to deduce the temperature at which the volume of a gas would approach zero: minus 273°C, or *absolute zero.* Of course, no gas can have zero volume, since all matter has mass and takes up space. Absolute zero, therefore, refers to the temperature at which the motion of molecules is at its absolute minimum according to the Kinetic-Molecular Theory. *Charles's Law* states that at constant pressure, the volume of a mass of gas is directly proportional to its absolute temperature ($V/T = k$). Charles's contemporary, the French physicist Joseph Gay-Lussac (1778–1850), also carried out experiments on the thermal expansion of gases. Gay-Lussac studied the relationship between pressure and temperature, and, in 1802, formulated a third law. *Gay-Lussac's Law* states that at constant volume the pressure of a gas is inversely proportional to its temperature ($P/T = k$). The three laws may be generalized for all ideal gases according to the following relationship: $PV/T = k$.

---

2. Examine the handout illustrations. Then complete the *Observations & Analysis* section.

CHARLES'S LAW

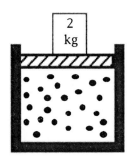

20 grams of gas
occupying 20 liters
at 273°C or 546K

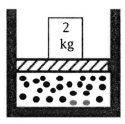

20 grams of gas
occupying 10 liters
at 0°C or 273K

20 grams of gas
occupying 5 liters
at –136.5°C or 136.5K

In the illustration, the volume of the gas decreases by 1/273 with every decrease of 1K.

GAY-LUSSAC'S LAW

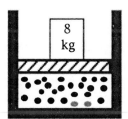

20 grams of gas
occupying 10 liters
at 273°C or 546K

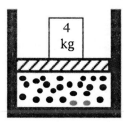

20 grams of gas
occupying 10 liters
at 0°C or 273K

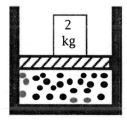

20 grams of gas
occupying 10 liters
at –136.5°C or 136.5K

In the illustration, the pressure of the gas decreases by 1/273 with every decrease of 1K.

Observations & Analysis

A gas is confined in a strong container at 40°C under a pressure of 114 cm of mercury. Calculate the temperature in degrees Celsius to which the gas must be heated to reach a pressure of 190 cm of mercury.

Lesson 82: Teacher Preparation

Basic Principle   The Kinetic-Molecular Theory describes the motion of atoms and molecules, and explains the properties of gases.

Competency   Students will define the values and meanings of standard temperature and pressure (STP).

Procedure

1. Give students time to read the information on *Standard Temperature and Pressure*.
2. Be sure students understand the concept of a standard as any measure used as a basis for comparison. Review the standard meter, kilogram, and liter as other standards used in physics and chemistry.
3. Give students time to complete the activity and the *Observations & Analysis* section.

Answers to Observations & Analysis

The initial temperature given is 323K (273 + 50). Standard conditions are 273K at 76 cm Hg. Since the temperature decreases, the volume at STP will be less than the initial volume. But the pressure is also decreasing, making the volume at STP greater than the initial volume. The volume at STP will depend upon which value is more influential. The temperature decreases by a factor of 273/323 and the volume is decreased by the same factor. The pressure is decreased by a factor of 76/100 so the volume is increased by a factor of 100/76.

Volume at STP:	500 ml	×	100/76	×	273/323	=	556 ml
	initial volume		pressure-change factor		temperature-change factor		final volume

Chemistry

STUDENT HANDOUT–LESSON 82

Basic Principle   The Kinetic-Molecular Theory describes the motion of atoms and molecules, and explains the properties of gases.

Objective   Define the values and meanings of standard temperature and pressure (STP).

Procedure

1. Read the information on *Standard Temperature and Pressure*.

Standard Temperature and Pressure

All measurements are based on some standard of comparison. Since the volume of a certain mass of gas depends on the pressure and temperature of the gas, it is clear that the volume of the gas has meaning only in relation to those specified pressures and temperatures. The standard reference conditions of temperature and pressure (STP), therefore, are set at the following arbitrary values: for temperature, 0°C (273K); for pressure, 76 cm Hg (1 atmosphere). If the volume of a gas is known under conditions that are different from those of standard conditions, the volume that the gas would occupy under standard conditions can be calculated using a combination of gas laws.

---

2. Complete the *Observations & Analysis* section.

Observations & Analysis

Five hundred milliliters of a gas are confined in a strong container at 50°C under a pressure of 100 cm of mercury. Calculate the volume of the gas at STP.

 **Chemistry**

Lesson 83: Teacher Preparation

Basic Principle   The Kinetic-Molecular Theory describes the motion of atoms and molecules, and explains the properties of gases.

Competency   Students will define the value and meaning of absolute zero: 0 Kelvin.

Procedure

1. Give students time to read the information on *Absolute Zero*.

2. Point out that the attempts to reach "super-cold" temperatures began with the liquefaction of air in the late 19th century. The Scottish chemist James Dewar (1842–1923) succeeded in liquefying hydrogen in 1898. Helium was liquified a short time later by the Dutch physicist Heike Kamerling Onnes (1853–1926) who studied under Robert Bunsen (1811–1899), the inventor of the Bunsen burner. Onnes founded the Cryogenic Laboratory in Heidelberg in 1894. Onnes also noticed that the electrical resistivity of metals decreased to nearly zero at very low temperature. The phenomenon later became known as *superconductivity*. Albert Einstein (1879–1955) and the Indian physicist Satyendra Nath Bose (1894–1974) predicted one striking behavior of matter at low temperatures. They suggested that at ranges of only billionths of a degree above absolute zero, chilled atoms that ceased moving would merge, due to quantum-mechanical effects, into a single "super atom" that behaved as though it were a single entity. The "super atom" is referred to as a "Bose–Einstein condensate." In 1995 two teams of physicists announced that they had created such a condensate.

3. Give students time to complete the *Observations & Analysis* section.

Answers to Observations & Analysis

1. Answers will vary, but should include the following main points: The Kinetic-Molecular Theory of matter states that atoms and molecules are in constant motion, having absorbed energy from their environment. As matter gives off energy, across a temperature gradient where heat flows from regions of higher temperature to regions of lower temperature, atoms and molecules slow down. In a theoretical region of space where there is no heat, atoms and molecules would be motionless.

2. Answers will vary, but should include the following main point: There is no region of space devoid of heat. Heat radiation permeates space.

3. Answers will vary, but should include the following main points: Matter cooled to nearly absolute zero would be comprised of molecules with minimal motion and, therefore, minimal momentum. Their collisions with other molecules would have little impact on those molecules. The molecules of "super-cold" fluid would flow more easily around one another.

Name _____   Date _____

Chemistry

STUDENT HANDOUT–LESSON 83

Basic Principle   The Kinetic-Molecular Theory describes the motion of atoms and molecules, and explains the properties of gases.

Objective   Define the value and meaning of absolute zero: 0 Kelvin.

Procedure

1. Read the information on *Absolute Zero*.

Absolute Zero

Absolute zero is the lowest possible temperature. It is a theoretical temperature whose calculated value is equal to 0 Kelvin (−273.16°C or −459.67°F). At absolute zero, all molecules become motionless for lack of energy, an idea that runs contrary to the laws of thermodynamics. Although absolute zero cannot actually be reached, scientists have been successful at cooling matter to temperatures approaching several billionths of one Kelvin. At this temperature matter would have maximum order, but neither volume nor entropy. A heat engine would be able to function at 100-percent efficiency. The study of extremely low temperature ranges is called *cryogenics*. Modern researchers studying the cryogenic behavior of matter have discovered such phenomena as superfluidity (i.e., the disappearance of viscosity in liquid helium) and superconductivity (i.e., the loss of electrical resistance).

---

2. Complete the *Observations & Analysis* section.

Observations & Analysis

1. Use the Kinetic-Molecular Theory of Matter to describe the theoretical conditions of matter at absolute zero.

   _____

   _____

   _____

   _____

2. Use the Kinetic-Molecular Theory of Matter to explain why it is not possible to cool matter to absolute zero.

   _____

   _____

   _____

   _____

   _____

   _____

   _____

3. Use the Kinetic-Molecular Theory of Matter to explain why matter cooled to nearly absolute zero would flow more easily than warmer matter.

   _____

   _____

   _____

   _____

   _____

   _____

   _____

Lesson 84: Teacher Preparation

Basic Principle   The Kinetic-Molecular Theory describes the motion of atoms and molecules, and explains the properties of gases.

Competency   Students will convert temperatures from one scale to another: Celsius, Kelvin, Fahrenheit.

Procedure   Give students time to read the information on *Temperature Scales* before completing the *Observations & Analysis* section.

Answers to Observations & Analysis

1.	47	320.78	118
2.	−6.4	266.6	20.5
3.	−8.3	264.7	17
4.	7.8	280.8	46
5.	40	313	104
6.	5	278	41
7.	15	288	59
8.	−180	93	−292
9.	−273	0	−459.4
10.	0	273	32

Name _____ **Date** _____

Chemistry

STUDENT HANDOUT–LESSON 84

Basic Principle   The Kinetic-Molecular Theory describes the motion of atoms and molecules, and explains the properties of gases.

Objective   Convert temperatures from one scale to another: Celsius, Kelvin, Fahrenheit.

Procedure

1. Read the information on *Temperature Scales*.

Temperature Scales

All temperature scales are arbitrary. A thermometer is a tool used to measure the temperature of a substance, the average kinetic energy of the particles that comprise it. The glass walls of a thermometer are made of atoms, as is the fluid inside the thermometer. The matter outside the thermometer is also made of atoms that are in constant motion. If the atoms surrounding a thermometer absorb energy, they will move faster and have more momentum. They will transfer that energy to other atoms with every collision. The glass atoms comprising the walls of the thermometer will absorb that energy and collide with the atoms in the thermometer fluid. As the atoms of the fluid move faster, the fluid will expand. Scientists mark the glass tube and read the fluid expansion in units called *degrees*. The three temperature scales used by scientists are the *Celsius*, *Kelvin*, and *Fahrenheit* scales invented by Anders Celsius (1701–1744), Lord Kelvin (1824–1907), and Gabriel Fahrenheit (1901–1954), respectively.

---

2. Study the handout illustrations and conversion formulas. Then complete the *Observations & Analysis* section.

TEMPERATURE SCALES

water boils	100	373	212
water freezes	0	273	32
	°C	K	°F

CONVERSION FORMULAS

To change Celsius to Fahrenheit:

$$°F = 9/5 \ (°C) + 32$$

To change Fahrenheit to Celsius:

$$°C = 5/9 \ (°F - 32)$$

Observations & Analysis

Change the following temperatures to readings on the other temperature scales as follows: 25°C = 350K = 77°F.

	°C	K	°F
1.	_____	_____	118
2.	_____	_____	20.5
3.	_____	_____	17
4.	_____	_____	46
5.	40	_____	_____
6.	5	_____	_____
7.	15	_____	_____
8.	−180	_____	_____
9.	_____	0	_____
10.	_____	273	_____

Chemistry

Lesson 85: Teacher Preparation

Basic Principle   Acids, bases, and salts are three classes of compounds that form ions in water solutions.

Competency   Students will list the properties of acids, bases, and salts.

Procedure

1. Give students time to read the information on *Acids, Bases, and Salts*.

2. Point out the German chemist Wilhelm Ostwald (1853–1932) and the Swedish chemist Svante Arrhenius (1859–1927) who demonstrated that when acids, bases, and salts are dissolved in water, they dissociated partially or completely into ions. Solutions of ions are good electrical conductors, and the substances that produce them are called *electrolytes*. They theorized that acids become electrolytes by producing hydrogen ions ($H+$), and bases become electrolytes by producing hydroxide ions ($OH-$).

3. Assist students in completing the *Observations & Analysis* section.

Answers to Observations & Analysis

1. Answers will vary, but should include the following main points: Acids, bases, and salts help water to conduct electricity by becoming electrolytes, charged ions, that can transfer charges through a solution.

2. Answers will vary, but should include the following main points: The corrosive properties of an acid can be neutralized by mixing it with a base. The reaction produces salt and water.

3. Answers will vary, but should include the following main points: The caustic properties of a base can be neutralized by mixing it with a acid. The reaction produces salt and water.

Chemistry

STUDENT HANDOUT–LESSON 85

Basic Principle   Acids, bases, and salts are three classes of compounds that form ions in water solutions.

Objective   List the properties of acids, bases, and salts.

Procedure

1. Read the information on *Acids, Bases, and Salts*.

Acids, Bases, and Salts

Acids are among the most common groups of chemical substances. They range from mildly to extremely corrosive, taste sour in low concentrations, can conduct electricity in solution, and turn litmus paper red. Acids also react with metals, sometimes violently, to liberate explosive hydrogen gas. Acids dissociate in water to produce hydrogen ions (H+) that can tear electrons from other chemical substances. This accounts for an acid's biting physical and reactive chemical properties. Hydrochloric acid (HCl), sulfuric acid (H_2SO_4), carbonic acid (H_2CO_3), and nitric acid (HNO_3) are the most well-known examples of acids. *Bases* are also very common chemical substances. They range from mildly to extremely caustic, taste bitter in low concentration, can conduct electricity in solution, and will turn litmus paper blue. All bases dissociate in water to produce hydroxide ions (OH–) that attract positively charged ions or dipole molecules in their vicinity. Sodium hydroxide (NaOH), magnesium hydroxide [$Mg(OH)_2$], ammonium hydroxide (NH_4OH), and potassium hydroxide (KOH) are the most well-known examples of bases. Reacting an acid with a base produces salt and water. An acid–base reaction is also called a *neutralization reaction*.

---

2. Examine the handout illustrations. Then complete the *Observations & Analysis* section.

ACID-BASE REACTIONS

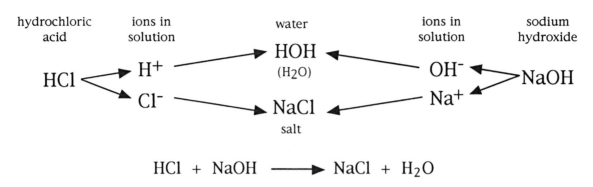

$$HCl + NaOH \longrightarrow NaCl + H_2O$$

Observations & Analysis

1. Explain how acids, bases, and salts help water to conduct electricity.

_____

_____

_____

_____

_____

_____

_____

2. Explain how the corrosive properties of acids can be neutralized.

_____

_____

_____

3. Explain how the caustic properties of bases can be neutralized.

_____

_____

_____

Lesson 86: Teacher Preparation

Basic Principle Acids, bases, and salts are three classes of compounds that form ions in water solutions.

Competency Students will identify acids as hydrogen-ion-donating and bases as hydrogen-ion-accepting substances.

Procedure

1. Give students time to read the information on the *Bronsted–Lowry Theory of Acids and Bases*.

2. Review the handout illustration to make sure students understand that a hydrogen ion dissociated from a molecule of hydrochloric acid in water solution is attracted to the exposed electron pairs on a water molecule. The result is the formation of hydronium (i.e., oxonium) and chloride ions. Review as well how the hydrogen proton from a dissociated water molecule is attracted by the exposed electron pair of an ammonia molecule. The result is the formation of ammonium and hydroxide ions.

3. Assist students in completing the *Observations & Analysis* section.

Answers to Observations & Analysis

1. Answers will vary, but should include the following main points: The Bronsted–Lowry theory of acids and bases describes all acids as proton donors, and bases as proton acceptors. This broadens Arrhenius's idea to include bases that do not necessarily contain a hydroxide ion. For example, ammonia (NH_3) can accept a proton to become an ammonium ion (NH_4^+), which behaves like a base.

2. Answers will vary, but should include the following main point: Water is an amphoteric compound because it can either accept or donate protons.

3. Answers will vary, but should include the following main point: The ammonium ion acts like an acid because it can donate a proton.

Chemistry

STUDENT HANDOUT–LESSON 86

Basic Principle Acids, bases, and salts are three classes of compounds that form ions in water solutions.

Objective Identify acids as hydrogen-ion-donating and bases as hydrogen-ion-accepting substances.

Procedure

1. Read the information on the *Bronsted–Lowry Theory of Acids and Bases*.

Bronsted–Lowry Theory of Acids and Bases

In 1923, the Danish chemist Johannes Bronsted (1879–1947) and the English chemist Thomas Lowry (1874–1936) proposed that an acid was any substance that gave up one or more protons (i.e., hydrogen ions, H+). If a single proton is donated by a molecule, then the acid is *monoprotic*; two protons per molecule and the acid is *diprotic*, and so on. They suggested that a base was any substance that accepted one or more protons (e.g., *monobasic*, *dibasic*, etc.). According to this idea, which broadened Svante Arrhenius's (1859–1927) concept of acids and bases, every acid produces a *conjugate* base by the loss of a proton. Since some acids can yield two or more protons by donating more than one proton, one at a time, certain substances can act as both acids and bases. These compounds are called *amphoteric* compounds.

---

2. Examine the handout illustrations. Then complete the *Observations & Analysis* section.

BRONSTED-LOWRY THEORY OF ACIDS AND BASES

$$H\text{:}Cl\text{:} \ + \ H\text{:}\overset{..}{O}\text{:}H \ \longrightarrow \ \left[H\text{:}\overset{..}{O}\text{:}H\atop H\right]^{+} \ + \ \text{:}\overset{..}{Cl}\text{:}^{-}$$

| acid | base | acid | base |

$$H\text{:}\overset{H}{\underset{H}{N}}\text{:} \ + \ H\text{:}\overset{..}{O}\text{:}H \ \longrightarrow \ \left[H\text{:}\overset{H}{\underset{H}{N}}\text{:}H\right]^{+} \ + \ \text{:}\overset{..}{O}\text{:}H^{-}$$

| base | acid | acid | base |

Observations & Analysis

1. Explain how the Bronsted–Lowry description of acids and bases differs from that of Arrhenius's.

_____

_____

_____

_____

_____

2. Explain why water is an amphoteric compound according to the Bronsted–Lowry description of acids and bases.

_____

_____

_____

_____

3. Explain why the ammonium ion (NH_4^+) can act as an acid according to the Bronsted–Lowry description of acids and bases.

_____

_____

_____

_____

Chemistry

Lesson 87: Teacher Preparation

Basic Principle   Acids, bases, and salts are three classes of compounds that form ions in water solutions.

Competency   Students will compare the relative strengths of different acids and bases using litmus paper.

Materials   pHydrion litmus paper dispenser with color legend; beakers labeled A, B, C, D, and E; mild solution of hydrochloric acid; white vinegar; distilled water; weak solution of dishwashing liquid; mild sodium hydroxide solution; paper towels; eyedroppers (5 per group); goggles

Procedure

1. Give students time to read the information on *Litmus and pH*.
2. Point out that in 1909, the Danish chemist Søren Sørensen (1868–1939) proposed that strong acids contained hydrogen ions in concentrations of about 1 gram of ion per liter of solution. Bases, he suggested, contained as little as 10^{-14} grams of dissociated hydrogen ion in one liter of solution. Sørensen defined the pH of a solution as the negative logarithm of hydrogen ion concentration [i.e., -log (H+)]. For example, a solution containing a 10^{-5} molar concentration of hydrogen ions has a pH equal to 5. Recall that log 100 = 2 (in base 10) because $10^2 = 100$. Sulfuric acid used in car batteries has a pH of about 2; citrus fruits have a pH of about 4; soil has a pH of about 7; soaps have a pH of about 10; and potash (KOH) has a pH of about 13.
3. Provide students with the following list of solutions from which they may choose to identify the "unknown" selection of solutions: mild solution of hydrochloric acid, white vinegar, distilled water, weak solution of dishwashing liquid, mild sodium hydroxide solution.
4. Assist students in completing the activity and the *Observations & Analysis* section.

Answers to Observations & Analysis

Observations will vary slightly.

A. red; 1–2; hydrochloric acid

B. reddish-orange; 2–3; vinegar

C. light green; 6–8; distilled water

D. greenish-blue; 10–12; dishwashing liquid

E. dark blue; 13–14; sodium hydroxide

Chemistry

STUDENT HANDOUT–LESSON 87

Basic Principle   Acids, bases, and salts are three classes of compounds that form ions in water solutions.

Objective   Compare the relative strengths of different acids and bases using litmus paper.

Materials   pHydrion litmus paper dispenser with color legend, unknown solutions provided by your instructor, paper towels, 5 eyedroppers, goggles

Procedure

1. Read the information on *Litmus and pH*.

Litmus and pH

The Irish chemist Robert Boyle (1627–1691) was one of the first to analyze the nature of acids, bases, and neutral solutions in an organized manner using plant extracts as chemical *indicators*. He extracted an organic chemical called *litmus dye* from species of lichen grown in the Netherlands: *Lecanora tartarea* and *Roccella tinctorum*. Boyle published his methods in 1664 in a book entitled *Experiments and Considerations Touching Colours*. Since then, litmus paper has been used to distinguish between the relative strengths of acids and bases. Litmus paper turns red in the presence of a strong acid, and blue in the presence of a strong base. Specially treated litmus paper will turn a variety of different hues depending upon the strength of specific acids or bases to which it is exposed. Litmus paper prepared to identify a range of acid and base strengths usually comes complete with a "color legend" that matches colors to the intensity of hydrogen ion ($H+$) and hydroxide ($OH–$) concentrations present in a solution. The scale used to compare the concentrations of these ions is called the *pH scale*.

PH SCALE

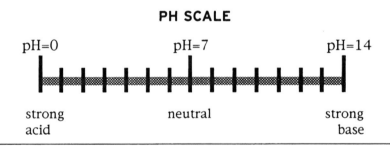

---

2. Place small strips of litmus paper on separate pieces of paper towel. Label the paper towels Test A, Test B, Test C, Test D, and Test E.

3. **WEAR GOGGLES** to protect your eyes against splattered fluids, and avoid getting the fluids on your clothing.

4. Use different eyedroppers to test a single drop of each solution provided by your instructor on the litmus paper.

5. Compare the color created by the sample drop against the "color legend" on the litmus paper dispenser. Record the color (e.g., red, pink, light green) and approximate pH (e.g., 1, 2, 3, etc.) of each solution in the spaces provided in the *Observations & Analysis* section. Make a guess as to the identity of the solution from the list of possibilities provided by your instructor.

6. Complete the *Observations & Analysis* section.

Observations & Analysis

Test A. Color: _____   Approximate pH: _____

　　　 Solution: _____

Test B. Color: _____   Approximate pH: _____

　　　 Solution: _____

Test C. Color: _____   Approximate pH: _____

　　　 Solution: _____

Test D. Color: _____   Approximate pH: _____

　　　 Solution: _____

Test E. Color: _____   Approximate pH: _____

　　　 Solution: _____

Lesson 88: Teacher Preparation

Basic Principle   Acids, bases, and salts are three classes of compounds that form ions in water solutions.

Competency   Students will titrate a base with an acid to compare their relative strengths.

Materials   small beakers, 10-mL graduated cylinders, 0.1 molar NaOH solution (i.e., 4 grams NaOH per liter pure distilled water), 0.1 molar HCl solution, small rubber or cork stoppers, eyedroppers (1 per group), phenolphthalein indicator solution, pHydrion paper, goggles

Procedure

1. Give students time to read the information on *Neutralization Reactions*.

2. Point out that if a neutralization is complete, the chemist will not be able to distinguish between the resulting solution and a salt-water solution. Complete neutralization is achieved by adding molar equivalents of an acid and base as determined by the neutralization equations that describe their interaction. In this activity, one-tenth molar solution of sodium hydroxide is neutralized by an equal volume of one-tenth molar hydrochloric acid. A neutralized solution need not have a pH of exactly 7, since the salts of strong acids and weak bases are slightly acidic. The salts of weak acids and strong bases are slightly basic.

3. Give students time to perform the activity before completing the *Observations & Analysis* section.

Answers to Observations & Analysis

1. 1–2; 13–14

2. Answers will vary, but should be close to 3 mL since the acid and base solutions were of equal molarity. Students can achieve this result by subtracting the starting volume of the base solution from the total volume of the acid–base mixture (6 mL – 3 mL = 3 mL).

3. $HCl + NaOH \longrightarrow NaCl + H_2O$

   Answers will vary, but should include the following main points: Since it took about the same amount of acid to neutralize an equivalent volume of base (i.e., 3 mL), and the ratio of the reactants in this chemical reaction is 1 : 1, then the unknown molarity of the base must be the same as the known molarity of the acid: 0.1 M.

Chemistry

STUDENT HANDOUT–LESSON 88

Basic Principle   Acids, bases, and salts are three classes of compounds that form ions in water solutions.

Objective   Titrate a base with an acid to compare their relative strengths.

Materials   2 small beakers, 10-mL graduated cylinders, NaOH solution of unknown concentration, 0.1 molar HCl, small rubber or cork stoppers, eyedroppers, phenolphthalein indicator solution, pHydrion paper, goggles

Procedure

1. Read the information on *Neutralization Reactions*.

Neutralization Reactions

Neutralizing an acid with a base is called a *neutralization reaction*. The general chemical equation for this type of chemical reaction is expressed as follows:

$$HX \quad + \quad YOH \quad \longrightarrow \quad HOH \quad + \quad XY$$
"acid"   "base"   "water"   "salt"

A neutralization reaction is a *double displacement* reaction that combines two harsh substances to form water and salt. Stomach antacids such as magnesium hydroxide (i.e., milk of magnesia) and calcium hydroxide (i.e., antacid tablets) neutralize excess stomach acid (i.e., hydrochloric acid) to provide relief. The manufacture of many kinds of materials involves the use of acids and bases as the neutralization reaction is one of the most common chemical reactions performed by modern industry. The relative strengths of acids and bases can be compared by *titration*. Titration is a technique employed to find the concentration of one compound in solution by mixing it with another compound. Since a base can be identified using a chemical indicator such as phenolphthalein, which turns purple in the presence of a base, the strength of the base can be approximated by adding a known concentration of acid until the indicator clears.

---

2. **WEAR GOGGLES** to protect your eyes against splattered fluids, and avoid getting the solution on clothing.

3. Use the two small beakers to obtain about 5 mL of 0.1 M HCl and 5 mL of the NaOH solution from your instructor.

4. Test each solution with litmus paper and record their pH.

5. Carefully pour 3 mL of the sodium hydroxide solution into the graduated cylinder.

6. Add one or two drops of the phenolphthalein indicator solution to the NaOH in the cylinder to turn the solution purple.

7. Slowly add 0.1 M hydrochloric acid, several drops at a time, to the colored base. When the solution begins to show signs of clearing, cap the cylinder with a small stopper, and shake it gently to mix the solution thoroughly.

8. Test the cleared solution with litmus paper.

9. Complete the *Observations & Analysis* section.

TITRATING A BASE WITH AN ACID

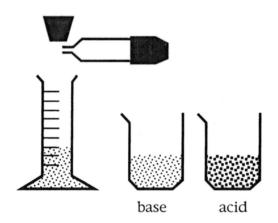

base   acid

Observations & Analysis

1. Record the pH of the acid and base in the beakers using the litmus paper.

   Acid pH: _____   Base pH: _____

2. How much of the 0.1 M HCl was required to neutralize the base? _____

3. Use your results and a chemical equation describing the reaction of hydrochloric acid with sodium hydroxide to estimate the concentration of sodium hydroxide used in this activity. Explain your reasoning.

   Chemical Equation: _____ + _____ ⟶ _____ + _____

   _____

   _____

   _____

   _____

   _____

   _____

   _____

Lesson 89: Teacher Preparation

Basic Principle Solutions are homogeneous mixtures of two or more substances.

Competency Students will distinguish between a solute and a solvent.

Procedure

1. Give students time to read the information on *Solutions*.

2. Point out that the French chemist Auguste Laurent (1807–1853) once surmised that chemistry is the study of substances that do not exist. What he meant to say was that no substance used by the chemist was ever absolutely pure. Even with modern filtering techniques, chemists are mindful of the impurities that contaminate their samples. They express the degree of contamination in parts per million or billion. Nevertheless, purity is a fundamental concept of chemistry, which refers to the homogeneity of a substance according to its capacity to yield reproducible effects under given conditions. A contemporary of Auguste Laurent, the French chemist Michel-Eugéne Chevreul (1786–1889), determined the first criteria for assessing the purity of a substance. Chevreul established melting point and boiling point as essential characteristics in the identification of any pure material. Since most substances dissolve well in water, water is sometimes called the *universal solvent*.

3. Give students time to complete the *Observations & Analysis* section.

Answers to Observations & Analysis

1. sugar; water
2. none; water
3. potassium hydroxide; water
4. sulfuric acid; water
5. assorted minerals; water

Chemistry

STUDENT HANDOUT–LESSON 89

Basic Principle   Solutions are homogeneous mixtures of two or more substances.

Objective   Distinguish between a solute and a solvent.

Procedure

1. Read the information on *Solutions*.

Solutions

Matter rarely exists in a pure state. Most materials are combined with different materials to form *mixtures*. A mixture is any combination of substances that can be separated by physical means. Mixtures can be sifted, filtered, or distilled to separate the materials making up the mixture. The substances themselves are not changed when they are separated in this manner. They are simply isolated from one another and purified. A *solution* is a liquid mixture. Solutions contain particles of *solute* dissolved in a liquid *solvent*. Most common liquids are mixtures. Even tap water is a mixture of water and a variety of minerals. A homogeneous solution contains a well-dissolved solute present in equal amounts throughout the solvent. Salt water is a homogeneous solution.

---

2. Complete the *Observations & Analysis* section.

Observations & Analysis

Identify the solute and solvent (if any) in each of the following liquid substances.

substance	solute	solvent
1. sugar water	sugar	water
2. pure ice water	water	water
3. potassium hydroxide water solution		
4. sulfuric acid solution		
5. tap water		

Lesson 90: Teacher Preparation

Basic Principle   Solutions are homogeneous mixtures of two or more substances.

Competency   Students will describe the usual effect of temperature on the amount of solute able to dissolve in a given solvent, and explain the dissolving process as a result of random molecular motion.

Procedure   Give students time to read the information on *Solubility* before completing the *Observations & Analysis* section.

Answers to Observations & Analysis

1. Answers will vary, but should include the following main points: All of the solutions are saturated. Each curve indicates the amount of solute at each given temperature below which the solute will remain in solution. Additional solute at each temperature will precipitate out of solution.

2. The same amount of solutes A and B saturate equal amounts of water at just less than 5°C. The same amount of solutes C and F saturate equal amounts of water at about 25°C. The same amount of solutes C and D saturate equal amounts of water at just less than 60°C.

3. The substance is probably solute B. According to the graph, approximately 200 grams of solute B dissolve in 100 mL of water at 75°C. This indicates that 100 grams of solute B would dissolve in 50 mL of water at the same temperature. This is exactly how the unknown solute behaved.

4. Answers will vary, but should include the following main points: The random molecular motion of molecules in solution causes the molecules to move from regions of high concentration to regions of lower concentration. This causes molecules to become evenly distributed throughout the solution.

Chemistry

STUDENT HANDOUT–LESSON 90

Basic Principle   Solutions are homogeneous mixtures of two or more substances.

Objective   Describe the usual effect of temperature on the amount of solute able to dissolve in a given solvent and explain the dissolving process as a result of random molecular motion.

Procedure

1. Read the information on *Solubility and Temperature*.

Solubility and Temperature

The amount of a solute that can be dissolved in a liquid solvent depends on the temperature of a solution. Increasing temperature usually increases the amount of material that can be dissolved in solution. *Solubility* is a measure of the amount of solute that can be dissolved in a solvent at a particular temperature. Scientists record the solubility of solutes in given solvents (i.e., usually water) using *solubility graphs*. A solubility graph shows the amount of solute needed to saturate a given volume of solvent at a particular temperature. Solubility tests are used to identify unknown samples of matter.

---

2. Examine the handout illustrations. Then complete the *Observations & Analysis* section.

SOLUBILITY GRAPH

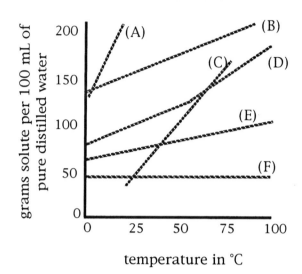

Observations & Analysis

1. Which solutions are saturated solutions? Explain your answer.

   _____

   _____

2. Which solutions become saturated at the same temperature with the same amount of solute? Explain your answer by giving the temperature and the amount of solute that saturates each pair of solutions.

   _____

   _____

3. A scientist finds that 100 grams of an unknown substance becomes saturated in 50 mL of pure water at 75°C. Which substance in the solubility graph is most probably similar to the unknown sample?

   _____

   _____

4. Explain the dissolving process as a result of random molecular motion.

   _____

   _____

   _____

   _____

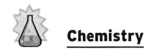

Lesson 91: Teacher Preparation

Basic Principle   Solutions are homogeneous mixtures of two or more substances.

Competency   Students will calculate the concentration of a solute in terms of mass of solute per unit mass of solvent, weight percentage of solute in solution, molarity, and molality.

Procedure   Give students time to read the information on *Measuring Solute Concentrations* before completing the *Observations & Analysis* section.

Answers to Observations & Analysis

1. Answers will vary, but should include the following main point: Mix 10 grams of table salt, sodium chloride (NaCl), with 100 grams of solvent (e.g., water).

2. Answers will vary, but should include the following main point: Mix 10 grams of table salt, sodium chloride (NaCl), with 90 grams of solvent (e.g., water) to make a 10% solution of salt-water by weight percentage in solution.

3. Answers will vary, but should include the following main point: The gram molecular weight of sodium chloride is 58 grams. Mix 58 grams of table salt, sodium chloride (NaCl), with 1 liter of solvent (e.g., water) to make a 1-molar solution of salt-water.

4. Answers will vary, but should include the following main point: The gram molecular weight of sodium chloride is 58 grams. Mix 58 grams of table salt, sodium chloride (NaCl), in 1,000 grams of ethyl alcohol to make a 1-molal solution of salt and ethyl alcohol.

Name _____   Date _____

Chemistry

STUDENT HANDOUT–LESSON 91

Basic Principle   Solutions are homogeneous mixtures of two or more substances.

Objective   Calculate the concentration of a solute in terms of mass of solute per unit mass of solvent, weight percentage of solute in solution, molarity, and molality.

Procedure

1. Read the information on *Measuring Solute Concentrations.*

Measuring Solute Concentrations

Chemists use a variety of standards to measure the concentrations of solutions. The *mass of a solute per unit mass of a solvent* is usually expressed as the number of grams of solute per 100 grams of a solvent (e.g., water). This measurement is useful in determining the concentration of a saturated solution at given temperatures. The *weight percentage of solute in solution* is given as the percent of solute in 100 grams of total solution. Thus, a 15% solution of fructose contains 15 grams of fructose in 85 grams of water (i.e., 15 + 85 = 100). This method helps to identify the amount of solute in a specific amount of solvent. The *molarity* of a solution is equal to the number of moles (i.e., gram molecular weight) of a solute per liter of solution. For example, 40 grams of sodium hydroxide (i.e., gram molecular weight of NaOH) dissolved in 1 liter of water is a 1 molar solution of sodium hydroxide. The *molality* of a solution is the number of moles of solute in 1,000 grams of solvent.

---

2. Examine the handout illustrations. Then complete the *Observations & Analysis* section.

Observations & Analysis

1. Write a procedure for mixing a solution of table salt and water that is 10 grams of solute per 100 grams of solvent.

   _____

   _____

   _____

   _____

2. Write a procedure for mixing a solution of table salt and water by weight percentage of solute in solution.

   _____

   _____

   _____

   _____

3. Write a procedure for mixing a solution of table salt and water that is a 1-molar solution of table salt.

   _____

   _____

   _____

   _____

4. Write a procedure for mixing a solution of table salt and alcohol that is a 1-molal solution.

   _____

   _____

   _____

   _____

Lesson 92: Teacher Preparation

Basic Principle   Energy is exchanged or transformed in all chemical reactions and physical changes of matter.

Competency   Students will describe temperature and heat flow in terms of the motion of atoms and molecules.

Procedure

1. Give students time to read the information on *Heat and Energy Transfer*.

2. Point out that improvements in thermometer technology made it possible for the Scottish chemist Joseph Black (1728–1799), who also discovered carbon dioxide, to accurately measure the *specific heat capacity* of different substances (i.e., the amount of heat energy that a substance can "store"). Using a newly invented mercury thermometer, Black defined *specific heat* as the amount of energy required to raise the temperature of a substance by 1°C. Iron, for example, requires 0.11 times the amount of heat needed to raise its temperature as much as the same mass of water. Iron is a much better conductor of heat. It does not store heat energy as well as water, but, instead, transfers heat readily to surrounding substances. Iron, therefore, has a lower specific heat than water. It was not until the work of Black's student, James Watt (1736–1819), and the discoveries of the American–English inventor Benjamin Thompson Rumford (1753–1814) that the notion of heat as a form of kinetic energy became a widely accepted alternative to the caloric theory. Following the invention of the steam engine, and James Watt's significant improvement of its design, scientists became acutely aware of the mechanical aspects of heat and heat transfer.

3. Give students time to complete the *Observations & Analysis* section.

Answer to Observations & Analysis

Answers will vary, but should include the following main points: As the atoms of metal absorb the radiant energy of the flame, they vibrate and collide more and more energetically with adjacent atoms. The thermometers touching the metal bar absorb some of that mechanical energy, as they are in contact with the atoms of the metal. The energy conducted from the metal to the glass and into the fluid of the thermometer causes the fluid to expand. The fluid expansion is recorded as an increase in temperature in all three thermometers, the thermometers closest to the flame heating up first as atoms move faster along the length of the metal bar.

Chemistry

STUDENT HANDOUT–LESSON 92

Basic Principle   Energy is exchanged or transformed in all chemical reactions and physical changes of matter.

Objective   Describe temperature and heat flow in terms of the motion of atoms and molecules.

Procedure

1. Read the information on *Heat and Energy Transfer*.

Heat and Energy Transfer

The ancient Greeks believed that heat was a fluid substance they called *caloric* that moved freely from hot objects to cold ones. The *caloric theory* proved valuable in explaining some phenomena, but was clearly weak at explaining others; and, by the start of the 19th century, scientists became less and less convinced that heat was a substance. They argued that heat could arise from the motion of the particles that made up matter, such as when you rub your cold hands together to make them warm. They knew that friction between two cold surfaces caused the production of heat. In 1798, the American–English inventor Benjamin Thompson Rumford (a.k.a, Count Rumford, 1753–1814) proposed that heat was a form of "mechanical energy." He explained that momentum, energy of motion (i.e., kinetic energy), was transferred from one particle of matter to another by collision and vibratory motion. He surmised that the *internal energy* of an object was the sum of the total vibratory motion of all of the particles comprising an object. Since it is impossible to directly measure the exact momentum of every particle in a substance, scientists refer to the *average kinetic energy* of millions of particles to describe the heat capacity of a material. *Temperature*, measured with a *thermometer*, is a measure of the average kinetic energy in the atoms and molecules of a substance. The glass walls of a thermometer, according to the Kinetic-Molecular Theory of Matter, are made of moving atoms just like the fluid inside the thermometer. If the atoms of some material (i.e., solid, liquid, or gas) surrounding the thermometer absorb energy, they will move faster and have more momentum. Their energy will be transferred to other atoms by collision. The thermometer will absorb that energy and the fluid inside the thermometer will expand; the individual molecules will move farther apart. Scientists mark the glass tube and read the fluid expansion in units called *degrees*. While a thermometer measures average kinetic energy, a *calorimeter* measures the *heat content* of a substance in *calories*. One *calorie* is the amount of energy needed to raise the temperature of one milliliter of water 1° Celsius. One thousand calories are equal to 1 Food Calorie. The energy released from a burning soda cracker containing 4 Food Calories will raise the temperature of one liter of water 4° Celsius.

2. Study the handout illustrations. Then complete the *Observations & Analysis* section.

HEAT TRANSFER AND THE KINETIC-MOLECULAR THEORY OF MATTER

Since all matter is made of tiny particles that are in constant motion, heat energy can be transferred in three different ways. Through a solid, the heat transfer by colliding particles is called *conduction*. In a fluid, either liquid or gas, the heat transfer by colliding particles is called *convection*. Energy is also given off by the rapid motion of electrons moving around inside atoms. This type of energy is called *radiation*. It is a form of low-frequency electromagnetic energy.

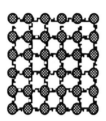
orderly
arrangement of
atoms in a solid

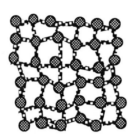
more disorderly
arrangement of atoms
in a liquid

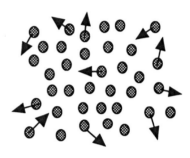
completely disordered,
randomly moving atoms
in a vapor

Observations & Analysis

A chemistry student secured a metal bar with ring stands and clamps and placed it horizontally over his lab table. He placed a Bunsen burner under the bar at one end. He then secured three thermometers at varying distances from the burner with additional clamps so that the bulb of each thermometer touched the bar. He then lit the burner and recorded the temperatures of the three thermometers for several minutes. Describe what the student probably observed and explain those observations according to the Kinetic-Molecular Theory of Matter.

_____

_____

_____

_____

_____

_____

_____

_____

_____

_____

_____

Lesson 93: Teacher Preparation

Basic Principle   Energy is exchanged or transformed in all chemical reactions and physical changes of matter.

Competency   Students will show that chemical processes can either release (exothermic) or absorb (endothermic) thermal energy.

Materials   ring stand and clamps, Celsius thermometers, glass stirring rod, 100-mL beaker, water, vinegar, baking soda, sodium hydroxide pellets, wax paper, goggles

Procedure

1. Give students time to read the information on the *Exothermic and Endothermic Reactions*.

2. Point out that a rise in thermometer temperature during a chemical reaction indicates that the molecules in the reaction have released heat. The reaction is, therefore, an *exothermic* reaction. A drop in thermometer temperature during a chemical reaction indicates that the molecules of the reaction have absorbed heat from the thermometer. The reaction is, therefore, an *endothermic* reaction. Draw the illustration to show how the amount of heat released from a reaction can be calculated from the energy content of the reactants and products.

Answers to Observations & Analysis

1. Answers will vary, but should include the following main points: The reaction of baking soda with vinegar is endothermic because there is an associated drop in thermometer temperature as the reaction takes place. This indicates that the reaction is absorbing heat.

2. Answers will vary, but should include the following main points: The dissolving of sodium hydroxide in water is exothermic because there is an associated rise in thermometer temperature as the reaction takes place. This indicates that the reaction is releasing heat.

Chemistry–Lesson 93 *(Continued)*

EXOTHERMIC

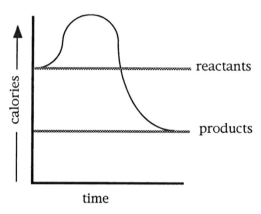

The exothermic reaction
releases calories of energy.

ENDOTHERMIC

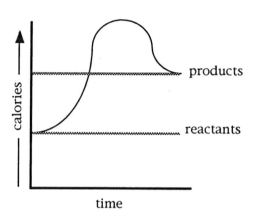

The endothermic reaction
absorbs calories of energy.

Name _____ Date _____

Chemistry

STUDENT HANDOUT–LESSON 93

Basic Principle   Energy is exchanged or transformed in all chemical reactions and physical changes of matter.

Objective   Show that chemical processes can either release (exothermic) or absorb (endothermic) thermal energy.

Materials   ring stand and clamps, Celsius thermometers, glass stirring rod, 100-mL beaker, water, vinegar, baking soda, sodium hydroxide pellets, wax paper, goggles

Procedure

1. Read the information about *Exothermic and Endothermic Reactions*.

Exothermic and Endothermic Reactions

All chemical reactions involve the liberation and absorption of heat. The Swiss–Russian chemist Germain Hess (1802–1850) discovered the law of *constant heat summation*—now called *Hess's Law*—summarizing how this happens. According to Hess's Law, the reactants and products in a chemical reaction always have a certain amount of energy. The heat liberated or absorbed by the reacting substances depends on the nature of those reactants and products, and not on the method used to get the reactants to change. If the reactants have more energy than the products, then the reaction must have released energy. This type of reaction is called an *exothermic reaction*. If the reactants have less energy than the products, then energy must have been absorbed during the chemical reaction. This type of reaction is called an *endothermic reaction*.

---

2. Fill a 100-mL beaker with 30 mL of water and place it on a ring stand.

3. Secure a Celsius thermometer to a ring stand and lower it into the beaker as shown in the diagram. Record the temperature in the *Observations & Analysis* section.

4. **WEAR GOGGLES** when mixing all solutions.

5. Add a half-dozen pellets of sodium hydroxide to the beaker and stir gently without hitting the thermometer.

6. Record in the *Observation & Analysis* section the temperature of the water after a minute of stirring.

7. Thoroughly rinse and dry the beaker, the thermometer, and the stirring rod.

8. Fill the 100-mL beaker with 30 ml of vinegar and place it on a ring stand.

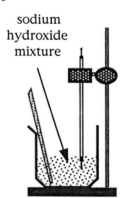

sodium hydroxide mixture

9. Lower the thermometer into the beaker as before. Record the temperature in the *Observations & Analysis* section.

10. **WEAR GOGGLES** when mixing all solutions.

11. Add one teaspoon of baking soda to the beaker and stir gently without hitting the thermometer.

12. After a minute of stirring, record the temperature of the water again in the *Observations & Analysis* section.

13. Thoroughly rinse and dry the beaker, the thermometer, and the stirring rod. Then complete the *Observations & Analysis* section.

Observations & Analysis

Initial temperature of water: _____
Final temperature of water and sodium hydroxide mixture: _____

Initial temperature of vinegar: _____
Final temperature of vinegar and baking soda mixture: _____

1. Which reaction was an endothermic reaction? Explain your answer.

_____
_____
_____
_____
_____
_____

2. Which reaction was an exothermic reaction? Explain your answer.

_____
_____
_____
_____
_____
_____

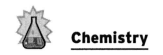

Lesson 94: Teacher Preparation

Basic Principle   Energy is exchanged or transformed in all chemical reactions and physical changes of matter.

Competency   Students will illustrate how energy is released when a material condenses or freezes, and absorbed when a material melts or evaporates.

Materials   ring stand and clamps, Ehrlenmeyer flask, Celsius thermometer, water, Bunsen burner, tongs, goggles, apron, heat-resistant gloves, 250-mL beaker, crushed ice, small test tube

Procedure

1. Give students time to read the information on *Latent Heat of Fusion and Vaporization.*

2. Point out that the energy released or absorbed during a phase change works to reorganize the molecules in the substance, rather than working to affect a change in the temperature of the thermometer.

3. Give students time to complete the activity and the *Observations & Analysis* section.

Answers to Observations & Analysis

1. Answers will vary, but should include the following main points: The graph shows that the temperature levels off as the water boils. This "plateau" represents the latent heat of vaporization used to overcome the attraction between liquid molecules.

2. Answers will vary, but should include the following main points: The graph shows that the temperature levels off as the water begins to freeze. This "plateau" represents the latent heat of fusion as heat transferred from the liquid to its surroundings allows the water molecules to get closer together to form a crystal.

Chemistry

STUDENT HANDOUT–LESSON 94

Basic Principle   Energy is exchanged or transformed in all chemical reactions and physical changes of matter.

Objective   Illustrate how energy is released when a material condenses or freezes, and absorbed when a material melts or evaporates.

Materials   ring stand and clamps, Ehrlenmeyer flask, Celsius thermometer, water, Bunsen burner, tongs, goggles, apron, heat-resistant gloves, 250-mL beaker, crushed ice, small test tube

Procedure

1. Read the information on *Latent Heat of Fusion and Vaporization*.

Latent Heat of Fusion and Vaporization

Latent heat is the heat transferred between a substance and its surroundings when the substance changes phase. The heat transferred to a solid when it melts is called *latent heat of fusion*. During melting, the temperature of the substance remains constant as absorbed heat works to overcome the attractive forces between the crystallized molecules. The heat transferred to a liquid when it vaporizes is called *latent heat of vaporization*. During vaporization, the temperature of the substance remains constant as absorbed heat works to overcome the attractive forces between the fluid molecules.

---

2. Pour 50 mL of water into an Ehrlenmeyer flask and place the flask onto a ring stand. Secure it with a clamp.

3. Secure a thermometer in a clamp and attach it to the ring stand. Be sure that the tip of the thermometer barely touches the surface of the water.

4. Make proper use of the Bunsen burner. **WEAR GOGGLES, AN APRON, AND HEAT-RESISTANT GLOVES TO PROTECT YOUR SKIN AND EYES FROM THE SCALDING HOT STEAM.**

5. Record the initial temperature at the bottom of the graph, turn on the Bunsen burner, and plot the temperature on the thermometer every 30 seconds. When the water reaches a vigorous boil, continue reading the thermometer for three more minutes. Clean up when the apparatus is cool.

6. Pour 1 mL of water into a small test tube and secure the test tube in a clamp. Place it in a 250-mL beaker. Surround the test tube with a mixture of ice and water (mostly ice).

7. Secure a thermometer in a clamp and lower it into the test tube so that it touches the surface of the water.

8. Record the temperature of the water at the top of the graph, then plot the temperature of the water every minute for 10 minutes.

9. Carefully remove the thermometer and test tube. Extreme cold can crack and splinter the glass. **DO NOT TOUCH BROKEN GLASS.** Examine the contents of the test tube. Ask your instructor to assist you in disposing of it.

10. Complete the *Observations & Analysis* section.

LIQUID TO VAPOR   **LIQUID TO SOLID**

Observations & Analysis

1. What happened to the temperature registered by the thermometer during the last three minutes of the demonstration once the water began to boil vigorously? Explain your observation.

   _____

   _____

   _____

   _____

   _____

2. What happened to the temperature registered by the thermometer during the last three minutes of the demonstration as the liquid cooled? Explain your observation.

   _____

   _____

   _____

   _____

   _____

Lesson 95: Teacher Preparation

Basic Principle   Energy is exchanged or transformed in all chemical reactions and physical changes of matter.

Competency   Students will solve problems of heat flow using known values of specific heat.

Procedure

1. Give students time to read the information on *Specific Heat*.
2. Assist them in completing the *Observations & Analysis* section.

Answers to Observations & Analysis

1. If 1 gram of this substance absorbs 0.73 calories, then—by definition of specific heat—*2 grams* of the substance will absorb 1.46 calories ($1.46 \div 0.73 = 2$).
2. If 1 gram of aluminum absorbs 0.22 calories, then—by definition of specific heat—it will require *6.16 calories* ($0.22 \times 7 \times 4 = 6.16$) to increase the temperature of 7 grams of aluminum by 4°C.
3. If 5 grams of a substance requires 2 calories to warm it 2°C, then 1 calorie will raise its temperature 1°C. Since specific heat is the number of calories needed to raise the temperature of 1 gram of a substance 1°C, then the specific heat of this substance is *0.2* ($1 \div 5 = 0.2$).

Name _____ Date _____

Chemistry

STUDENT HANDOUT–LESSON 95

Basic Principle   Energy is exchanged or transformed in all chemical reactions and physical changes of matter.

Objective   Solve problems of heat flow using known values of specific heat.

Procedure

1. Read the information on *Specific Heat*.

Specific Heat

The *specific heat* of a substance is the number of calories required to increase the temperature of 1 gram of that substance 1° Celsius. The specific heat of water is 1.0 (i.e., 1 calorie per gram usually measured at 20°C). The specific heat of iron is 0.11, meaning that 0.11 calorie of heat will warm 1 gram of iron 1°C. While specific heat varies slightly with temperature, the variation—in most cases—is negligible.

Specific Heat of Some Common Substances*

water	1.00	air	0.24
aluminum	0.22	brass	0.09
copper	0.09	glass	0.20
gold	0.03	ice	0.50
iron	0.11	lead	0.03
silver	0.06	zinc	0.09

*approximated to nearest hundredths place

---

2. Complete the *Observations & Analysis* section.

Observations & Analysis

1. The specific heat of a substance is 0.73. How many grams of the substance will absorb 1.46 calories?

2. How many calories of heat are required to warm 7 grams of aluminum 4°C?

3. What is the specific heat of 5 grams of a substance if it requires 2 calories to warm it 2°C?

Lesson 96: Teacher Preparation

Basic Principle   Chemical reaction rates depend on factors that influence the frequency of collision among reactant molecules.

Competency   Students will explain that the rate of reaction is the decrease in concentration of reactants, or the increase in the concentration of products with time.

Procedure

1. Give students time to read the information on *Reaction Rates*.

2. Point out that the rate of change in concentration of reactants and products during a chemical reaction is a function of time and other factors (e.g., temperature, pressure, the presence of a catalyst). To say that the reaction rate of any given chemical reaction is directly proportional to the concentration of reactants and products is an oversimplification, since not all collisions between molecules is effective in causing chemical change. Reaction rates are a function of additional factors that make them empirically-determined proportionality constants. In the example here, the reaction rates of a reaction between H_2 and Cl_2 can be expressed as $r = k[H_2][Cl_2]$ where k is the proportionality constant.

$$H_2 + Cl_2 \longrightarrow 2HCl$$

3. Give students time to complete the *Observations & Analysis* section.

Answers to Observations & Analysis

1. Answers will vary, but should include the following main points: As the concentration of reactants decreases, the number of collisions between reactant molecules decreases as a percentage of all colliding molecules in the reaction. The production of products is, thereby, slowed.

2. Answers will vary, but should include the following main points: As the concentration of products increases, the number of collisions between reactant molecules decreases as a percentage of all colliding molecules in the reaction. The production of products is, thereby, slowed.

Chemistry

STUDENT HANDOUT–LESSON 96

Basic Principle Chemical reaction rates depend on factors that influence the frequency of collision among reactant molecules.

Objective Explain that the rate of reaction is the decrease in concentration of reactants, or the increase in the concentration of products with time.

Procedure

1. Read the information on *Reaction Rates*.

Reaction Rates

Chemical reactions proceed at different speeds. The rate at which reactions occur are determined by a number of factors: the concentration of the reactants, the concentration of the products, the temperature of the reactants, and the presence of a catalyst. Reactions taking place in the gaseous state will be affected by pressure. Reactions taking place in the solid phase will be affected by the size of the reactant particles. Reaction rate is expressed in terms of substance concentrations: moles per liter per second of reactants consumed or products formed. During a reaction at constant temperature and pressure, reaction rates decrease with time as the concentration of the reactants decrease and the concentration of the products increase. The Kinetic-Molecular Theory of Matter explains these effects as dependent on the rates of collisions between reactant and product molecules.

---

2. Complete the *Observations & Analysis* section.

RATES OF REACTION

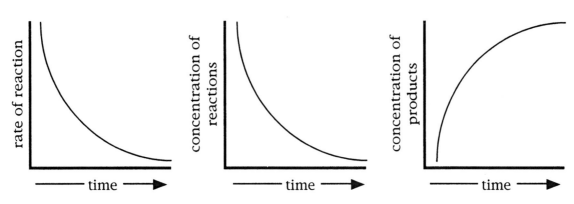

Observations & Analysis

1. Use the Kinetic-Molecular Theory of Matter to explain why reaction rates decrease as the concentration of reactants decreases.

_____

_____

_____

_____

_____

_____

_____

_____

_____

2. Use the Kinetic-Molecular Theory of Matter to explain why reaction rates decrease as the concentration of products increases.

_____

_____

_____

_____

_____

_____

_____

_____

_____

Lesson 97: Teacher Preparation

Basic Principle   Chemical reaction rates depend on factors that influence the frequency of collision among reactant molecules.

Competency   Students will show how reaction rates depend on such factors as concentration, temperature, and pressure.

Procedure   Give students time to read the information on *Factors Influencing Reaction Rates* before completing the *Observations & Analysis* section.

Answers for Observations & Analysis

1. Answers will vary, but should include the following main points: If the concentration of reactants is increased, then the number of collisions between reactant molecules increased per unit time. Since reactant molecules must collide to produce a product, an increase in the number of collisions per unit time increases the reaction rate (i.e., the production of products).

2. Answers will vary, but should include the following main points: If the temperature of reactants is increased, then the reactants gain energy. Their rate of motion is, therefore, increased, a condition that increases the number of collisions between molecules per unit time. Since reactant molecules must collide to produce a product, an increase in the number of collisions per unit time increases the reaction rate.

3. Answers will vary, but should include the following main points: If the pressure of reactants is increased, then the reactants are in closer proximity to one another. Since reactant molecules must collide to produce a product, a decrease in the distance between moving molecules results in an increase in the number of collisions between them per unit time. This condition increases the reaction rate.

Name _____   Date _____

Chemistry

STUDENT HANDOUT–LESSON 97

Basic Principle   Chemical reaction rates depend on factors that influence the frequency of collision among reactant molecules.

Objective   Show how reaction rates depend on such factors as concentration, temperature, and pressure.

Procedure

1.   Read the information on *Factors Influencing Reaction Rates*.

Factors Influencing Reaction Rates

Increasing the concentration of reactants increases the number of effective collisions that would be successful in producing products. Increasing the temperature of the reactants increases the kinetic energy of reacting molecules, thereby increasing the number of effective collisions between reacting molecules per unit time. Increasing the pressure exerted on the reactants brings them into closer proximity, thereby increasing the number of effective collisions between reacting molecules per unit time.

---

2.   Complete the *Observations & Analysis* section.

Observations & Analysis

1. Use the Kinetic-Molecular Theory of Matter to explain why increasing the concentration of reactants would increase the rate of a chemical reaction.

_____

_____

_____

_____

_____

_____

_____

_____

2. Use the Kinetic-Molecular Theory of Matter to explain why increasing the temperature of reactants would increase the rate of a chemical reaction.

_____

_____

_____

_____

_____

_____

_____

_____

3. Use the Kinetic-Molecular Theory of Matter to explain why increasing the pressure exerted on reactants would increase the rate of a chemical reaction.

_____

_____

_____

_____

_____

_____

_____

_____

Lesson 98: Teacher Preparation

Basic Principle   Chemical reaction rates depend on factors that influence the frequency of collision among reactant molecules.

Competency   Students will show how reaction rates depend on such factors as concentration, temperature, and pressure.

Procedure

1. Give students time to read the information on *Catalysts*.

2. Explain that catalysts do not necessarily affect the equilibrium of a reaction while reducing the activation energy needed to "spark" the reaction. Acids can act as catalysts in the formation of organic compounds (e.g., esters made from organic acids and alcohols) or in the hydrolysis of water. In many cases, only a small amount of catalyst is required to produce a huge change in reaction rate. A single molecule of the enzyme triose-phosphate isomerase can catalyse the reaction of 400,000 reactant molecules per second. Point out that catalysts can be either *homogeneous* (i.e., in the same phase as the reactants) or *heterogeneous* (i.e., in a different phase from the reactants).

3. Give students time to complete the *Observations & Analysis* section.

Answer to Observations & Analysis

Answers will vary, but should include the following main points: A catalyst increases the rate of a chemical reaction by bringing reactant molecules into closer proximity, thereby maximizing the effectiveness of molecular collisions that produce a product. The activation energy needed to "spark" a reaction in the presence of a catalyst is, therefore, less than that required in the absence of the catalyst.

Chemistry

STUDENT HANDOUT–LESSON 98

Basic Principle   Chemical reaction rates depend on factors that influence the frequency of collision among reactant molecules.

Objective   Show how reaction rates depend on such factors as concentration, temperature, and pressure.

Procedure

1. Read the information on *Catalysts*.

Catalysts

A *catalyst* is any substance that increases the rate of a chemical reaction. During the reaction, the catalyst itself remains unchanged. One example of a catalyst is the effect of platinum on the reaction of hydrogen and oxygen, two gases that do not normally react at room temperature. If a small amount of finely powdered platinum is added to the reactants, they combust rapidly to form water. Platinum acts as a catalyst by providing a "surface" on which the hydrogen and oxygen molecules are drawn into close proximity. The presence of a catalyst provides the reactants with an alternative pathway with a lower activation energy. Catalysts involved in biochemical pathways are proteins called *enzymes*.

---

2. Complete the *Observations & Analysis* section.

DECREASING ACTIVATION ENERGY WITH A CATALYST

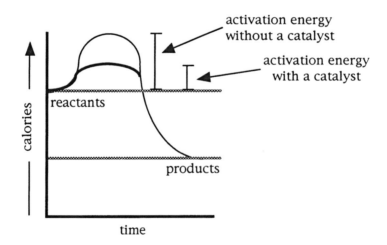

Copyright © 2005 by John Wiley & Sons, Inc.

ACTION OF A CATALYST

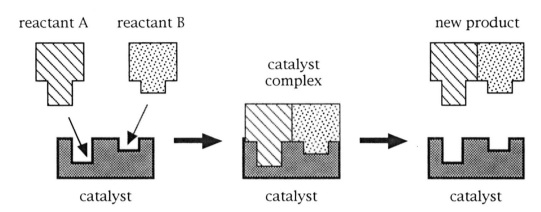

Observations & Analysis

Explain how a catalyst increases the rate of a chemical reaction.

_____

_____

_____

_____

_____

_____

_____

_____

 **Chemistry**

Lesson 99: Teacher Preparation

Basic Principle   Chemical equilibrium is a dynamic process at the molecular level.

Competency   Students will show that equilibrium is established when forward and reverse reaction rates are equal.

Procedure

1. Give students time to read the information on *Chemical Equilibrium.*

2. Point out that in a reversible reaction, the products begin forming as soon as the reactants are mixed. The reaction rate of the reactants remains high as long as the concentration of reactants is high; the reverse reaction that reforms the reactants by reaction between the products remains low as long as the concentration of products remains low. At some point, which is dependent upon temperature, the two reaction rates become equal and a state of equilibrium is reached. There is no net change in the concentrations of either the reactants or products during equilibrium.

3. Give students time to complete the *Observations & Analysis* section.

Answer to Observations & Analysis

Answers will vary, but should include the following main points: As reactant molecules collide, product molecules are produced. At the start of the reaction, the probability of reactant molecules colliding to form product molecules is greater than the probability of product molecules colliding to reform reactant molecules. This is because there are more reactant molecules than product molecules in the mixture. When the concentrations of the products reach a certain level, the probability of collisions between products to reform reactants becomes equal to the probability of collisions between reactants to form products. The forward and backward reaction rates reach dynamic equilibrium.

Chemistry

STUDENT HANDOUT–LESSON 99

Basic Principle   Chemical equilibrium is a dynamic process at the molecular level.

Objective   Show that equilibrium is established when forward and reverse reaction rates are equal.

Procedure

1. Read the information on *Chemical Equilibrium.*

Chemical Equilibrium

Many chemical reactions are easily reversible. That is, the products of the reaction can react to form the original reactants with as much facility as the reactants that formed the products. *Chemical equilibrium* refers to that circumstance of a reversible chemical reaction during which there is no net change in the reaction mixture. The concentrations of the reactants and products in the mixture remain constant. Although the individual molecules in the reaction continue to react, the number of "forward reactions" is equal to the number of "backward reactions." The equilibrium is dynamic. Different chemical reactions have different *equilibrium constants* that relate the concentrations of reactants and products at specific temperatures and pressures. In the equation, the equilibrium constant, *K*, relates the concentration of the reactants, AB and CD, to the products, AC and BD.

$$K = [AC]^a[BD]^b/[AB]^c[CD]^d$$

---

2. Complete the *Observations & Analysis* section.

REVERSIBLE CHEMICAL REACTIONS IN EQUILIBRIUM*

forward reaction

$$a\text{AB} \quad + \quad b\text{CD} \quad \rightleftharpoons \quad c\text{AC} \quad + \quad d\text{BD}$$

backward reaction

*a, b, c, and d are coefficients

Observations & Analysis

Use the Kinetic-Molecular Theory of Matter to describe a reversible chemical reaction that is in equilibrium.

_____

_____

_____

_____

_____

_____

_____

_____

_____

_____

Lesson 100: Teacher Preparation

Basic Principle   Chemical equilibrium is a dynamic process at the molecular level.

Competency   Students will use Le Chatelier's Principle to predict the effect of changes in concentration, temperature, and pressure on chemical reactions in equilibrium.

Procedure   Give students time to read the information on *Le Chatelier's Principle* before completing the *Observations & Analysis* section.

Answers to Observations & Analysis

1. Answers will vary, but should include the following main points: When the temperature is raised on an exothermic reaction that has reached chemical equilibrium, the additional temperature favors the endothermic reaction and the concentration of products decreases until the reaction returns to equilibrium.

2. Answers will vary, but should include the following main points: When a catalyst is introduced in an exothermic reaction that has reached chemical equilibrium, the concentrations of the products remain unchanged.

Chemistry

STUDENT HANDOUT–LESSON 100

Basic Principle   Chemical equilibrium is a dynamic process at the molecular level.

Objective   Use Le Chatelier's Principle to predict the effect of changes in concentration, temperature, and pressure on chemical reactions in equilibrium.

Procedure

1. Read the information on *Le Chatelier's Principle*.

Le Chatelier's Principle

If a reaction in chemical equilibrium is subjected to changes in temperature or pressure, then the equilibrium will minimize the effect of the change. This principle was first formulated by the French physical chemist Henri Louis Le Chatelier (1850–1936). The principle can be illustrated in the reversible reaction between nitrogen gas, N_2, and hydrogen gas, H_2.

$$N_2 + 3H_2 \rightleftharpoons 2NH_3 \qquad\qquad \Delta H = -50 \text{ kJ}$$

The reaction is an exothermic reaction that releases about 50 kilojoules (kJ) of heat. The decomposition of ammonia, NH_3, is endothermic, a reaction in which 50 kJ of heat is absorbed. If the temperature of the reaction is raised after it has reached dynamic equilibrium, then the mixture absorbs heat, favoring the endothermic reaction and counteracting the rise in temperature.

---

2. Study the chart on *The Effects of Changes in Concentration, Temperature, and Pressure on Chemical Equilibrium*. Then complete the *Observations & Analysis* section.

**THE EFFECTS OF CHANGES IN CONCENTRATION,
TEMPERATURE, AND PRESSURE ON CHEMICAL EQUILIBRIUM**

Reaction:	AB + CD ⟶ AC + BD (exothermic)		
	(larger volume) (smaller volume)		
external change	**rate of reaction**	**equilibrium mixture**	**equilibrium constant**
increased temperature	increased	> AB + CD	changed
decreased temperature	decreased	> AC + BD	changed
increased pressure	increased for gaseous reactions	> AC + BD	unchanged
decreased pressure	decreased for gaseous reactions	> AB + CD	unchanged
addition of a catalyst	increased	unchanged	unchanged

Observations & Analysis

1. Use Le Chatelier's Principle to describe the effects on the concentration of products in an exothermic reaction that has reached chemical equilibrium when the temperature of the mixture is raised.

   _____

   _____

   _____

   _____

2. Use Le Chatelier's Principle to describe the effects on the concentration of products in an exothermic reaction that has reached chemical equilibrium when a catalyst is added to the mixture.

   _____

   _____

   _____

   _____

Lesson 101: Teacher Preparation

Basic Principle   The bonding characteristics of carbon lead to many different molecules with varied sizes, shapes, and chemical properties, providing the chemical basis of life.

Competency   Students will show that large polymers such as carbohydrates, lipids, proteins, and nucleic acids are formed by repetitive combinations of smaller subunits.

Procedure

1. Give students time to read the information on *Acids, Bases, and Salts*.

2. Draw the illustration showing *The Miller–Urey Experiment*.

3. Point out that four billion years ago, planet Earth was not as it appears today. The planet's crust and atmosphere were raging hot with active volcanoes spotting the landscape, flooding the land with molten metal, and filling the skies with plumes of carbon dioxide (CO_2), ammonia (NH_3) , and methane (CH_4). There was little free oxygen (O_2) in the atmosphere; most of that elementary substance combined with hydrogen to form water (H_2O) or joined with metals to form metal oxides. About three billion years ago, however, things changed. The electrical energy from lightning discharges in the atmosphere helped to combine these basic molecules into the raw materials needed to form living organisms: carbohydrates, lipids, proteins, and nucleic acids. In the 1950s, American chemists Stanley Lloyd Miller (b. 1930) and Harold Clayton Urey (1893–1981) performed a series of experiments to show how the "organic synthesis" of large macromolecules can take place.

4. Give students time to complete the *Observations & Analysis* section.

Answer to Observations & Analysis

Answers will vary, but should include the following main points: Carbohydrates, lipids, proteins, and nucleic acids are all formed from simpler subunits by the same chemical process: dehydration synthesis. Carbohydrates are formed from saccharides. Lipids are formed from fatty acids and glycerol. Proteins are formed from amino acids. Nucleic acids are composed of nucleotides made of nitrogenous bases, deoxyribose and ribose sugars, and phosphates.

THE MILLER-UREY EXPERIMENT

In the Miller and Urey experiment, volcanic gases present on the primitive Earth are reacted in an electrical discharge chamber and condensed to liquid in a cooling jacket. The liquid is drawn into boiling water by a vacuum where the molecules in the liquid can be collected and examined. The building-block molecules of life—carbohydrates, fats, proteins, and nucleic acids—can be formed in this way.

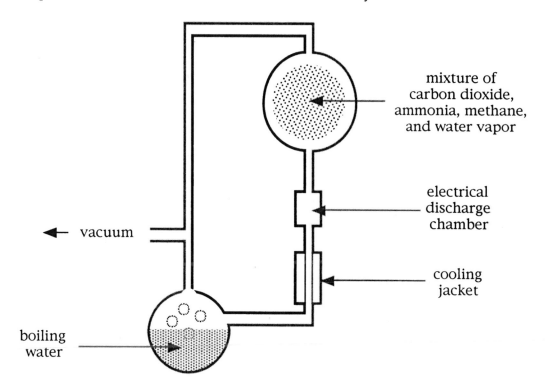

mixture of carbon dioxide, ammonia, methane, and water vapor

electrical discharge chamber

cooling jacket

vacuum

boiling water

Chemistry

STUDENT HANDOUT–LESSON 101

Basic Principle   The bonding characteristics of carbon lead to many different molecules with varied sizes, shapes, and chemical properties providing the chemical basis of life.

Objective   Show that large polymers such as carbohydrates, lipids, proteins, and nucleic acids are formed by repetitive combinations of smaller subunits.

Procedure

1. Read the information on *The Polymers of Life.*

The Polymers of Life

Large molecules such as *carbohydrates, lipids, proteins,* and *nucleic acids* are polymers comprised of repeating patterns of simpler subunits. *Carbohydrates* (e.g., sugars and starches) that give living organisms energy to burn are made of simple sugars such as glucose. Simple sugars are collectively called *saccharides.* Saccharides combine to form complex macromolecules in a polymerization reaction called *dehydration synthesis.* During dehydration synthesis, a molecule of water (2 hydrogen atoms and 1 oxygen atom) is removed from adjacent glucose molecules to form a polysaccharide. Both complex sugars and starches (e.g, plant cellulose) are polysaccharides. *Lipids* (e.g., fats) that help to form cell membranes, an organism's protective tissues, and serve as a secondary source of energy are formed in similar fashion. Like carbohydrates, lipids are produced by dehydration synthesis. In the process, three *fatty acid* molecules are linked to a molecule of *glycerol* to form the substance commonly called fat. *Proteins* that catalyse biochemical reactions (e.g., enzymes) and give an organism its structure (e.g., bones, muscles, blood vessels) are also produced by dehydration synthesis from simpler subunits called *amino acids.* There are only about twenty different amino acids that give rise to the millions of macromolecular proteins that exist in nature. *Nucleic acids* such as *deoxyribonucleic acid (DNA)* that carry the hereditary features of living organisms are also formed by dehydration synthesis from simpler subunits called *nucleotides.* The nucleotides of a DNA macromolecule are held together in a chain made of alternating phosphates and deoxyribose sugars arranged in a coded sequence that carries instructions for the production of specific proteins.

---

2. Examine the handout illustrations. Then complete the *Observations & Analysis* section.

FORMATION OF A CARBOHYDRATE

FORMATION OF A LIPID

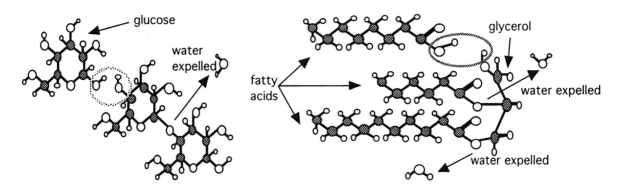

FORMATION OF A PROTEIN

FORMATION OF A NUCLEIC ACID

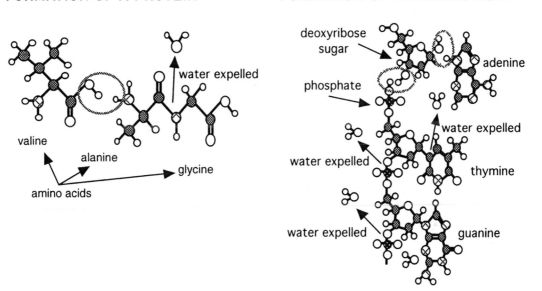

Observations & Analysis

Compare and contrast the chemical characteristics of carbohydrates, lipids, proteins, and nucleic acids.

_____

_____

_____

_____

_____

_____

_____

_____

 **Chemistry**

Lesson 102: Teacher Preparation

Basic Principle   The bonding characteristics of carbon lead to many different molecules with varied sizes, shapes, and chemical properties, providing the chemical basis of life.

Competency   Students will identify the subunits of carbohydrates, lipids, proteins, and nucleic acids.

Procedure

    1. Give students time to read the information on *The Building Blocks of Life*.

    2. Assist students in completing the *Observations & Analysis* section.

Answers to Observations & Analysis

    1. See the diagram.

    2. D, C, B, A

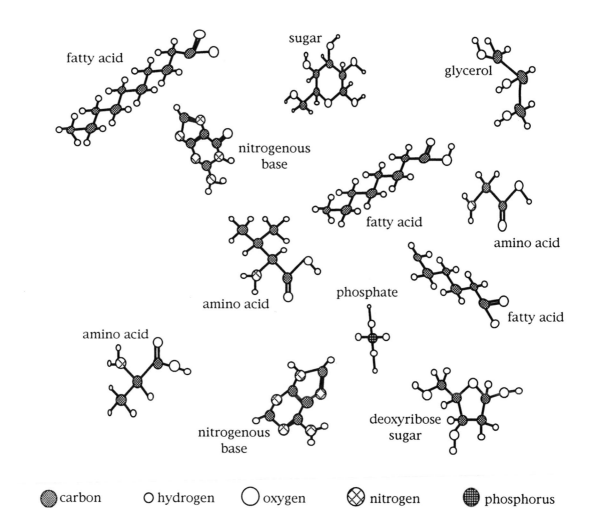

fatty acid

sugar

glycerol

nitrogenous base

fatty acid

amino acid

amino acid

phosphate

fatty acid

amino acid

nitrogenous base

deoxyribose sugar

● carbon   ○ hydrogen   ⊘ oxygen   ⊗ nitrogen   ⊕ phosphorus

Chemistry

STUDENT HANDOUT–LESSON 102

Basic Principle   The bonding characteristics of carbon lead to many different molecules with varied sizes, shapes, and chemical properties, providing the chemical basis of life.

Objective   Identify the subunits of carbohydrates, lipids, proteins, and nucleic acids.

Procedure

1. Read the information on *The Building Blocks of Life*.

The Building Blocks of Life

Biochemistry is the study of the chemistry of living organisms (i.e., organic chemistry). The basic elements comprising all living things are carbon, hydrogen, oxygen, nitrogen, and phosphorus. Because of the bonding characteristics of carbon, which allows atoms of that element to form any number of covalent arrangements with other atoms, these five elements can be combined millions of ways to form the polymers of life: carbohydrates, lipids, proteins, and nucleic acids.

---

2. Examine the handout illustrations. Then complete the *Observations & Analysis* section.

Observations & Analysis

1. Identify each of the molecules shown as a saccharide, amino acid, fatty acid, glycerol, deoxyribose sugar, phosphate, or nitrogenous base.

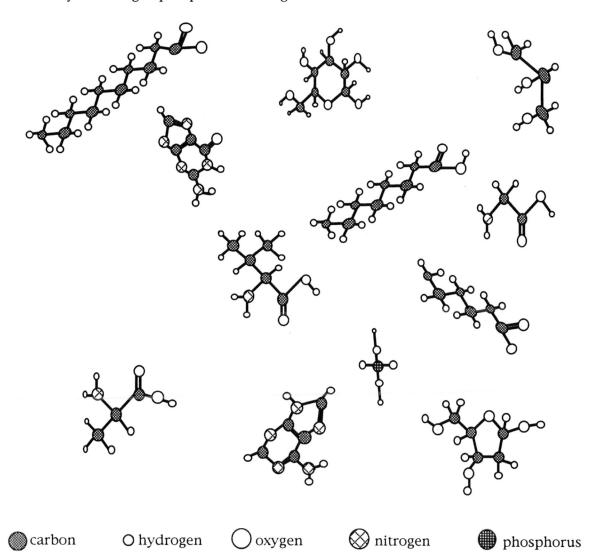

⬤ carbon   ○ hydrogen   ◯ oxygen   ⊗ nitrogen   ⬤ phosphorus

2. Choose the letter of the subunit that comprises each polymer of life.

_____ carbohydrate   (A) nitrogenous base

_____ lipid   (B) amino acid

_____ protein   (C) fatty acids and glycerol

_____ nucleic acid   (D) saccharide

Lesson 103: Teacher Preparation

Basic Principle   Nuclear processes are those in which the atomic nucleus changes, including radioactive decay of naturally occurring and artificial isotopes, nuclear fission, and nuclear fusion.

Competency   Students will explain that protons and neutrons are held together by powerful nuclear forces much stronger than the electromagnetic repulsion between protons.

Procedure

1. Give students time to read the information on *The Strong Nuclear Force*.
2. Review the Rutherford–Bohr Model of the atom, which pictures the atom as a concentrated nucleus of positively charged protons surrounded by negatively charged electrons orbiting in distant energy shells. Make sure students understand the relationships depicted by Coulomb's Law and that the expression is an inverse square law similar to Newton's Law of Gravity ($F = G \bullet m_1 m_2 / r_2$).
3. Give students time to complete the *Observations & Analysis* section.

Answers to Observations & Analysis

1. Answers will vary, but should include the following main points: According to Coulomb's Law, the electromagnetic force between charged particles increases as the product of the individual charges, and decreases as the square of the distance between them. Unlike charges (i.e., + and –) attract one another while like charges (i.e., + and + , – and –) are repelled according to this relationship.
2. Answers will vary, but should include the following main points: In order for particles of like electrostatic charge to remain in close proximity to one another, as they do in the atomic nucleus, the force that holds them in place must be stronger than their mutual electrostatic repulsion.

RUTHERFORD-BOHR MODEL OF THE ATOM

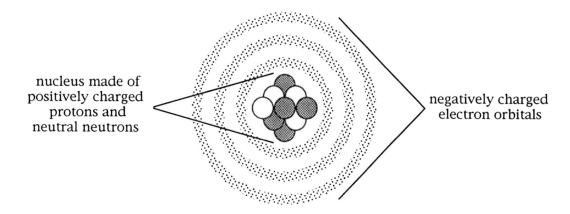

nucleus made of positively charged protons and neutral neutrons

negatively charged electron orbitals

Name _____ Date _____

Chemistry

STUDENT HANDOUT–LESSON 103

Basic Principle Nuclear processes are those in which the atomic nucleus changes, including radioactive decay of naturally occurring and artificial isotopes, nuclear fission, and nuclear fusion.

Objective Explain that protons and neutrons are held together by powerful nuclear forces much stronger than the electromagnetic repulsion between protons.

Procedure

1. Read the information on *The Strong Nuclear Force.*

The Strong Nuclear Force

When the experiments of Ernst Rutherford (1871–1937) determined that the positively charged nucleus was composed of a compact nucleus of positively charged protons, physicists were at a loss to explain how the nucleus held together. Since the repulsive force between positive charges increases as the distance between them decreases, according to Coulomb's Law, how is it that the individual positively charged protons in the nucleus stay together? In the representation of Coulomb's Law here, "F" is the force between individual positively charged particles, "q_1" is the charge of one particle, "q_2" is the charge on the second particle, and "r" is the distance between them.

$$\text{Coulomb's Law: } F \approx \frac{q_1 q_2}{r^2}$$

Physicists, therefore, surmised that there must be a force that overcomes the repulsive forces of protons, a force that acts at distances that cannot exceed 10^{-15} meters (i.e., the approximate size of an atomic nucleus). They called this force the *strong nuclear force.*

---

2. Complete the *Observations & Analysis* section.

Observations & Analysis

1. Use Coulomb's Law to explain how charged particles, both positive and negative, behave when they encounter one another.

_____

_____

_____

_____

_____

_____

_____

_____

2. Considering that the atomic nucleus is composed of individual positively charged particles called protons, why must physicists conclude that a force stronger than the electromagnetic force is responsible for holding the atomic nucleus together?

_____

_____

_____

_____

_____

_____

_____

_____

_____

_____

_____

_____

Lesson 104: Teacher Preparation

Basic Principle   Nuclear processes are those in which the atomic nucleus changes, including radioactive decay of naturally occurring and artificial isotopes, nuclear fission, and nuclear fusion.

Competency   Students wil explain that energy released during nuclear fission and fusion is much greater than the energy released during chemical reactions.

Procedure

1. Give students time to read the information on *Nuclear Energy vs. Chemical Energy* before completing the *Observations & Analysis* section.

2. Point out that the energy released by electrons as they jump from higher electron orbitals to lower ones corresponds to the energy of the electromagnetic waves (e.g., light waves) being radiated. This energy can be calculated using the formula of Max Planck (1858–1947), the "father of quantum mechanics": $E = hf$, where "E" is energy, "h" is Planck's constant (6.626×10^{-34} Js), and "f" is the frequency of light being radiated. By all accounts, these energies are many magnitudes less than the energy released during a nuclear reaction, which is calculated using Einstein's formula: $E = mc^2$.

Answer to Observations & Analysis

Answers will vary, but should include the following main points: Electrons moving from one orbital to another in a Rutherford–Bohr atom absorb and release energies in accordance with Maxwell's Laws of Electromagnetism and can be calculated using Planck's formula: $E = hf$. Since chemistry involves the trading and sharing of valence electrons, the energy released in chemical reactions is substantially lower than the energy released in a nuclear reaction. In a nuclear reaction, the enormous amount of energy stored under the influence of the strong force corresponds to the huge amount of work that was done to fuse positively charged particles together into a space measuring the size of the atomic nucleus.

Chemistry

STUDENT HANDOUT–LESSON 104

Basic Principle   Nuclear processes are those in which the atomic nucleus changes, including radioactive decay of naturally occurring and artificial isotopes, nuclear fission, and nuclear fusion.

Objective   Explain that energy released during nuclear fission and fusion is much greater than the energy released during chemical reactions.

Procedure

1. Read the information on *Nuclear Energy vs. Chemical Energy*.

> ### Nuclear Energy vs. Chemical Energy
>
> The energy stored in an atomic nucleus, constrained by the short-acting, strong nuclear force, is enormous compared to the energy released by electrons moving from one electron energy level to another. This is because the strong force must overcome the electrostatic repulsion between positively charged protons inside the nucleus. The movement of electrons outside the atomic nucleus are governed by the laws of electromagnetism derived by James Clerk Maxwell (1831–1879). The laws governing the fission and fusion of atomic nuclei are derived from Albert Einstein's (1879–1955) Theory of Relativity. Einstein explained that a small amount of mass can be converted to energy according to his famous relations, $E = mc^2$; where, "E" is energy, "m" is mass, and "c" is the speed of light (i.e., 300,000 km/s). The energy released from a splitting atomic nucleus (i.e., fission) releases energy in accordance with this formula. The energy released from the joining of subatomic particles (i.e., fusion) can also be calculated using Einstein's formulas and corresponds roughly to the huge amounts of energy required to overcome the electrostatic repulsion of the like-charged particles being fused.

2. Complete the *Observations & Analysis* section.

Observations & Analysis

Use the Rutherford–Bohr Model of the atom to explain why chemical reactions release less energy than nuclear reactions.

_____

_____

_____

_____

_____

_____

_____

_____

_____

_____

_____

_____

_____

_____

_____

_____

_____

_____

_____

Lesson 105: Teacher Preparation

Basic Principle   Nuclear processes are those in which the atomic nucleus changes, including radioactive decay of naturally occurring and artificial isotopes, nuclear fission, and nuclear fusion.

Competency   Students will calculate the energy released per gram of material in a nuclear reaction using the formula $E = mc^2$.

Procedure

1. Give students time to read the information on $E = mc^2$.
2. Review the CGS/MKS system for coupling the correct units of measure (i.e., grams used with centimeters, kilograms used with meters) so that students do not mix units of measure. In the *Observations & Analysis* question, the speed of light must be converted to centimeters if students choose to use grams instead of kilograms. The speed of light must be converted to meters per second if students decide to use kilograms in their calculations.
3. Give students time to complete the *Observations & Analysis* section.

Answers to Observations & Analysis

$$E \;=\; mc^2$$
$$\;=\; (1 \text{ kg}) \times (3 \times 10^8 \text{ m/s}) \times (3 \times 10^8 \text{ m/s})$$
$$\;=\; 9 \times 10^{16} \text{ kg} \bullet \text{m}^2/\text{s}^2$$
$$\;=\; 9 \times 10^{16} \text{ joules } (\div \ 1{,}000 \text{ grams in sample} = 9 \times 10^{13} \text{ joules/gram})$$

OR

$$E \;=\; mc^2$$
$$\;=\; (1 \times 10^3 \text{ g}) \times (3 \times 10^{10} \text{ cm/s}) \times (3 \times 10^{10} \text{ cm/s})$$
$$\;=\; 9 \times 10^{23} \text{ g} \bullet \text{cm}^2/\text{s}^2$$
$$\;=\; 9 \times 10^{23} \text{ ergs } (\div \ 1{,}000 \text{ grams in sample} = 9 \times 10^{20} \text{ ergs/gram})$$

Name _____ Date _____

Chemistry

STUDENT HANDOUT–LESSON 105

Basic Principle   Nuclear processes are those in which the atomic nucleus changes, including radioactive decay of naturally occurring and artificial isotopes, nuclear fission, and nuclear fusion.

Objective   Calculate the energy released per gram of material in a nuclear reaction using the formula $E = mc^2$.

Procedure

1. Read the information on $E = mc^2$.

$E = mc^2$

Albert Einstein's (1879–1955) famous formula, $E = mc^2$, illustrates the equivalency of matter and energy. According to Einstein's Special Theory of Relativity, from which the formula is derived, matter and energy are manifestations of the same physical phenomenon: Matter can be converted to energy and vice versa. The equation can be used to calculate the amount of energy released in *nuclear fission* and *fusion* reactions. The former occurs in nuclear reactors and with the detonation of an atomic bomb (i.e., the fission of uranium-235). The latter occurs in stars and with the detonation of a hydrogen bomb (i.e., fusion of hydrogen). In this equation, "E" is energy, in joules or ergs, "m" is mass in kilograms or grams, and "c" is the speed of light measured at 300,000 kilometers per second or 300,000,000 meters per second.

---

2. Complete the *Observations & Analysis* section.

Observations & Analysis

Calculate the energy that would be released from the total obliteration of a one-kilogram chunk of uranium-235. Assume that every atom of uranium is converted to pure energy.

Lesson 106: Teacher Preparation

Basic Principle   Nuclear processes are those in which the atomic nucleus changes, including radioactive decay of naturally occurring and artificial isotopes, nuclear fission, and nuclear fusion.

Competency   Students will identify naturally occurring isotopes of radioactive elements as well as those formed by nuclear reactions.

Procedure

1. Give students time to read the information on *Isotopes*.

2. Draw the illustrations and review the difference between nuclear fission and fusion. Explain that while radioactive isotopes exist naturally in nature, they usually make up an extremely small percentage of the more pervasive form of the same element. For example, the radioactive isotope carbon-14 makes up a miniscule percentage of the total amount of carbon, mostly carbon-12, in the environment. However, huge numbers of radioactive isotopes are created in artificial nuclear reaction, such as those that take place in nuclear reactors and with the detonation of nuclear weapons.

3. Give students time to complete the *Observations & Analysis* section.

Answers to Observations & Analysis

symbol	number of protons	number of neutrons	symbol	number of protons	number of neutrons
$_{1}H^{1}$	1	0	$_{1}H^{2}$	1	1
$_{3}Li^{7}$	3	4	$_{3}Li^{6}$	3	3
$_{6}C^{12}$	6	6	$_{6}C^{14}$	6	8
$_{8}O^{16}$	8	8	$_{8}O^{18}$	8	10
$_{26}Fe^{54}$	26	28	$_{26}Fe^{57}$	26	31
$_{50}Sn^{112}$	50	62	$_{50}Sn^{124}$	50	74
$_{56}Ba^{137}$	56	81	$_{56}Ba^{141}$	56	85
$_{36}Kr^{84}$	36	48	$_{36}Kr^{92}$	36	56
$_{84}Po^{210}$	84	126	$_{84}Po^{214}$	84	130
$_{92}U^{238}$	92	146	$_{92}U^{235}$	92	143

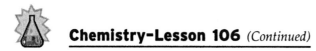

NUCLEAR FISSION

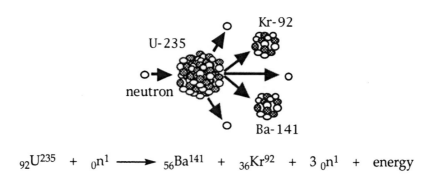

$$_{92}U^{235} \quad + \quad _0n^1 \quad \longrightarrow \quad _{56}Ba^{141} \quad + \quad _{36}Kr^{92} \quad + \quad 3\ _0n^1 \quad + \quad \text{energy}$$

NUCLEAR FUSION

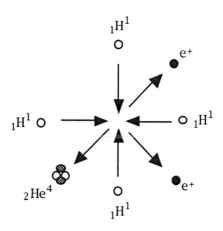

$$4\ _1H^1 \quad \longrightarrow \quad _2He^4 \quad + \quad 2\ e^+ \quad + \quad \text{energy (where } e^+ \text{ is a "positron")}$$

Chemistry

STUDENT HANDOUT–LESSON 106

Basic Principle   Nuclear processes are those in which the atomic nucleus changes, including radioactive decay of naturally occurring and artificial isotopes, nuclear fission, and nuclear fusion.

Objective   Identify naturally occurring isotopes of radioactive elements as well as those formed by nuclear reactions.

Procedure

1. Read the information on *Isotopes*.

Isotopes

In all chemical reactions, atoms of the same element react in exactly the same way. But not all atoms of the same chemical element are exactly alike. For example, some carbon atoms weigh more than other carbon atoms. While carbon nuclei all contain the same number of protons, they may contain different numbers of neutrons. Atoms with the same atomic number (i.e., number of protons) but differing atomic masses (i.e., different numbers of neutrons) are called *isotopes*. Most isotopes are radioactive. That is, they disintegrate, losing subatomic particles from their nucleus. Any radioactive isotope can be identified using a device called a *Geiger counter*. A Geiger counter, invented by the German physicist Hans Geiger (1882–1945) in 1908, can detect the presence of the charged subatomic particles emitted by an unstable nucleus. The rate at which atomic nuclei disintegrate is the same for atoms of the same element. Radioactive isotopes of the same element fall apart in the same amount of time. The time it takes for half of the atoms in an isotope to disintegrate is called the *half-life* of that isotope. Different isotopes have different half-lives. Below is a list of the half-lives of various radioactive isotopes.

RADIOACTIVE HALF-LIVES

tritium: 12.26 years
carbon-14: 5,730 years
oxygen-20: 14 seconds
potassium-40: 1,280,000,000 years
cobalt-60: 5.26 years
uranium-235: 710,000,000 years

Radioactive elements can exist naturally or can be created by nuclear fission and fusion reactions.

---

2. Study the handout before completing the *Observations & Analysis* section.

Observations & Analysis

Use the Periodic Table of Elements to determine the number of protons and neutrons in each isotope listed in the chart. **NOTE:** The atomic number in each symbol is written as a subscript to the lower left of each symbol. The atomic mass is written as a superscript to the upper right of each symbol.

symbol	number of protons	number of neutrons	symbol	number of protons	number of neutrons
$_1H^1$			$_1H^2$		
$_3Li^7$			$_3Li^6$		
$_6C^{12}$			$_6C^{14}$		
$_8O^{16}$			$_8O^{18}$		
$_{26}Fe^{54}$			$_{26}Fe^{57}$		
$_{50}Sn^{112}$			$_{50}Sn^{124}$		
$_{56}Ba^{137}$			$_{56}Ba^{141}$		
$_{36}Kr^{84}$			$_{36}Kr^{92}$		
$_{84}Po^{210}$			$_{84}Po^{214}$		
$_{92}U^{238}$			$_{92}U^{235}$		

Lesson 107: Teacher Preparation

Basic Principle   Nuclear processes are those in which the atomic nucleus changes, including radioactive decay of naturally occurring and artificial isotopes, nuclear fission, and nuclear fusion.

Competency   Students will identify the three most common forms of radioactive decay (alpha, beta, and gamma) and show how the nucleus changes with each type of decay.

Procedure

1. Give students time to read the information on *Radioactive Decay*.
2. Point out that the discovery of radioactivity was accidental. In 1896, the French physicist Henri Becquerel (1852–1908) wrapped a piece of uranium ore in dark paper and left it in a closed drawer with some photographic film. Upon developing the film, he discovered blurry images on his photographs indicating that the film had been exposed to light. After further investigation, Becquerel concluded that the "light" was being emitted by the uranium ore. In 1898, the Polish-born physicist Manya Sklodowska (a.k.a. Marie Curie, 1867–1934) discovered two new radioactive ores: polonium and radium. She shared the Nobel Prize in Physics for these discoveries with her husband, the French physicist Pierre Curie (1859–1906) in 1903. The English physicist Ernst Rutherford (1871–1937) identified alpha and beta particles during his research on the structure of the atomic nucleus. And, the German-born American physicist Albert Einstein (1879–1955) determined the amount of energy that can be released by atomic particles when they are transmuted to pure energy. Einstein's work led the Italian-born American physicist Enrico Fermi (1901–1954) to invent the first atomic reactor in Chicago in 1942. Fermi's success was a prelude to the building of the atomic bomb, a program code-named The Manhattan Project and coordinated by the American physicist Robert Oppenheimer (1904–1967).
3. Assist students in completing the *Observations & Analysis* section.

Answers to Observations & Analysis

1. $_1n^0$ (a neutron)
2. $_{86}Rn^{222}$
3. $_{84}Po^{214}$
4. $_7N^{14}$
5. $_{90}Th^{234}$
6. $_{86}Rn^{222}$ (no change)

Name _____ **Date** _____

Chemistry

STUDENT HANDOUT–LESSON 107

Basic Principle   Nuclear processes are those in which the atomic nucleus changes, including radioactive decay of naturally occurring and artificial isotopes, nuclear fission, and nuclear fusion.

Objective   Identify the three most common forms of radioactive decay (alpha, beta, and gamma) and show how the nucleus changes with each type of decay.

Procedure

1. Read the information on *Radioactive Decay*.

Radioactive Decay

The disintegration of atomic nuclei is called *radioactivity*. There are three basic kinds of radioactivity: *alpha particles*, *beta particles*, and *gamma rays*. Alpha particles are composed of two protons and two neutrons and cannot be distinguished from the nuclei of helium atoms. Alpha particles are expelled from the atomic nuclei of large atoms like uranium, which are highly unstable even in their natural state. Losing an alpha particle changes the uranium atom to a thorium atom with two fewer protons and a mass that is reduced by four. The nuclei of other atoms give off beta particles that have the same mass and charge as negatively charged electrons. A nucleus that gives off a beta particle increases the atom's atomic number by one, which changes the atom to that of another element. This is the result of a neutron being transformed into a proton inside the nucleus. During beta decay, the change in the atom's mass is negligible (i.e., the mass of an electron is 1/1870th of a proton). Gamma decay involves the emission of a highly energic (i.e., high frequency) photon from the nucleus. Gamma decay changes neither the atomic number nor atomic mass of the atom.

---

2. Complete the *Observations & Analysis* section.

Student Handout–Lesson 107 *(Continued)*

Observations & Analysis

Refer to the Periodic Table of Elements to show the missing product of each nuclear equation.

1. p^+ + beta particle $\longrightarrow$ _____

2. $_{88}Ra^{226} \longrightarrow$ alpha particle + _____

3. $_{83}Bi^{214} \longrightarrow$ beta particle + _____

4. $_{6}C^{14} \longrightarrow$ beta particle + _____

5. $_{92}U^{238} \longrightarrow$ alpha particle + _____

6. $_{86}Rn^{222} \longrightarrow$ gamma ray + _____

THE PERIODIC TABLE OF ELEMENTS

	atomic number
6	chemical symbol
C	
(12)	atomic mass

PHYSICAL PROPERTIES

Families 1-2 are light metals.
Families 3-7 are brittle.
Families 8-11 are ductile.
Family 12 is low boiling.
Families 13-17 are nonmetals.
Family 18 is inert.

	alkali metals IA (1)	alkaline metals IIA (2)	IIIA (3)	IVA (4)	VA (5)	VIA (6)	VIIA (7)	VIIIA (8)	(9)	(10)	IB (11)	IIB (12)	IIIB (13)	IVB (14)	VB (15)	VIB (16)	halogens VIIB (17)	noble gases VIIIB (18)
1	1 H 1																	2 He (4)
2	3 Li (7)	4 Be (9)											5 B (11)	6 C (12)	7 N (14)	8 O (16)	9 F (19)	10 Ne (20)
3	11 Na (23)	12 Mg (24)											13 Al (27)	14 Si (28)	15 P (31)	16 S (32)	17 Cl (35)	18 Ar (40)
4	19 K (39)	20 Ca (40)	21 Sc (45)	22 Ti (48)	23 V (51)	24 Cr (52)	25 Mn (55)	26 Fe (56)	27 Co (59)	28 Ni (59)	29 Cu (63)	30 Zn (65)	31 Ga (70)	32 Ge (73)	33 As (75)	34 Se (79)	35 Br (80)	36 Kr (84)
5	37 Rb (85)	38 Sr (88)	39 Y (89)	40 Zr (91)	41 Nb (93)	42 Mo (96)	43 Tc (97)	44 Ru (101)	45 Rh (103)	46 Pd (106)	47 Ag (108)	48 Cd (112)	49 In (114)	50 Sn (119)	51 Sb (122)	52 Te (128)	53 I (127)	54 Xe (131)
6	55 Cs (133)	56 Ba (137)	"L" series	72 Hf (178)	73 Ta (181)	74 W (184)	75 Re (186)	76 Os (190)	77 Ir (192)	78 Pt (195)	79 Au (197)	80 Hg (201)	81 Tl (204)	82 Pb (207)	83 Bi (209)	84 Po (210)	85 At (210)	86 Rn (222)
7	87 Fr (223)	88 Ra (226)	"A" series	104 Ku (251)	105 Ha (260)													

"L" or Lanthanide Series

57 La (139)	58 Ce (140)	59 Pr (141)	60 Nd (144)	61 Pm (145)	62 Sm (150)	63 Eu (152)	64 Gd (157)	65 Tb (159)	66 Dy (163)	67 Ho (165)	68 Er (167)	69 Tm (169)	70 Yb (173)	71 Lu (175)

"A" or Actinide Series

89 Ac (227)	90 Th (232)	91 Pa (231)	92 U (238)	93 Np (237)	94 Pu (242)	95 Am (243)	96 Cm (247)	97 Bk (249)	98 Cf (251)	99 Es (254)	100 Fm (257)	101 Md (256)	102 No (254)	103 Lr (257)

* The **atomic number** is equal to the number of protons in the nucleus of an atom.
* The **atomic mass** is equal to the total number of protons and neutrons in the nucleus of an atom.
* The **atomic mass** is the mass in grams of 6×10^{23} atoms of an element.

actinium: Ac
aluminum: Al
americium: Am
antimony: Sb
argon: Ar
arsenic: As
astatine: At
barium: Ba
berkyllium: Bk
beryllium: Be
bismuth: Bi

boron: B
bromium: Br
cadmium: Cd
calcium: Ca
californium: Cf
carbon: C
cerium: Ce
cesium: Cs
chlorine: Cl
chromium: Cr
cobalt: Co

copper: Cu
curium: Cm
dysprosium: Dy
ensteinium: Es
erbium: Er
europium: Eu
fermium: Fm
fluorine: F
francium: Fr
gadolinium: Gd
gallium: Ga

germanium: Ge
gold: Au
hahnium: Ha
hafnium: Hf
helium: He
holmium: Ho
hydrogen: H
indium: In
iodine: I
iridium: Ir
iron: Fe

krypton: Kr
kurchatovium: Ku
lanthanium: La
lawrencium: Lr
lead: Pb
lithium: Li
lutetium: Lu
magnesium: Mg
manganese: Mn
mendelevium: Md
mercury: Hg

molybdenum: Mo
neodymium: Nd
neon: Ne
neptunium: Np
nickel: Ni
niobium: Nb
nitrogen: N
nobelium: No
osmium: Os
oxygen: O
palladium: Pd

phosphorus: P
platinum: Pt
plutonium: Pu
polonium: Po
potassium: K
praseodymium: Pr
promethium: Pm
protactinium: Pa
radium: Ra
radon: Rn
rhenium: Re

rhodium: Rh
rubidium: Rb
ruthenium: Ru
samarium: Sm
scandium: Sc
selenium: Se
silicon: Si
silver: Ag
sodium: Na
strontium: Sr
sulfur: S

tantalium: Ta
technetium: Tc
tellurium: Te
terbium: Tb
thallium: Tl
thorium: Th
thulium: Tm
tin: Sn
titanium: Ti
tungsten: W
uranium: U

vanadium: V
xenon: Xe
ytterbium: Yb
yttrium: Y
zinc: Zn
zirconium: Zr

TENTH-GRADE LEVEL

Chemistry

PRACTICE TEST

Chemistry

PRACTICE TEST

General Directions: Use the Periodic Table of Elements to assist you in answering these questions.

Directions: Use the Answer Sheet to darken the letter of the choice that best answers each question.

1. How is the position of an element on the Periodic Table related to its atomic number and mass?

   (A) Atomic mass and number increase down and to the right.

   (B) Atomic mass and number increase up and to the left.

   (C) Atomic mass and number decrease down and to the right.

   (D) Atomic mass and number decrease from right to left.

2. Which of the following can be used to assess the position and reactivity of an element on the Periodic Table?

   (A) valence number

   (B) atomic number

   (C) atomic mass

   (D) period number

3. Which of the following chemical families contain mostly metals?

   (A) 1, 2, and 3

   (B) 12, 13, and 14

   (C) 15, 16, and 17

   (D) 16, 17, and 18

4. Which of the following chemical families contain metalloids?

   (A) 1 and 2

   (B) 7 and 8

   (C) 14 and 15

   (D) 17 and 18

5. Which of the following chemical families contain mostly nonmetals?

   (A) 1 and 2

   (B) 7 and 8

   (C) 14 and 15

   (D) 17 and 18

6. Which chemical family contains halogens?

   (A) 1

   (B) 6

   (C) 12

   (D) 17

7. Which family of elements reacts most violently with water and halogens?

   (A) alkali metals

   (B) alkaline earth metals

   (C) transition metals

   (D) noble gases

8. Which family of elements reacts with halogens to form ionic compounds with the following general chemical formula: AB_2?

   (A) alkali metals

   (B) alkaline earth metals

   (C) transition metals

   (D) noble gases

9. How is the position of an element on the Periodic Table related to its electronegativity?

   (A) Electronegativity increases down and to the right.

   (B) Electronegativity increases up and to the right.

   (C) Electronegativity increases down and to the left.

   (D) Electronegativity increases up and to the left.

10. Which model of the atom was used to explain evidence suggesting that the atomic nucleus is much smaller in size than the atom as a whole?

   (A) Dalton's Model

   (B) Thomson's Model

   (C) Rutherford's Model

   (D) Bohr's model

11. Which fundamental force governs the behavior of atoms during chemical reactions?

   (A) strong force

   (B) electromagnetism

   (C) weak force

   (D) gravity

12. How do atoms form ions?

   (A) They lose electrons.

   (B) They gain electrons.

   (C) They share electrons.

   (D) both A and B

13. How do atoms form covalent bonds?

   (A) They lose electrons.

   (B) They gain electrons.

   (C) They share electrons.

   (D) both A and B

14. Which of the following compounds is most probably held together by an ionic bond?

   (A) H_2O

   (B) $C_6H_{12}O_6$

   (C) LiBr

   (D) SiO_2

15. Which of the following compounds is most probably held together by one or more covalent bonds?

   (A) NaCl

   (B) $Mg(OH)_2$

   (C) C_2H_5OH

   (D) RbF

16. Which of the following family of elements is most able to form large molecules held together by covalent bonds?

   (A) 2

   (B) 4

   (C) 6

   (D) 8

17. Which of the following forces is responsible for the stability of an ionic crystal such as NaCl?

    (A) covalent bonding between atoms

    (B) covalent bonding between molecules

    (C) electrostatic attraction between ions

    (D) van der Waal's forces

18. Which of the following best explains how solids differ from liquids and liquids differ from gases?

    (A) Special Theory of Relativity

    (B) Law of Conservation of Matter and Energy

    (C) Atomic-Molecular Theory

    (D) Law of Gravity

19. Which of the following is the correct electron-dot structure of a neutral sodium atom?

    (A) Na•

    (B) •Na•

    (C) $\vdots$Na•

    (D) $\vdots$Na$\vdots$

20. What happens when a scientist captures all of the products of a chemical reaction?

    (A) The products always have less calories than the reactants.

    (B) The products always have more calories than the reactants.

    (C) The products sometimes have the same mass as the reactants.

    (D) The products always have the same mass as the reactants.

21. Which of the following is a balanced chemical equation?

    (A) $HCl + NaOH \longrightarrow NaCl + 2H_2O$

    (B) $2HNO_3 + NaOH \longrightarrow NaNO_3 + H_2O$

    (C) $H_2SO_4 + NH_4OH \longrightarrow (NH_4)_2SO_4 + H_2O$

    (D) $H_2CO_3 + 2RbOH \longrightarrow Rb_2CO_3 + 2H_2O$

22. Which of the following best summarizes the concept of a "mole"?

    (A) smallest part of a molecule

    (B) number of molecules or reactants needed to start a chemical reaction

    (C) number of molecules of products produced in a chemical reaction

    (D) Avogadro's number of atoms or molecules of vaporized substance in one liter of volume

23. What is the mass of one mole of H_2SO_4?

    (A) 7 grams

    (B) 9 grams

    (C) 78 grams

    (D) 98 grams

24. How many moles of water are present in 54 grams of water?

    (A) 1

    (B) 2

    (C) 3

    (D) 4

25. A chemist combined 45 grams of NaOH with 36 grams of HCl. How many grams of NaCl remained unreacted?

    (A) none

    (B) 5

    (C) 10

    (D) 15

26. How many grams of sugar will be produced in the photosynthetic reaction of 84 grams of CO_2 and 54 grams of H_2O?

    (A) 45 grams

    (B) 90 grams

    (C) 180 grams

    (D) 360 grams

27. Which of the following explains the observable pressure created by a gas on a surface?

    (A) the random motion of the molecules comprising the surface

    (B) the Earth's gravitational attraction for the gas molecules

    (C) the random molecular motion of gas molecules in collision with the surface

    (D) the chemical properties of the gas

28. Which phenomenon best describes the fact that a room will smell of perfume minutes after a bottle of perfume is opened?

    (A) osmosis

    (B) diffusion

    (C) conduction

    (D) catalysis

29. Which principle summarizes the observation that a gas at constant temperature will increase in pressure if its volume decreases?

    (A) Boyle's Law

    (B) Charles's Law

    (C) Gay-Lussac's Law

    (D) Le Chatelier's Principle

30. Which of the following explains why chemists use standard temperatures and pressures when conducting chemical reactions?

    (A) Chemical reactions are temperature dependent.

    (B) Chemical reactions are neither temperature nor pressure dependent.

    (C) Chemical reactions can only occur at standard temperature and pressure.

    (D) Chemical reactions are irreversible at standard temperature and pressure.

31. What is the theoretical temperature at which molecules cease to move?

    (A) standard temperature

    (B) ambient temperature

    (C) relative temperature

    (D) absolute zero

32. Which of the following is equal to absolute zero?

    (A) –273°C

    (B) –273°F

    (C) –273 K

    (D) –273 J

33. Which of the following is equal to 10°C?

    (A) 50°F

    (B) 50 K

    (C) 100°C

    (D) 100 K

34. Which of the following is equal to 41°F?

    (A) 5°C

    (B) 5 K

    (C) 20°C

    (D) 20 K

35. Which of the following is equal to 373 K?

    (A) 100°C

    (B) 212°F

    (C) both A and B

    (D) neither A nor B

36. Which of the following describes a property of acids?

    (A) Acids react with metals to produce hydrogen.

    (B) Acids taste bitter.

    (C) Acids do not conduct electricity in solution.

    (D) Acids turn litmus blue.

37. Which of the following best describes a property of bases?

    (A) Bases react with metals to produce oxygen.

    (B) Bases taste sour.

    (C) Bases do not conduct electricity in solution.

    (D) Bases turn litmus blue.

38. Which of the following best describes a property of a salt?

    (A) Salts react with metals to produce halogens.

    (B) Salts have no taste.

    (C) Salts conduct electricity in solution.

    (D) Salts turn litmus blue.

39. How do chemists conceive of an acid in solution?

    (A) Acids are hydrogen-ion-donating molecules.

    (B) Acids are hydrogen-ion-accepting molecules.

    (C) Acids are poorly dissociating ionic compounds.

    (D) Acids are polyatomic ions.

40. How do chemists conceive of a base in solution?

    (A) Bases are hydrogen-ion-donating molecules.

    (B) Bases are hydrogen-ion-accepting molecules.

    (C) Bases are poorly dissociating ionic compounds.

    (D) Bases are polyatomic ions.

41. Which of the following is true of all strong acids?

    (A) They dissociate poorly in solution.

    (B) They dissociate well in solution.

    (C) They do not dissociate.

    (D) They readily form covalent bonds with molecules of solvent.

42. Which pH indicates a strong acid in solution?

    (A) pH = 3

    (B) pH = 5

    (C) pH = 7

    (D) pH = 9

43. Which pH indicates a strong base in solution?

    (A) pH = 5

    (B) pH = 7

    (C) pH = 9

    (D) pH = 11

44. Which pH indicates a salt in solution?

    (A) pH = 6

    (B) pH = 7

    (C) pH = 8

    (D) pH = 9

45. Which of the following best describes a solute?

    (A) a substance mixed with water

    (B) water

    (C) a low boiling liquid

    (D) a low melting metal

46. Which of the following best describes a solvent?

    (A) a substance mixed with water

    (B) water

    (C) a low boiling liquid

    (D) a low melting metal

47. How would a chemist express the concentration in grams per liter of 58 grams of NaCl in 500 mL of water?

    (A) 29 grams/liter

    (B) 58 grams/liter

    (C) 97 grams/liter

    (D) 116 grams/liter

48. How would a chemist express the molarity (M) of 58 grams of NaCl in 500 mL of water?

    (A) 0.5 M

    (B) 1.0 M

    (C) 1.5 M

    (D) 2.0 M

49. How would a chemist express the percent composition of 36 grams of HCl dissolved in 64 mL of water?

    (A) 18%

    (B) 36%

    (C) 56%

    (D) 100%

50. Which of the following describes heat flow through a solid?

    (A) conduction

    (B) convection

    (C) radiation

    (D) dissolution

51. Which of the following describes heat flow through a liquid or gas?

    (A) conduction

    (B) convection

    (C) radiation

    (D) dissolution

52. Which of the following describes heat flow through a vacuum?

    (A) conduction

    (B) convection

    (C) radiation

    (D) dissolution

53. Which of the following best describes an endothermic reaction?

    (A) The calorie content of the products is greater than that of the reactants.

    (B) The calorie content of the products is less than that of the reactants.

    (C) The products are the result of the creation of matter.

    (D) The products are the result of the destruction of matter.

54. Which of the following best describes an exothermic reaction?

    (A) The calorie content of the products is greater than that of the reactants.

    (B) The calorie content of the products is less than that of the reactants.

    (C) The products are the result of the creation of matter.

    (D) The products are the result of the destruction of matter.

Directions: Use the graph to answer questions 55, 56, and 57.

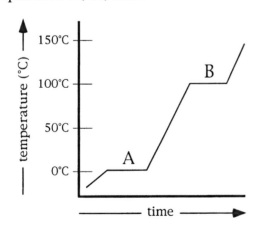

55. What is probably happening to this substance at point A?

    (A) It is freezing.

    (B) It is melting.

    (C) It is vaporizing.

    (D) It is condensing.

56. What is probably happening to this substance at point B?

    (A) It is freezing.

    (B) It is melting.

    (C) It is vaporizing.

    (D) It is condensing.

57. Which of the following substances behaves like the sample shown in the graph?

    (A) hydrogen gas

    (B) liquid helium

    (C) frozen methane

    (D) water

58. Five grams of an unknown metal requires 0.5 calorie of heat to warm it 2°C. What is the specific heat of the metal?

    (A) 0.05

    (B) 0.10

    (C) 0.15

    (D) 0.20

Directions: Refer to the graphs to answer questions 59, 60, and 61.

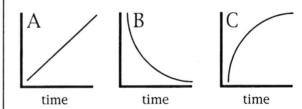

59. Which graph shows a change over time in the concentration of reactants in a chemical reaction: A, B, or C?

60. Which graph shows a change over time in the concentration of products in a chemical reaction: A, B, or C?

61. Which graph shows the reaction rate of a typical chemical reaction over time: A, B, or C?

62. What would happen to the concentration of molecular hydrogen in the following chemical reaction if the ambient temperature decreased?

$$2H_2 + O_2 \longrightarrow 2H_2O$$

(A) It would increase more rapidly.

(B) It would decrease more rapidly.

(C) It would remain constant.

(D) It would increase, then decrease.

63. What would happen to the concentration of molecular hydrogen in the following chemical reaction if the ambient pressure increased?

$$2H_2 + O_2 \longrightarrow 2H_2O$$

(A) It would increase more rapidly.

(B) It would decrease more rapidly.

(C) It would remain constant.

(D) It would increase, then decrease.

64. What would happen to the concentration of molecular hydrogen in the following chemical reaction if the concentration of molecular oxygen increased?

$$2H_2 + O_2 \longrightarrow 2H_2O$$

(A) It would increase more rapidly.

(B) It would decrease more rapidly.

(C) It would remain constant.

(D) It would increase, then decrease.

65. What would happen to the concentration of molecular hydrogen in the following chemical reaction if a platinum catalyst were added to the reaction?

$$2H_2 + O_2 \longrightarrow 2H_2O$$

(A) It would increase more rapidly.

(B) It would decrease more rapidly.

(C) It would remain constant.

(D) It would increase, then decrease.

66. Which best describes a chemical reaction in equilibrium?

(A) The molarity of the reactants equals the molarity of the products.

(B) The heat content of the reactants is equal to the heat content of the products.

(C) Activation energy is not required to produce the products of the reaction.

(D) The forward and reverse reaction rates are equal.

67. Predict the effect of an increase in temperature on a chemical reaction in equilibrium.

(A) The reaction will stop.

(B) The reaction will move to minimize the effect of the change.

(C) The reaction will move to maximize the production of products.

(D) The reaction will move to maximize the production of reactants.

68. Which of the following processes best describes the formation of proteins?

    (A) polymerization

    (B) neutralization

    (C) decomposition

    (D) replacement

69. Which of the following biochemical subunits comprises a protein?

    (A) saccharide

    (B) amino acid

    (C) fatty acid

    (D) nucleotide

70. Which of the following biochemical subunits comprises a carbohydrate?

    (A) saccharide

    (B) amino acid

    (C) fatty acid

    (D) nucleotide

71. Which of the following biochemical subunits comprises a lipid?

    (A) saccharide

    (B) amino acid

    (C) fatty acid

    (D) nucleotide

72. Which of the following biochemical subunits comprises a nucleic acid?

    (A) saccharide

    (B) amino acid

    (C) fatty acid

    (D) nucleotide

73. Which force holds the nucleus of an atom together?

    (A) strong force

    (B) weak force

    (C) electromagnetic force

    (D) gravity

74. Which of the following best describes an alpha particle?

    (A) nucleus of a helium atom

    (B) electron

    (C) photon

    (D) gluon

75. Which of the following best describes a beta particle?

    (A) nucleus of a helium atom

    (B) electron

    (C) photon

    (D) gluon

76. Which of the following best describes a gamma ray?

    (A) nucleus of a helium atom

    (B) electron

    (C) photon

    (D) gluon

77. Which best describes what happens to the nucleus of an atom when it loses an alpha particle?

    (A) The atomic number of the nucleus is reduced by 2 while its mass is reduced by 4.

    (B) The atomic number of the nucleus is increased by 1 while its mass remains unchanged.

    (C) The atomic number and mass remain unchanged.

    (D) The atomic number is reduced by 1 while its mass is increased by 1.

78. Which of the following allowed scientists to derive the amount of energy released during a nuclear reaction?

    (A) Special Theory of Relativity

    (B) Uncertainty Principle

    (C) Kinetic-Molecular Theory

    (D) Maxwell's Equations

79. Which of the following best describes an isotope?

    (A) atoms with the same number of protons and neutrons

    (B) atoms with the same number of protons and a greater number of neutrons

    (C) atoms with the same number of protons and a different number of neutrons

    (D) atoms with a different number of protons and the same number of neutrons

80. Which of the following would be the product of a nuclear reaction in which an alpha particle is emitted from an atom of uranium-238?

    (A) $_{92}U^{234}$

    (B) $_{93}Np^{237}$

    (C) $_{90}Th^{234}$

    (D) The uranium-238 would remain unchanged.

Chemistry

PRACTICE TEST: ANSWER SHEET

Name _____   Date _____   Period _____

Darken the circle above the letter that best answers the question.

#	A B C D	#	A B C D	#	A B C D	#	A B C D
1.	○ ○ ○ ○	21.	○ ○ ○ ○	41.	○ ○ ○ ○	61.	○ ○ ○ ○
2.	○ ○ ○ ○	22.	○ ○ ○ ○	42.	○ ○ ○ ○	62.	○ ○ ○ ○
3.	○ ○ ○ ○	23.	○ ○ ○ ○	43.	○ ○ ○ ○	63.	○ ○ ○ ○
4.	○ ○ ○ ○	24.	○ ○ ○ ○	44.	○ ○ ○ ○	64.	○ ○ ○ ○
5.	○ ○ ○ ○	25.	○ ○ ○ ○	45.	○ ○ ○ ○	65.	○ ○ ○ ○
6.	○ ○ ○ ○	26.	○ ○ ○ ○	46.	○ ○ ○ ○	66.	○ ○ ○ ○
7.	○ ○ ○ ○	27.	○ ○ ○ ○	47.	○ ○ ○ ○	67.	○ ○ ○ ○
8.	○ ○ ○ ○	28.	○ ○ ○ ○	48.	○ ○ ○ ○	68.	○ ○ ○ ○
9.	○ ○ ○ ○	29.	○ ○ ○ ○	49.	○ ○ ○ ○	69.	○ ○ ○ ○
10.	○ ○ ○ ○	30.	○ ○ ○ ○	50.	○ ○ ○ ○	70.	○ ○ ○ ○
11.	○ ○ ○ ○	31.	○ ○ ○ ○	51.	○ ○ ○ ○	71.	○ ○ ○ ○
12.	○ ○ ○ ○	32.	○ ○ ○ ○	52.	○ ○ ○ ○	72.	○ ○ ○ ○
13.	○ ○ ○ ○	33.	○ ○ ○ ○	53.	○ ○ ○ ○	73.	○ ○ ○ ○
14.	○ ○ ○ ○	34.	○ ○ ○ ○	54.	○ ○ ○ ○	74.	○ ○ ○ ○
15.	○ ○ ○ ○	35.	○ ○ ○ ○	55.	○ ○ ○ ○	75.	○ ○ ○ ○
16.	○ ○ ○ ○	36.	○ ○ ○ ○	56.	○ ○ ○ ○	76.	○ ○ ○ ○
17.	○ ○ ○ ○	37.	○ ○ ○ ○	57.	○ ○ ○ ○	77.	○ ○ ○ ○
18.	○ ○ ○ ○	38.	○ ○ ○ ○	58.	○ ○ ○ ○	78.	○ ○ ○ ○
19.	○ ○ ○ ○	39.	○ ○ ○ ○	59.	○ ○ ○ ○	79.	○ ○ ○ ○
20.	○ ○ ○ ○	40.	○ ○ ○ ○	60.	○ ○ ○ ○	80.	○ ○ ○ ○

Chemistry

KEY TO PRACTICE TEST

#	Ans	#	Ans	#	Ans	#	Ans
1.	A	21.	D	41.	B	61.	B
2.	A	22.	D	42.	A	62.	B
3.	A	23.	D	43.	D	63.	B
4.	C	24.	C	44.	B	64.	B
5.	D	25.	B	45.	A	65.	B
6.	D	26.	B	46.	B	66.	D
7.	A	27.	C	47.	D	67.	B
8.	B	28.	B	48.	D	68.	A
9.	B	29.	A	49.	B	69.	B
10.	C	30.	A	50.	A	70.	A
11.	B	31.	D	51.	B	71.	C
12.	D	32.	A	52.	C	72.	D
13.	C	33.	A	53.	A	73.	A
14.	C	34.	A	54.	B	74.	A
15.	C	35.	C	55.	B	75.	B
16.	B	36.	A	56.	C	76.	C
17.	C	37.	D	57.	D	77.	A
18.	C	38.	C	58.	A	78.	A
19.	A	39.	A	59.	B	79.	C
20.	D	40.	B	60.	C	80.	C

Appendix

Preparing Your Students for Standardized Proficiency Tests

Even as the debate over the value and fairness of standardized tests continues, standardized tests are an annual event for millions of students. In most school districts the results of the tests are vitally important. Scores may be used to determine if students are meeting district or state guidelines, they may be used as a means of comparing the scores of the district's students to local or national norms, or they may be used to decide a student's placement in advanced or remedial classes. No matter how individual scores are used in your school, students deserve the chance to do well. They deserve to be prepared.

By providing students with practice in answering the kinds of questions they will face on a standardized test, an effective program of preparation can familiarize students with testing formats, refresh skills, build confidence, and reduce anxiety, all critical factors that can affect scores as much as basic knowledge. Just like the members of an orchestra rehearse to get ready for a concert, the dancer trains for the big show, and the pianist practices for weeks before the grand recital, preparing students for standardized tests is essential.

To be most effective a test-preparation program should be comprehensive, based on skills your students need to know, and enlist the support of parents. Because students often assume the attitudes of their parents regarding tests—for example, nervous parents frequently make their children anxious—you should seek as much parental involvement in your test preparations as possible. Students who are encouraged by their parents and prepared for tests by their teachers invariably do better than those who come to the testing session with little preparation and support.

WHAT PARENTS NEED TO KNOW ABOUT STANDARDIZED TESTS

While most parents will agree it is important for their children to do well on standardized tests, many feel there is little they can do to help the outcome. Consequently, aside from encouraging their children to "try your best," they feel there is nothing more for them to do. Much of this feeling arises from parents not fully understanding the testing process.

To provide the parents of your students with information about testing, consider sending home copies of the following reproducibles:

- The Uses of Standardized Tests
- Test Terms
- Common Types of Standardized Tests
- Preparing Your Child for Standardized Tests

You may wish to send these home in a packet with a cover letter (a sample of which is included) announcing the upcoming standardized tests.

THE USES OF STANDARDIZED TESTS

Schools administer standardized tests for a variety of purposes. It is likely that your child's school utilizes the scores of standardized tests in at least some of the following ways.

- Identify strengths and weaknesses in academic skills.

- Identify areas of high interest, ability, or aptitude. Likewise identify areas of average or low ability or aptitude.

- Compare the scores of students within the district to each other as well as to students of other districts. This can be done class to class, school to school, or district to district. Such comparisons help school systems to evaluate their curriculums and plan instruction and programs.

- Provide a basis for comparison of report card grades to national standards.

- Identify students who might benefit from advanced or remedial classes.

- Certify student achievement, for example, in regard to receiving awards.

- Provide reports on student progress.

TEST TERMS

Although standardized tests come in different forms and may be designed to measure different skills, most share many common terms. Understanding these "test terms" is the first step to understanding the tests.

- *Achievement tests* measure how much students have learned in a particular subject area. They concentrate on knowledge of subject matter.

- *Aptitude tests* are designed to predict how well students will do in learning new subject matter in the future. They generally measure a broad range of skills associated with success. Note that the line between aptitude and achievement tests is often indistinct.

- *Battery* refers to a group of tests that are administered during the same testing session. For example, separate tests for vocabulary, language, reading, spelling, and mathematics that comprise an achievement test are known as the *test battery*.

- *Correlation coefficient* is a measure of the strength and direction of the relationship between two items. It can be a positive or negative number.

- *Diagnostic tests* are designed to identify the strengths and weaknesses of students in specific subject areas. They are usually given only to students who show exceptional ability or serious weakness in an area.

- *Grade equivalent scores* are a translation of the score attained on the test to an approximate grade level. Thus, a student whose score translates to a grade level of 4.5 is working at roughly the midyear point of fourth grade. One whose score equals a grade level of 8.0 is able to successfully complete work typically given at the beginning of eighth grade.

- *Individual student profiles* (also referred to as *reports*) display detailed test results for a particular student. Some of these can be so precise that the answer to every question is shown.

- *Item* is a specific question on a test.

- *Mean* is the average of a group of scores.

- *Median* is the middle score in a group of scores.

- *Mode* is the score achieved most by a specific group of test takers.

- *Normal distribution* is a distribution of test scores in which the scores are distributed around the mean and where the mean, median, and mode are the same. A normal distribution, when displayed, appears bell-shaped.

- *Norming population* is the group of students (usually quite large) to whom the test was given and on whose results performance standards for various age or grade levels are based. *Local norms* refer to distributions based on a particular school or school district. *National norms* refer to distributions based on students from around the country.

• *Norm-referenced tests* are tests in which the results of the test may be compared with other norming populations.

• *Percentile rank* is a comparison of a student's raw score with the raw scores of others who took the test. The comparison is most often made with members of the norming population. Percentile rank enables a test taker to see where his or her scores rank among others who take the same test. A percentile rank of 90, for example, means that the test taker scored better than 90% of those who took the test. A percentile rank of 60 means the test taker scored better than 60% of those who took the test. A percentile rank of 30 means he or she scored better than only 30% of those who took the test, and that 70% of the test takers had higher scores.

• *Raw score* is the score of a test based on the number correct. On some tests the raw score may include a correction for guessing.

• *Reliability* is a measure of the degree to which a test measures what it is designed to measure. A test's reliability may be expressed as a reliability coefficient that typically ranges from 0 to 1. Highly reliable tests have reliability coefficients of 0.90 or higher. Reliability coefficients may take several forms. For example, parallel-form reliability correlates the performance on two different forms of a test; split-half reliability correlates two halves of the same test; and test-retest reliability correlates test scores of the same test given at two different times. The producers of standardized tests strive to make them as reliable as possible. Although there are always cases of bright students not doing well on a standardized test and some students who do surprisingly well, most tests are quite reliable and provide accurate results.

• *Score* is the number of correct answers displayed in some form. Sometimes the score is expressed as a *scaled score,* which means that the score provided by the test is derived from the number of correct answers.

• *Standard deviation* is a measure of the variability of test scores. If most scores are near the mean score, the standard deviation will be small; if scores vary widely from the mean, the standard deviation will be large.

• *Standard error of measurement* is an estimate of the amount of possible measurement error in a test. It provides an estimate of how much a student's true test score may vary from the actual score he or she obtained on the test. Tests that have a large standard error of measurement may not accurately reflect a student's true ability. The standard error of measurement is usually small for well-designed tests.

- *Standardized tests* are tests that have been given to students under the same conditions. They are designed to measure the same skills and abilities for everyone who takes them.

- *Stanine scores* are scores expressed between the numbers 1 and 9 with 9 being high.

- *Validity* is the degree to which a test measures what it is supposed to measure. There are different kinds of validity. One, content validity, for example, refers to the degree to which the content of the test is valid for the purpose of the test. Another, predictive validity, refers to the extent to which predictions based on the test are later proven accurate by other evidence.

COMMON TYPES OF STANDARDIZED TESTS

Most standardized tests are broken down into major sections that focus on specific subjects. Together these sections are referred to as a *battery*. The materials and skills tested are based on grade level. The following tests are common throughout the country; however, not all schools administer every test.

- *Analogy tests* measure a student's ability to understand relationships between words (ideas). Here is an example: Boy is to man as girl is to woman. The relationship, of course, is that a boy becomes a man and a girl becomes a woman. Not only does an analogy test the ability to recognize relationships, it tests vocabulary as well.

- *Vocabulary tests* determine whether students understand the meaning of certain words. They are most often based on the student's projected grade-level reading, comprehension, and spelling skills.

- *Reading comprehension tests* show how well students can understand reading passages. These tests appear in many different formats. In most, students are required to read a passage and then answer questions designed to measure reading ability.

- *Spelling tests* show spelling competence, based on grade-level appropriate words. The tests may require students to select a correctly spelled word from among misspelled words, or may require students to find the misspelled word among correctly spelled words.

- *Language mechanics tests* concentrate on capitalization and punctuation. Students may be required to find examples of incorrect capitalization and punctuation as well as examples of correct capitalization and punctuation in sentences and short paragraphs.

- *Language expression tests* focus on the ability of students to use words correctly according to the standards of conventional English. In many "expression" tests, effective structuring of ideas is also tested.

- *Writing tests* determine how effectively students write and can express their ideas. Usually a topic is given and students must express their ideas on the topic.

Common Types of Standardized Tests *(Continued)*

- *Mathematics problem-solving tests* are based on concepts and applications, and assess the ability of students to solve math problems. These tests often include sections on number theory, interpretation of data and graphs, and logical analysis.

- *Mathematics computation tests* measure how well students can add, subtract, multiply, and divide. While the difficulty of the material depends on grade level, these tests generally cover whole numbers, fractions, decimals, percents, and geometry.

- *Science tests* measure students' understanding of basic science facts and the methodology used by scientists in the development of theoretical models that explain natural phenomena.

- *Social studies tests* measure students' understanding of basic facts in social studies.

PREPARING YOUR CHILD
FOR STANDARDIZED TESTS

As a parent, there is much you can do to help your son or daughter get ready for taking a standardized test.

During the weeks leading up to the test . . .

- Attend parent-teacher conferences and find out how you can help your child succeed in school.

- Assume an active role in school. Seeing your commitment to his or her school enhances the image of school in your child's eyes.

- Find out when standardized tests are given and plan accordingly. For example, avoid scheduling doctor or dentist appointments for your child during the testing dates. Students who take standardized tests with their class usually do better than students who make up tests because of absences.

- Monitor your child's progress in school. Make sure your child completes his or her homework and projects. Support good study habits and encourage your child to always do his or her best.

- Encourage your child's creativity and interests. Provide plenty of books, magazines, and educational opportunities.

- Whenever you speak of standardized tests, speak of them in a positive manner. Emphasize that while these tests are important, it is not the final score that counts, but that your child tries his or her best.

During the days immediately preceding the test . . .

- Once the test has been announced, discuss the test with your child to relieve apprehension. Encourage your son or daughter to take the test seriously, but avoid being overly anxious. (Sometimes parents are more nervous about their children's tests than the kids are.)

- Help your child with any materials his or her teacher sends home in preparation for the test.

- Make sure your child gets a good night's sleep each night before a testing day.

- On the morning of the test, make sure your child wakes up on time, eats a solid breakfast, and arrives at school on time.

- Remind your child to listen to the directions of the teacher carefully and to read directions carefully.

- Encourage your child to do his or her best.

COVER LETTER TO PARENTS
ANNOUNCING STANDARDIZED TESTS

Use the following letter to inform the parents of your students about upcoming standardized tests in your school. Feel free to adjust the letter according to your needs.

Dear Parents/Guardians,

    On _____(dates)_____ , our class will be taking the _____(name of test)_____. During the next few weeks students will work on various practice tests to help prepare for the actual test.

    You can help, too. Please read the attached materials and discuss the importance of the tests with your child. By supporting your child's efforts in preparation, you can help him or her attain the best possible scores.

    Thank you.

                    Sincerely,

                    (Name)

WHAT STUDENTS NEED TO KNOW
ABOUT STANDARDIZED TESTS

The mere thought of taking a standardized test frightens many students, causing a wide range of symptoms from mild apprehension to upset stomachs and panic attacks. Since even low levels of anxiety can distract students and undermine their achievement, you should attempt to lessen their concerns.

Apprehension, anxiety, and fear are common responses to situations that we perceive as being out of our control. When students are faced with a test on which they don't know what to expect, they may worry excessively that they won't do well. Such emotions, especially when intense, almost guarantee that they will make careless mistakes. When students are prepared properly for a test, they are more likely to know "what to expect." This reduces negative emotions and students are able to enter the testing situation with confidence, which almost always results in better scores.

The first step to preparing your students for standardized tests is to mention the upcoming tests well in advance—at least a few weeks ahead of time—and explain that in the days leading up to the test, the class will be preparing. Explain that while they will not be working with the actual test, the work they will be doing is designed to help them get ready. You may wish to use the analogy of a sports team practicing during the pre-season. Practices help players sharpen their skills, anticipate game situations, and build confidence. Practicing during the pre-season helps athletes perform better during the regular season.

You might find it useful to distribute copies of the following reproducibles:

- Test-taking Tips for Students
- Test Words You Should Know

Hand these out a few days before the testing session. Go over them with your students and suggest that they take them home and ask their parents to review the sheets with them on the night before the test.

Name _____ Date _____ Section _____

TEST-TAKING TIPS FOR STUDENTS

1. Try your best.

2. Be confident and think positively. People who believe they will do well usually do better than those who are not confident.

3. Fill out the answer sheet correctly. Be careful that you darken all circles. Be sure to use a number 2 pencil unless your teacher tells you otherwise.

4. Listen carefully to all directions and follow them exactly. If you don't understand something, ask your teacher.

5. Read all questions and their possible answers carefully. Sometimes an answer may at first seem right, but it isn't. Always read all answers before picking one.

6. Try to answer the questions in order, but don't waste too much time on hard questions. Go on to easier ones and then go back to the hard ones.

7. Don't be discouraged by hard questions. On most tests for every hard question there are many easy ones.

8. Try not to make careless mistakes.

9. Budget your time and work quickly.

10. Be sure to fill in the correct answer spaces on your answer sheet. Use a finger of your non-writing hand to keep your place on the answer space.

11. Look for clues and key words when answering questions.

12. If you become "stuck" on a question, eliminate any answers you know are wrong and then make your best guess of the remaining answers. (Do this only if there is no penalty for guessing. Check with your teacher about this.)

13. Don't leave any blanks. Guess if you are running out of time. (Only do this if unanswered questions are counted wrong. Check with your teacher.)

14. Double-check your work if time permits.

15. Erase completely any unnecessary marks on your answer sheet.

TEST WORDS YOU SHOULD KNOW

The words below are used in standardized tests. Understanding what each one means will help you when you take your test.

all	double-check	opposite
always	end	order
answer sheet	error	oval
best	example	part
blank	fill in	passage
booklet	finish	pick
bubble	following	punctuation
capitalization	go on	question
check	item	read
choose	language expression	reread
circle	language mechanics	right
column	mark	row
complete	match	same as
comprehension	missing	sample
continue	mistake	section
correct	name	select
definition	never	stop
details	none	topic
directions	not true	true
does not belong	number 2 pencil	vocabulary

CREATING A POSITIVE
TEST-TAKING ENVIRONMENT

Little things really do matter when students take standardized tests. Students who are consistently encouraged to do their best throughout the year in the regular classroom generally achieve higher scores on standardized tests than students who maintain a careless attitude regarding their studies. Of course, motivating students to do their best is an easy thing to suggest, but not such an easy goal to accomplish.

There are, fortunately, some steps you can take to foster positive attitudes on the part of your students in regard to standardized tests. Start by discussing the test students will take, and explain how the results of standardized tests are used. When students understand the purpose of testing, they are more likely to take the tests seriously. Never speak of tests in a negative manner, for example, saying that students must work hard or they will do poorly. Instead, speak in positive terms: by working hard and trying their best they will achieve the best results.

To reduce students' concerns, assure them that the use of practice tests will improve their scores. Set up a thorough test-preparation schedule well in advance of the tests, based upon the needs and abilities of your students. Avoid cramming preparation into the last few days before the test. Cramming only burdens students with an increased workload and leads to anxiety and worry. A regular, methodical approach to preparation is best, because this enables you to check for weaknesses in skills and offer remediation.

The value of preparation for standardized tests cannot be understated. When your students feel that they are prepared for the tests, and that you have confidence in them, they will feel more confident and approach the tests with a positive frame of mind. Along with effective instruction throughout the year, a focused program of test preparation will help ensure that your students will have the chance to achieve their best scores on standardized tests.

LaVergne, TN USA
11 May 2010
182275LV00001B/5/P